LINDSAY KEMENY

7 MIGHTY MOVES

Reading Resources

Ready-to-Use Tools and Templates to Transform Your Teaching

SCHOLASTIC

For my students, who inspire me to be a better teacher every day.

Senior Vice President and Publisher: Tara Welty
Editorial Director: Sarah Longhi
Editor-in-Chief: Raymond Coutu
Development Editor: Maria L. Chang
Production Editor: Danny Miller
Assistant Editor: Samantha Unger
Cover design: Tannaz Fassihi
Interior design: Maria Lilja
Illustrations: Doug Jones and Rob McClurkan

Photos: 63–88 by Adam Chinitz, copyright © Scholastic Inc. Additional images © Getty Images, Shutterstock.com, and Scholastic Inc. Icons by The Noun Project.

Credits: 244: "Days of Adventures" from *Leveled Poems for Small-Group Reading Lessons* © 2014 by Pamela Chanko. Used by permission of Scholastic Inc.; 245–246, 248–251: "Scary Things," "My Lunch Box," "My Teddy," "The Substitute Teacher," "What Does It Mean to Be Responsible?," and "All About Us" from *The Big Book of Classroom Poems* © 2004 Kathleen M. Hollenbeck. Used by permission of Scholastic Inc.; 247: "Amazing Changes" by Dexter Twisdale © Scholastic Inc. Used by permission; 252: "Mary's Lamb" by Sarah Josepha Hale, 1830; 253: "Three Little Kittens" by Eliza Lee Cabot Follen, 1843. All rights reserved.

ISBN 978-1-5461-5251-4

1 2 3 4 5 6 7 8 9 10 184 34 33 32 31 30 29 28 27 26 25

Scholastic Inc., 557 Broadway, New York, NY 10012

Acknowledgments

I'm so grateful to my husband and children for supporting me on this project. They have been so patient as I've devoted time to writing, reviewing, and revising. Thank you a million times! I love you all so much! Also, the unwavering support of my parents is something I'll always cherish. Thank you!

I'm thankful for my students, both past and present. They inspire my work and I feel so lucky to teach them every day. Dear students, thank you for making me smile, challenging me, and helping me grow into the best teacher I can be.

The support of so many educators means the world to me! I sincerely appreciate the kind comments, messages, and reviews I receive from around the world. Thank you! I'm often nervous to release my ideas, thoughts, and resources. Your continued encouragement keeps me going and helps me have the courage to continue to share.

A special thanks to all the teachers who are bravely sharing the wonderful things happening in your classrooms. I urge you to continue. We need more teachers leading from the classroom! May your passion continue to ignite and illuminate classrooms worldwide. I'm also grateful to the organizations that provide platforms for teachers to be heard and celebrated.

I could not have completed this book without the amazing work of the Scholastic team: Ray Coutu, Maria Chang, Sarah Longhi, Tara Welty, Tannaz Fassihi, Maria Lilja, Samantha Unger, Danny Miller, and so many others. Thank you for your attention to detail and all your amazing contributions. Ray, your calm demeanor and wise counsel has helped me regain my composure more than once. Thank you!

Finally, many thanks to those who endorsed my book: Renata M. Archie, Belkys Benison, Jake Daggett, Erin Eighmy, Angie Hanlin, and Yvette Manns. I'm incredibly grateful and honored to have your recommendation.

Contents

Introduction

When my son was diagnosed with dyslexia, it sparked a flame inside me to find out all I could about dyslexia and effective reading instruction for all students. Witnessing my son's struggles with self-esteem and depression because of his reading difficulties triggered a strong desire within me to prevent other children from feeling the way he did. As I dove into the research, I realized how much I didn't know about the most effective methods to teach children how to read. As my knowledge of the science of reading increased, I began to implement the strategies I was learning. As a result, I began witnessing the healing of my son's heart as he made progress. As his reading improved, so did his self-esteem.

I also began implementing those strategies, or "mighty moves," in my classroom. The difference was enormous. I saw, and continue to see, phenomenal growth in my students' reading abilities. The knowledge and experience I've gained empower me to guide my students effectively. I feel so much more confident as a teacher, and I want to help all teachers feel this way. Every child deserves a teacher who understands the science of reading.

When I was writing *7 Mighty Moves*, I felt a mix of nervousness and excitement. Would my explanations be clear? Would teachers find value in what I had to share? But my unwavering desire to help other educators propelled me forward. I've been very touched by the positive response to the book. As I traveled across the country to train teachers on the 7 Mighty Moves, the next step became clear: a companion resource to the professional book. I knew I could do even more to help teachers as they strive to implement effective literacy instruction in their classrooms.

7 Mighty Moves Reading Resources provides practical, ready-to-use routines and resources to help you implement each of the 7 Moves listed below and explained in depth in my first book, *7 Mighty Moves*, and I encourage you to read that one first. Not only does that book explain each move in depth, but it also explains the research behind it and some of my favorite ways to implement it in the classroom.

THE 7 MIGHTY MOVES		
	FROM	**TO**
MOVE 1	teaching phonemic awareness randomly	teaching it with intention
MOVE 2	teaching phonics incidentally and haphazardly	teaching it explicitly and systematically
MOVE 3	teaching cueing strategies	teaching decoding strategies
MOVE 4	using predictable texts for beginning readers	using decodable texts for beginning readers
MOVE 5	encouraging whole-word memorizing of "sight words"	encouraging decoding of high-frequency words
MOVE 6	expecting fluency to improve on its own	expecting it to improve with meaningful practice opportunities
MOVE 7	neglecting vocabulary and background knowledge	embracing them to improve comprehension

Sometimes the sheer volume of "extras" available online can feel overwhelming. Sorting through countless worksheets and reproducibles can be time-consuming and leave you questioning their effectiveness. This book aims to give you a one-stop shop to all the templates, lesson plans, and reminder cards you need to implement the strategies you've learned in *7 Mighty Moves*. I believe in making the most of every minute in my classroom and avoid wasting time on resources that might not be useful. That belief extends to this book as well. I included only resources that I myself would use in the classroom, with the goal of providing the most practical, powerful tools.

How to Use This Book

Think of this book as a literacy coach that reminds you of the important points in my original book and guides you as you implement the moves. Along the way I share my classroom-tested teaching tips as well as scaffolds for students who need more help and extension ideas for students who need to be challenged. The key to success with these resources is in how you use them. You get to decide which tools and templates work best for your students, when to use them, and how to tailor them to children's specific needs. That's where the science of reading meets the art of teaching!

You don't need to read this book in order, from cover to cover. Feel free to go straight to the move you or your students need most. Start by reading the move's introduction to get an overview of it, then delve into the resources and choose the ones that best suit your needs. If you have more time, read the corresponding move in *7 Mighty Moves* to expand and solidify your understanding.

How It's Organized

This book is organized by the 7 Mighty Moves. Each move begins with a quick overview and key points I discuss in my original book. A sidebar follows, listing teaching materials needed for implementing that move. Those materials include reproducible templates, word lists, picture cards, student practice pages, high-frequency word lessons, poems for fluency practice, and so many more! All the materials are available in the book and online at the book's companion website: scholastic.com/7mmreadingresources.

Each resource is presented in a predictable, user-friendly format.

An opening paragraph introduces the resource and explains how and why it works.

Differentiation Tips offer scaffolds for additional support and extension ideas for advanced learners.

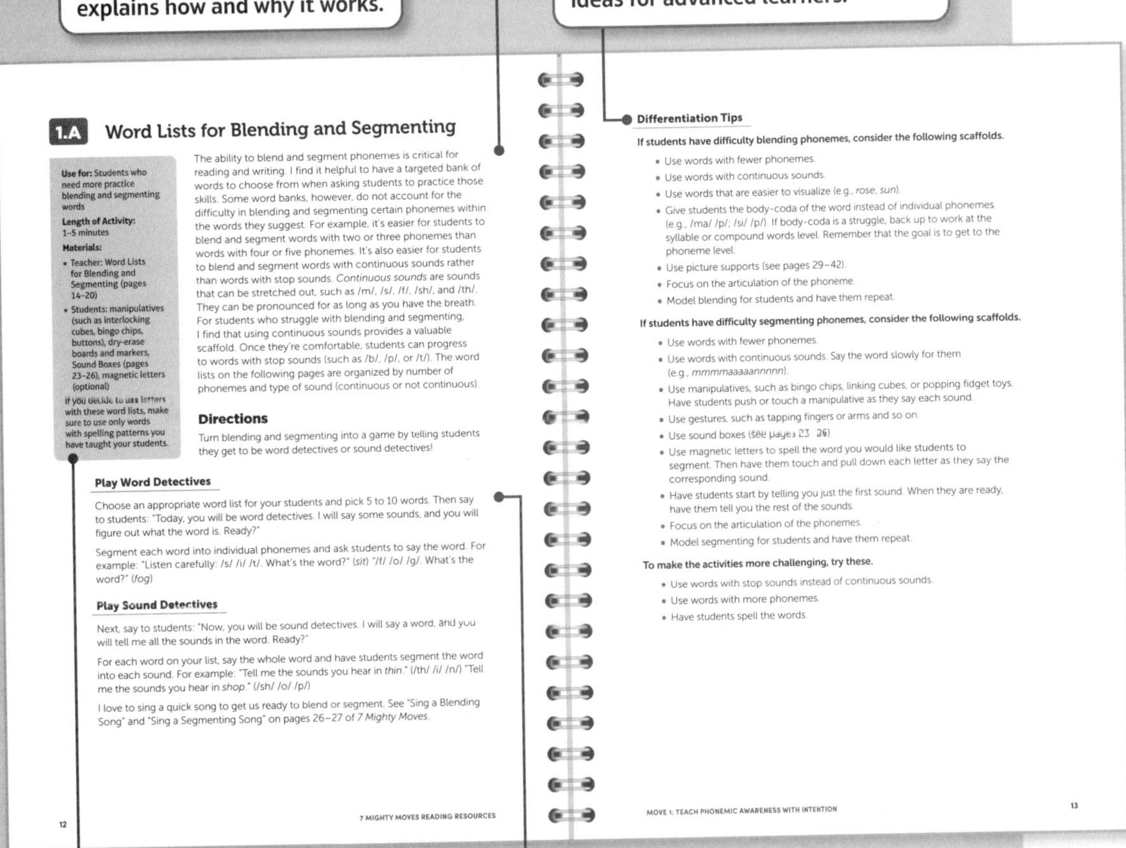

1.A Word Lists for Blending and Segmenting

Use for: Students who need more practice blending and segmenting words

Length of Activity: 1–5 minutes

Materials:

- Teacher: Word Lists for Blending and Segmenting (pages 14–20)
- Students: manipulatives (such as interlocking cubes, bingo chips, buttons), dry-erase boards and markers, Sound Boxes (pages 23–26), magnetic letters (optional)

If you decide to use letters with these word lists, make sure to use only words with spelling patterns you have taught your students.

The ability to blend and segment phonemes is critical for reading and writing. I find it helpful to have a targeted bank of words to choose from when asking students to practice those skills. Some word banks, however, do not account for the difficulty in blending and segmenting certain phonemes within the words they suggest. For example, it's easier for students to blend and segment words with two or three phonemes than words with four or five phonemes. It's also easier for students to blend and segment words with continuous sounds rather than words with stop sounds. *Continuous sounds* are sounds that can be stretched out, such as /m/, /s/, /f/, /sh/, and /th/. They can be pronounced for as long as you have the breath. For students who struggle with blending and segmenting, I find that using continuous sounds provides a valuable scaffold. Once they're comfortable, students can progress to words with stop sounds (such as /b/, /p/, or /t/). The word lists on the following pages are organized by number of phonemes and type of sound (continuous or not continuous).

Directions

Turn blending and segmenting into a game by telling students they get to be word detectives or sound detectives!

Play Word Detectives

Choose an appropriate word list for your students and pick 5 to 10 words. Then say to students: "Today, you will be word detectives. I will say some sounds, and you will figure out what the word is. Ready?"

Segment each word into individual phonemes and ask students to say the word. For example: "Listen carefully: /s/ /i/ /t/. What's the word?" (*sit*) "/f/ /o/ /g/. What's the word?" (*fog*)

Play Sound Detectives

Next, say to students: "Now, you will be sound detectives. I will say a word, and you will tell me all the sounds in the word. Ready?"

For each word on your list, say the whole word and have students segment the word into each sound. For example: "Tell me the sounds you hear in *thin*." (/th/ /i/ /n/) "Tell me the sounds you hear in *shop*." (/sh/ /o/ /p/)

I love to sing a quick song to get us ready to blend or segment. See "Sing a Blending Song" and "Sing a Segmenting Song" on pages 26–27 of *7 Mighty Moves*.

12 7 MIGHTY MOVES READING RESOURCES

Differentiation Tips

If students have difficulty blending phonemes, consider the following scaffolds.

- Use words with fewer phonemes.
- Use words with continuous sounds.
- Use words that are easier to visualize (e.g., *rose, sun*).
- Give students the body-coda of the word instead of individual phonemes (e.g., /ma/ /p/; /si/ /p/). If body-coda is a struggle, back up to work at the syllable or compound words level. Remember that the goal is to get to the phoneme level.
- Use picture supports (see pages 29–42).
- Focus on the articulation of the phoneme.
- Model blending for students and have them repeat.

If students have difficulty segmenting phonemes, consider the following scaffolds.

- Use words with fewer phonemes.
- Use words with continuous sounds. Say the word slowly for them (e.g., *mmmmaaaaannnnn*).
- Use manipulatives, such as bingo chips, linking cubes, or popping fidget toys. Have students push or touch a manipulative as they say each sound.
- Use gestures, such as tapping fingers or arms and so on.
- Use sound boxes (see pages 23–26).
- Use magnetic letters to spell the word you would like students to segment. Then have them touch and pull down each letter as they say the corresponding sound.
- Have students start by telling you just the first sound. When they are ready, have them tell you the rest of the sounds.
- Focus on the articulation of the phonemes.
- Model segmenting for students and have them repeat.

To make the activities more challenging, try these.

- Use words with stop sounds instead of continuous sounds.
- Use words with more phonemes.
- Have students spell the words.

MOVE 1: TEACH PHONEMIC AWARENESS WITH INTENTION 13

Sidebars provide at-a-glance details, such as target students, estimated activity time, and materials.

Easy-to-follow directions help you implement the resource.

I truly hope you enjoy this book and find it valuable and practical!

MOVE 1

Teach Phonemic Awareness With Intention

Move 1 downloadables are available here.

Earlier in my career, hearing a child correctly identify the sounds in a word, but then blend those sounds incorrectly, perplexed me. For example, given the word *tap*, a child may correctly identify the letter sounds /t/ /a/ /p/, but then say *pat* or *tam*, or even something completely unrelated, like *hop*. Now I understand that this indicates a weakness in phonemic awareness (PA) and that I need to work on it with that student. Mystery solved!

Learning that phonemic awareness is critical for students' reading success was a turning point for me. As a result, I made several adjustments in my instruction. The first move I made was to learn exactly what phonemic awareness is and to set aside time to teach it intentionally. *Phonemic awareness* is the understanding that spoken language can be broken down into *phonemes*, or individual speech sounds. I learned to focus my PA time on phoneme-level activities rather than on larger units of sound (syllables, onsets, rimes) because this directly impacts reading and writing. Students need to be able to blend those individual phonemes together to read, and they need to segment (or pull apart) those small units of sound to spell.

A growing body of research shows that we can bypass instruction in the larger units (syllables, onsets, rimes) and start right at the phoneme level (Brady, 2020; Blachman et al., 1999). However, if I have students who struggle with blending individual phonemes, then I will back up my instruction to include those larger units, such as syllables, to help prepare them for the work at the phoneme level. (See One Student's Story: Max, Part 1, in *7 Mighty Moves*, page 22.) The difference is that I know I need to focus on helping those students get down to the phoneme level as quickly as possible.

Another move I made was to intentionally add letters to my phonemic awareness instruction. Yes, we *can* combine phonics and phonemic awareness. The National Reading Panel (2000) states that manipulating letters during phonemic awareness instruction is more powerful for improving reading outcomes than instruction that is strictly oral. We need to explicitly show students how the sounds they hear connect with the letters on the page.

Let's review key points about Move 1.

- Phonemic awareness is a critical component of reading instruction.
- Phonemic awareness and letter knowledge are reliable predictors of future literacy performance.
- The most common source of reading difficulties is poor phonemic awareness.
- Phonemic awareness is the conscious awareness of phonemes (individual speech sounds) in spoken words.
- Blending and segmenting are the most critical phonemic awareness skills because they are necessary for reading and spelling.
- There are 44 phonemes of English, which can be categorized into vowel and consonant phonemes. We can discuss these phonemes by their place and manner of articulation.
- Students need to develop an awareness of individual phonemes and how they connect to graphemes, their written representations.
- Phonemic awareness is best taught in short and frequent sessions.
- We need to get to the phoneme level quickly.
- Students develop an awareness of the external units before the internal units.
- We can and should connect our phonemic awareness instruction with letters.
- Science continuously evolves, and so must we.

MOVE 1: Routines and Resources

RESOURCE		PAGE
1.A	Word Lists for Blending and Segmenting	12
1.B	Sound Boxes for Segmenting	21
1.C	Picture Cards for Additional Support	27
1.D	Word Chains for Decoding and Encoding	43

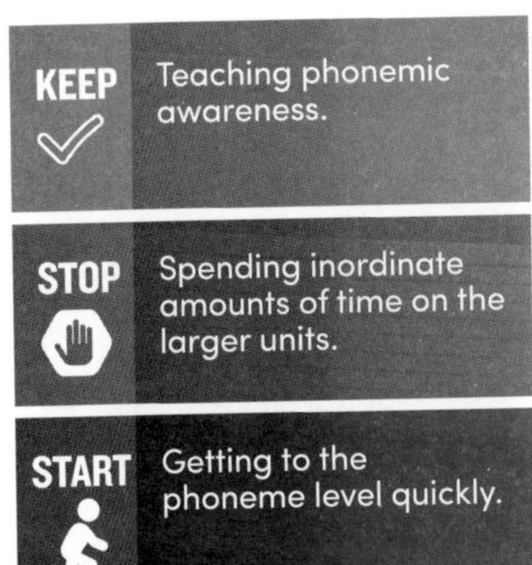

Terms to Know

Phoneme: individual speech sound

Grapheme: a letter or group of letters that represent an individual phoneme

Phonemic Awareness: the understanding that spoken language can be broken down into phonemes

Phonological Awareness: the umbrella term for the knowledge of sounds in spoken language, which includes larger chunks of sounds as well as phonemes

Phonological Sensitivity: the awareness of the larger units of speech in spoken sounds

Phonics: the method we use to teach letter-sound combinations

Blending: a procedure in which a student combines individual sounds that make up a word to decode and pronounce it

Segmenting: a procedure in which a student breaks down a word into its individual sounds

Syllable: a unit of speech that includes one vowel sound

Onset: the sounds that come before the vowel in a syllable (e.g., *sh* in *ship*)

Rime: the vowel plus the consonants that follow in a syllable (e.g., *ip* in *ship*)

Body: everything up to and including the vowel in a syllable (e.g., *su* in *sun*)

Coda: any consonants after the vowel sound in a syllable (e.g., *n* in *sun*)

Word Lists for Blending and Segmenting

Use for: Students who need more practice blending and segmenting words

Length of Activity: 1–5 minutes

Materials:

- Teacher: Word Lists for Blending and Segmenting (pages 14–20)
- Students: manipulatives (such as interlocking cubes, bingo chips, buttons), dry-erase boards and markers, Sound Boxes (pages 23–26), magnetic letters (optional)

If you decide to use letters with these word lists, make sure to use only words with spelling patterns you have taught your students.

The ability to blend and segment phonemes is critical for reading and writing. I find it helpful to have a targeted bank of words to choose from when asking students to practice those skills. Some word banks, however, do not account for the difficulty in blending and segmenting certain phonemes within the words they suggest. For example, it's easier for students to blend and segment words with two or three phonemes than words with four or five phonemes. It's also easier for students to blend and segment words with continuous sounds rather than words with stop sounds. *Continuous sounds* are sounds that can be stretched out, such as /m/, /s/, /f/, /sh/, and /th/. They can be pronounced for as long as you have the breath. For students who struggle with blending and segmenting, I find that using continuous sounds provides a valuable scaffold. Once they're comfortable, students can progress to words with stop sounds (such as /b/, /p/, or /t/). The word lists on the following pages are organized by number of phonemes and type of sound (continuous or not continuous).

Directions

Turn blending and segmenting into a game by telling students they get to be word detectives or sound detectives!

Play Word Detectives

Choose an appropriate word list for your students and pick 5 to 10 words. Then say to students: "Today, you will be word detectives. I will say some sounds, and you will figure out what the word is. Ready?"

Segment each word into individual phonemes and ask students to say the word. For example: "Listen carefully: /s/ /i/ /t/. What's the word?" (*sit*) "/f/ /o/ /g/. What's the word?" (*fog*)

Play Sound Detectives

Next, say to students: "Now, you will be sound detectives. I will say a word, and you will tell me all the sounds in the word. Ready?"

For each word on your list, say the whole word and have students segment the word into each sound. For example: "Tell me the sounds you hear in *thin*." (/th/ /i/ /n/) "Tell me the sounds you hear in *shop*." (/sh/ /o/ /p/)

I love to sing a quick song to get us ready to blend or segment. See "Sing a Blending Song" and "Sing a Segmenting Song" on pages 26–27 of *7 Mighty Moves*.

Differentiation Tips

If students have difficulty blending phonemes, consider the following scaffolds.

- Use words with fewer phonemes.
- Use words with continuous sounds.
- Use words that are easier to visualize (e.g., *rose, sun*).
- Give students the body-coda of the word instead of individual phonemes (e.g., /ma/ /p/; /si/ /p/). If body-coda is a struggle, back up to work at the syllable or compound words level. Remember that the goal is to get to the phoneme level.
- Use picture supports (see pages 29–42).
- Focus on the articulation of the phoneme.
- Model blending for students and have them repeat.

If students have difficulty segmenting phonemes, consider the following scaffolds.

- Use words with fewer phonemes.
- Use words with continuous sounds. Say the word slowly for them (e.g., *mmmmaaaaannnnn*).
- Use manipulatives, such as bingo chips, linking cubes, or popping fidget toys. Have students push or touch a manipulative as they say each sound.
- Use gestures, such as tapping fingers or arms and so on.
- Use sound boxes (see pages 23–26).
- Use magnetic letters to spell the word you would like students to segment. Then have them touch and pull down each letter as they say the corresponding sound.
- Have students start by telling you just the first sound. When they are ready, have them tell you the rest of the sounds.
- Focus on the articulation of the phonemes.
- Model segmenting for students and have them repeat.

To make the activities more challenging, try these.

- Use words with stop sounds instead of continuous sounds.
- Use words with more phonemes.
- Have students spell the words.

Words With 2 Phonemes			
CV Continuous Sounds	CV Stop Sounds	VC Continuous Sounds	VC Stop Sounds
fee	bee	ace	ache
hay*	boo	aim	add
he*	bow	am	age
hi*	boy	ash	ape
knee	bye	ear	app
lay	chew	eel	at
lie	cow	ice	ate
low	day	if	each
may	do	in	eat
me	doe	of	egg
moo	go	off	itch
mow	goo	oil	oak
my	guy	on	oat
new	jay	own	ode
no	Joe	us	ouch
ray	Kay		out
row	key		ugh
say	paw		up
see	pay		
she	pie		
shoe	pow		
show	tea		
sigh	tie		
so	toe		
way	toy		
we	two		
who*			
why			
you			

*Although the /h/ sound is considered continuous, it can be challenging for students to blend. Be mindful of that when selecting words.

Words With 3 Phonemes

Start and End With Continuous Sounds

face	life	name	shine
fan	line	nine	size
fin	love	nose	sun
fire	main	rain	them
fish	man	ran	thin
five	math	real	this
fun	maze	rhyme	thumb
ham*	mile	rim	van
hen*	mine	roll	vase
hill*	miss	room	whale
him*	mom	rose	win
home	moon	run	with
lamb	moose	save	yes
laugh	mouth	shave	zoom
leaf	move	shin	

*Although the /h/ sound is considered continuous, it can be challenging for students to blend. Be mindful of that when selecting words.

Words With 3 Phonemes			
Start With Continuous Sounds; End With Stop Sounds			
fat	lock	road	sick
feet	log	rob	sip
fig	look	rock	sit
fit	lot	rod	soap
fog	mad	rug	sob
food	map	sack	sock
hat*	mark	sad	sod
hid*	mat	sap	thick
hit*	met	sat	vet
hog*	mud	seed	vote
hot*	mug	set	wait
lake	nap	shade	wave
lap	net	shape	web
late	note	shark	weed
leap	rag	shed	week
leg	rat	sheep	wet
let	read	ship	wide
lick	red	shop	wig
like	rib	shout	wipe
lip	rip	shut	zip

*Although the /h/ sound is considered continuous, it can be challenging for students to blend. Be mindful of that when selecting words.

Words With 3 Phonemes

Start With Stop Sounds; End With Continuous Sounds		Start and End With Stop Sounds	
ball	guess	bag	dug
bath	gum	bat	get
bell	jam	beach	goat
bone	kiss	bed	good
bus	pail	big	got
bush	pan	bike	jet
buzz	pass	bite	job
can	path	book	joke
cash	pen	bud	keep
cave	pin	bug	kit
chase	puff	cage	pack
chin	tail	cap	peek
comb	tan	cape	peg
cone	teeth	cat	pet
cool	ten	chick	pig
dim	tin	chip	pipe
dime	toes	chop	pit
dish	tool	coat	pop
does	tooth	cook	pot
doll		cup	tack
game		dad	tag
gas		date	tap
gem		dig	tip
give		dog	top
goes		dot	tub

Words With 3 or 4 Phonemes (Beginning Consonant Clusters)			
3 Phonemes	**4 Phonemes**		
blue	black	freeze	smell
claw	blog	frog	smile
clue	brag	from	smoke
crow	brain	fruit	snack
cry	bread	glad	snail
draw	breath	glass	snake
dry	bright	grass	sneeze
flaw	broom	great	snug
flea	brown	green	spell
fly	brush	grip	spin
fray	clap	place	stack
free	class	plane	stage
fry	clip	plate	steak
gray	clop	please	steep
grow	crab	plot	stop
play	crack	plum	stove
plow	crash	prize	swan
pray	crib	prop	sweep
ski	crop	prune	sweet
sky	crumb	skate	swim
snow	dress	skid	throat
spy	drip	skip	throne
stay	drive	slam	track
three	drone	slap	train
through	drop	sleep	trap
throw	drum	slick	trash
tray	flag	slide	treat
tree	flame	slim	trick
try	flip	slip	trip
	flop	smash	

Words With 4 Phonemes (Ending Consonant Clusters)

bags	dump	lamp	rest
baked	felt	last	roast
band	film	launch	round
beast	finch	least	salt
belt	find	leaves	sand
bench	fist	left	self
bend	forks	lift	send
bent	found	lips	shelf
best	games	lunch	shield
birds	hand	mask	shorts
boats	hats	melt	tent
build	haunt	mend	test
bump	held	milk	thank
bunch	hills	mind	think
burst	hint	most	thirst
called	hold	must	west
camp	hopped	paint	wind
charms	hunch	pant	wink
cold	jump	pinch	yawned
cost	kind	pond	yelled
damp		ranch	
dogs		rats	

Words With 5 Phonemes (Consonant Clusters)		
blank	draft	sleeves
blast	drench	slept
blend	drift	slump
blink	drink	smells
blocked	friend	snacks
branch	front	spend
brand	frost	spoiled
brisk	glance	stacked
bronze	grand	stamp
brunch	grant	stand
clamp	ground	stomp
climbs	plant	stump
crabs	plump	swept
craft	prance	swift
cramp	prince	tripped
crawled	print	trucks
crept	shrimp	trunk
crisp	skunk	twist
crust	slant	

Sound Boxes for Segmenting

1.B

Sound boxes are a useful tool for phonemic awareness instruction. Use them to help students listen for and segment the phonemes, or sounds, in a word. They help draw students' attention to the number of phonemes in a word rather than focus on the number of letters.* You can give students a sound box with room for the exact number of phonemes in the word, or you can give them a box with more room and have them use only as much space as they need. Choose words from your phonics lesson, the decodable books students will read, or the word lists for resource 1.A (pages 14–20).

* If you have students spell the word, make sure it's a word whose spelling you have taught.

Use for: Students who need more practice segmenting and spelling words

Length of Activity: 3–5 minutes

Materials:

- Students: Sound Boxes (pages 23–26),* manipulatives such as interlocking cubes, bingo chips, or buttons

*Consider laminating these pages so students can use dry-erase markers on them.

Directions

Say the Sounds

Choose 5 to 10 words to give students practice in oral segmentation. Students will say each sound as they push a manipulative into each sound box. For example, you might tell them: "Say the sounds in the word *snap*. Put a chip in each box as you say each sound." The student then says:

/s/ (pushing a chip into the first box);

/n/ (pushing another chip into the second box);

/a/ (pushing another chip into the third box);

/p/ (pushing another chip into the fourth box).

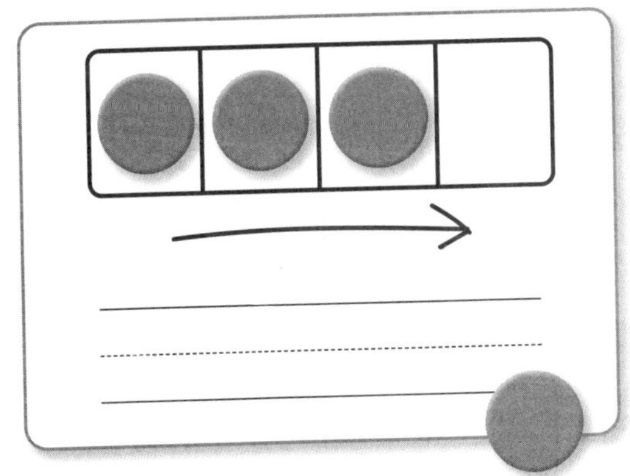

Extension: After students push a manipulative into each sound box, have them say the sounds again as they remove the manipulative and write the corresponding spelling in each box. Make sure they say the sound as they write each spelling. You might say: "Now, let's say the sounds again as we write the letters." The student then says:

/s/ (removing the chip in the first box and writing *s*);

/n/ (removing the chip in the second box and writing *n*);

/a/ (removing the chip in the third box and writing *a*);

/p/ (removing the chip in the fourth box and writing *p*).

Differentiation Tips

If students have difficulty, consider the following scaffolds.

- Use words with fewer phonemes.
- Use words with continuous sounds.
- Say the word slowly for them as you point to each box for each sound.
- Have the children say the first sound only. When ready, have them tell you the rest of the sounds.
- Use magnetic letters instead of having students write the letters.
- Focus on the articulation of the phonemes.
- Model segmenting for students and have them repeat.

To make the activity more challenging, try these.

- Use words with stop sounds instead of continuous sounds.
- Use words with more phonemes, especially words with consonant clusters.
- Use words with more challenging spellings. (Make sure you have taught the spellings.)

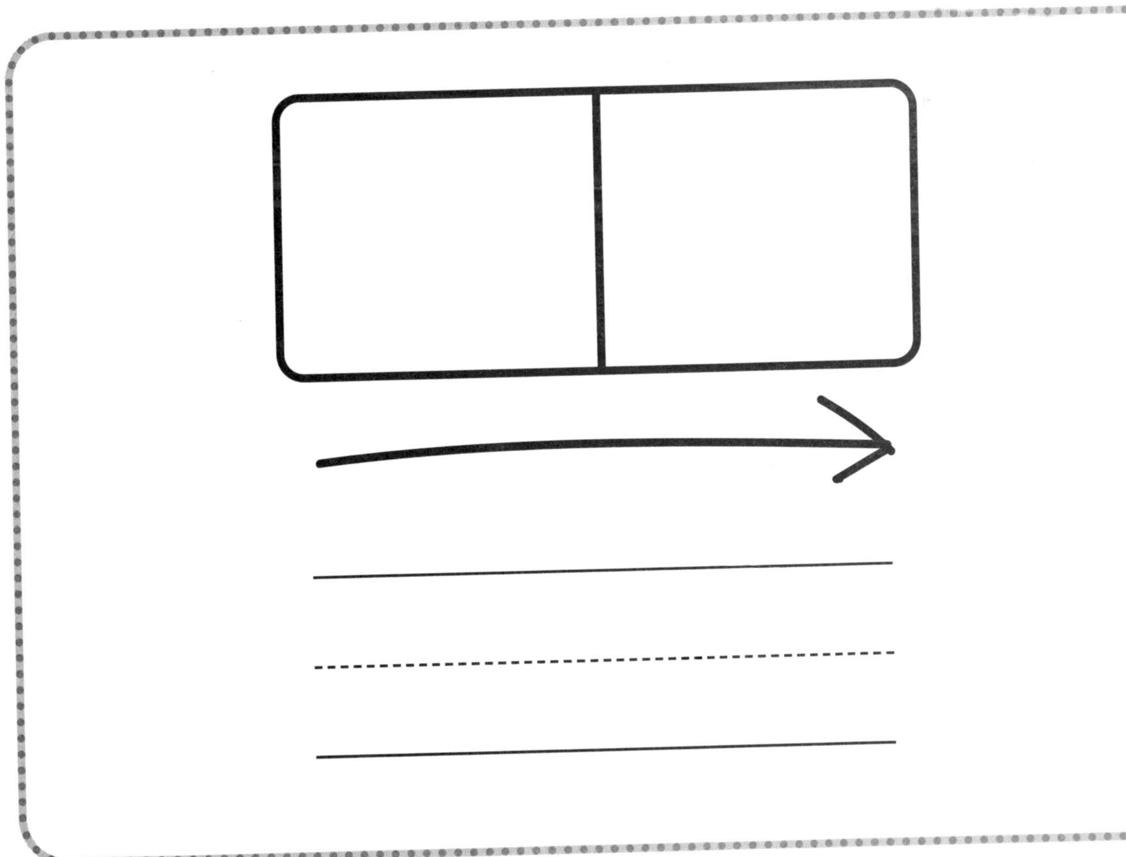

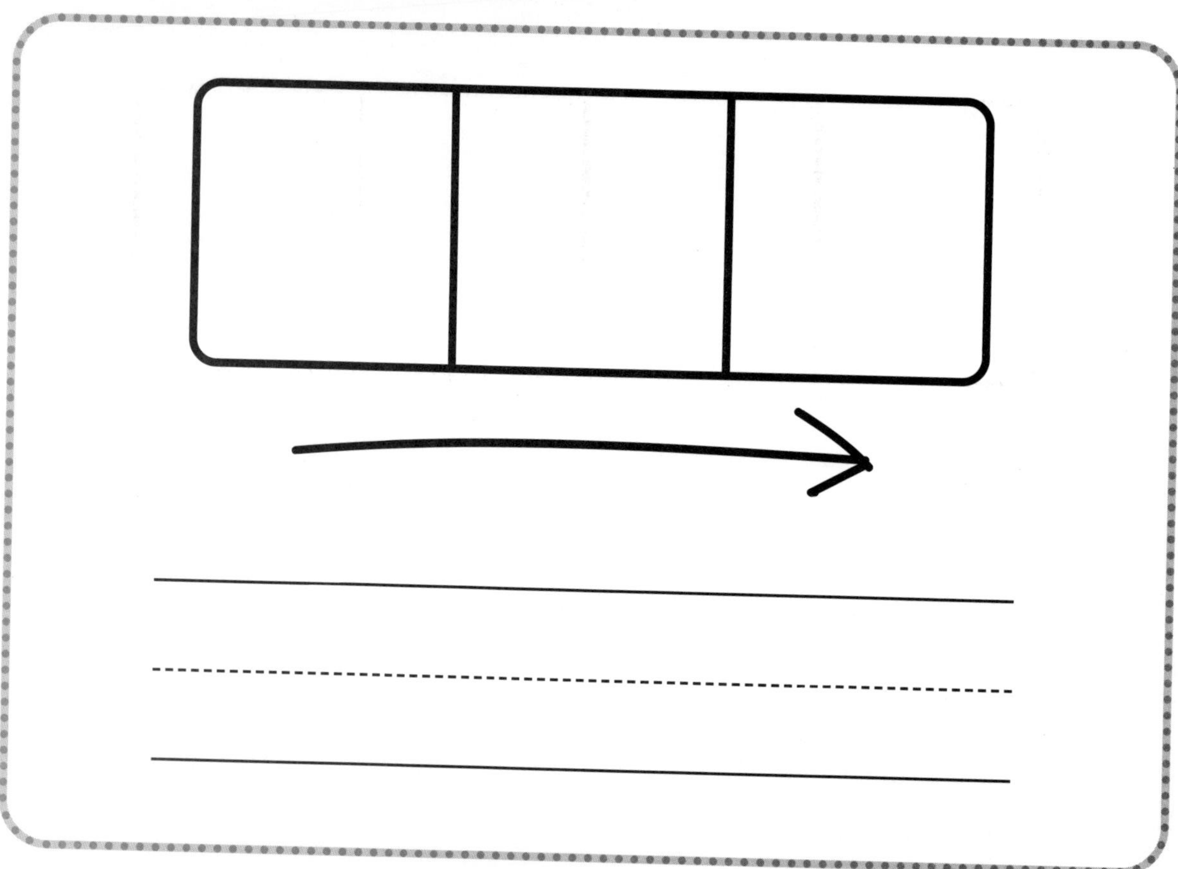

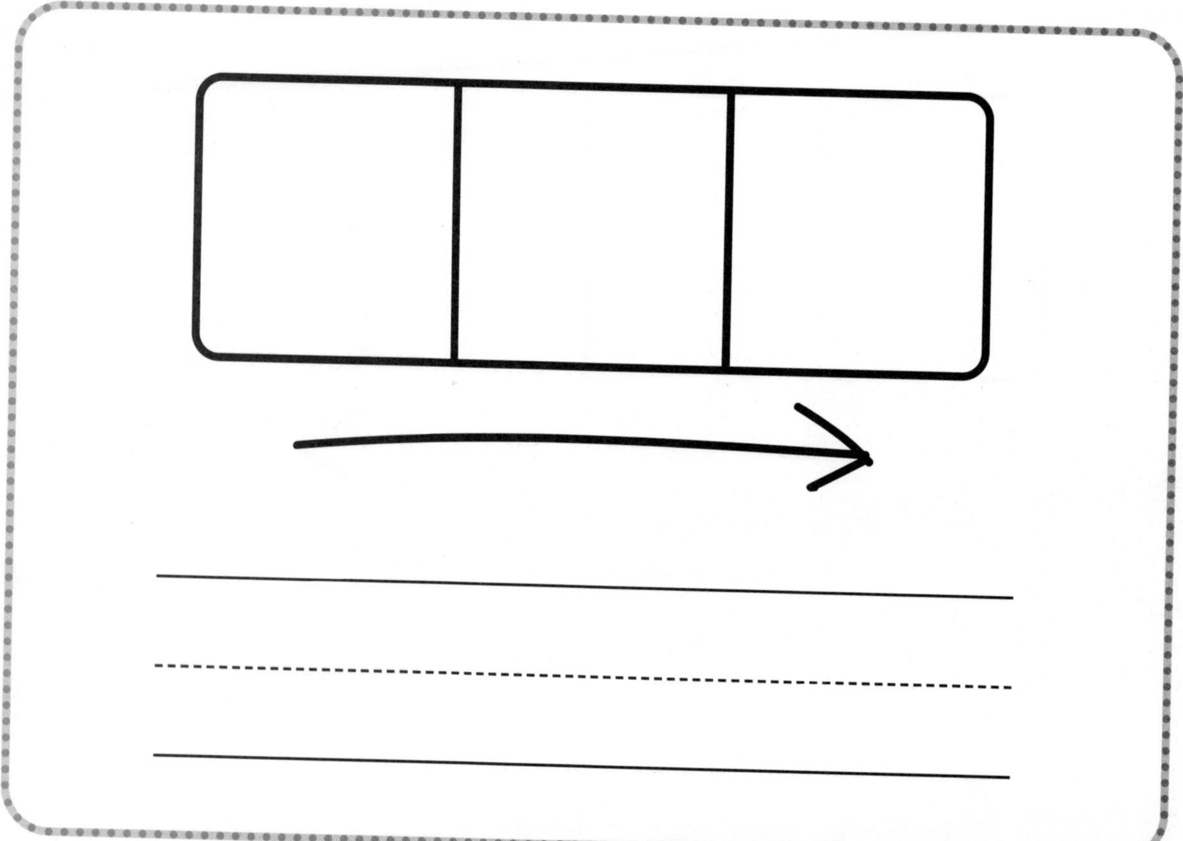

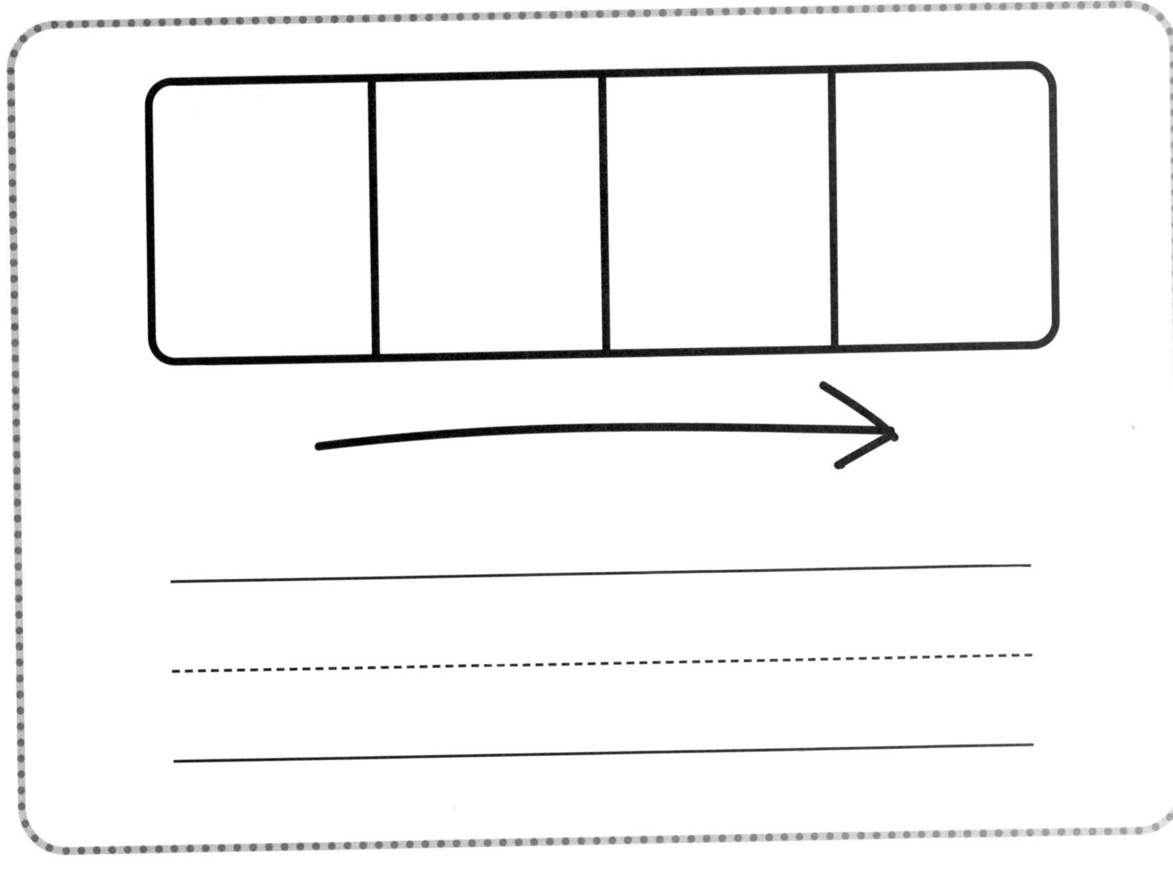

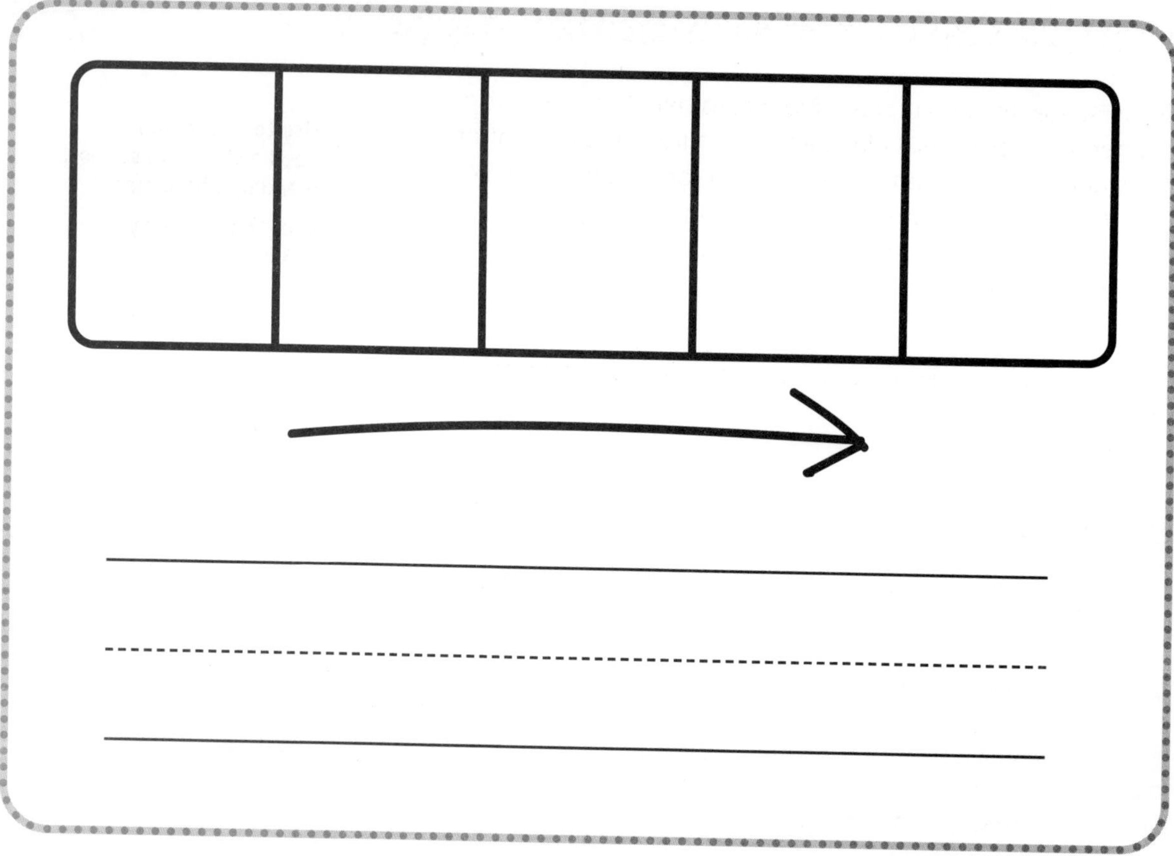

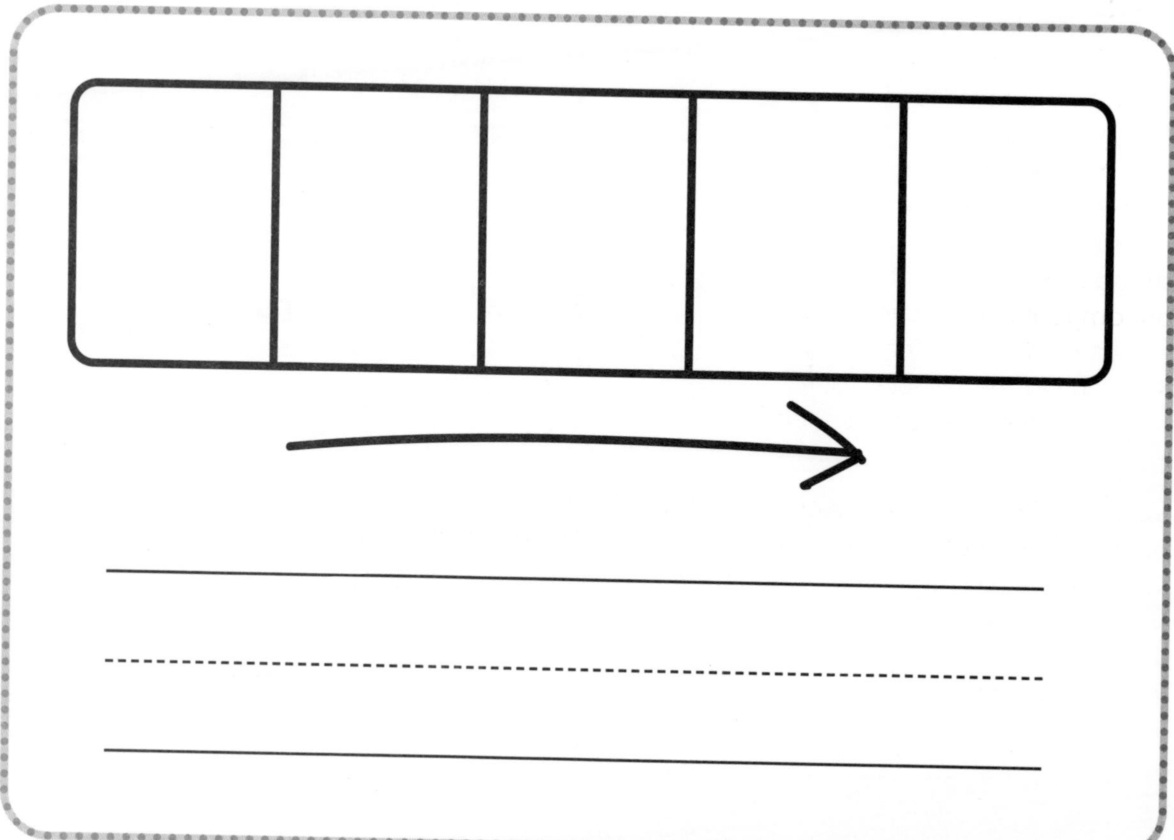

Picture Cards for Additional Support

Some students need picture support to help them develop phonemic awareness. I place a few picture cards in front of them and then segment the sounds for one picture, for example, /s/ /u/ /n/. Students then blend the sounds to say the word and point to the picture that matches. I find this is an especially great strategy for students who are learning the English language.

Once students begin to grasp blending and have learned some letters, I use the picture cards with words underneath to reinforce phoneme-grapheme correspondences as well as blending. Yes, we *can* connect phonemic awareness with letters.

Use for: Students who need much more support blending phonemes

Length of Activity: 2–3 minutes

Materials:

- Students: Picture Cards (pages 29–42)

Directions

Use picture cards to help students who are struggling with phonemic awareness tasks. (Additional picture cards are available online.)

Match the Sounds to the Picture

Set out two to six picture cards on the table. Tell students that you will say the sounds in a word, and they will blend the sounds to say the word. Then they will point to the picture that matches the word.

Remember, the goal is to get to the phoneme level because that directly impacts reading and writing. Start with the two-phoneme word cards. If students can blend these easily, move on to the three-phoneme word cards. If students struggle to blend two-phoneme words, use the CVC picture cards and tell students the word's body-coda for them to blend. For example, say, *su n*. If they continue to struggle, move to multisyllable or compound word cards: the easiest cards to use (pages 38–42). You say the syllables (*side walk*), and the child blends them into the word.

Variation: Print out two copies of six picture cards and place each card face down on the table. Students play a matching game. Each time they turn over a card, they segment the sounds for the picture they uncovered.

Differentiation Tips

If students have difficulty blending phonemes, consider the following scaffolds.

- Use words with fewer phonemes.
- Use words with continuous sounds.
- Model for students and have them repeat.
- Tell students the words for each picture beforehand.
- Say the body-coda of the word instead of individual phonemes (e.g., /ma/ /p/; /si/ /p/).*
- Use the multisyllable picture cards. If students still struggle with body-coda, back up to syllables. You will say the syllables in a word (*pur ple*), and students will blend them and point to the picture that matches.*
- Use the compound word picture cards. If students struggle with blending syllables, back up to compound words. You will say the words in a compound word (*butter fly*), and students will blend the words and point to the picture that matches.*

* Don't focus on larger units for too long. The goal is to get back to the phoneme level.

To make the activity more challenging, try these.

- Use words with stop sounds instead of continuous sounds.
- Use words with more phonemes.
- Use the picture cards with the words shown (pages 34–37) so students work on both phonics and phonemic awareness together.
- Take the picture supports away and move on to a different activity.

Words With 2 Phonemes

Start With Continuous Sounds (CV)

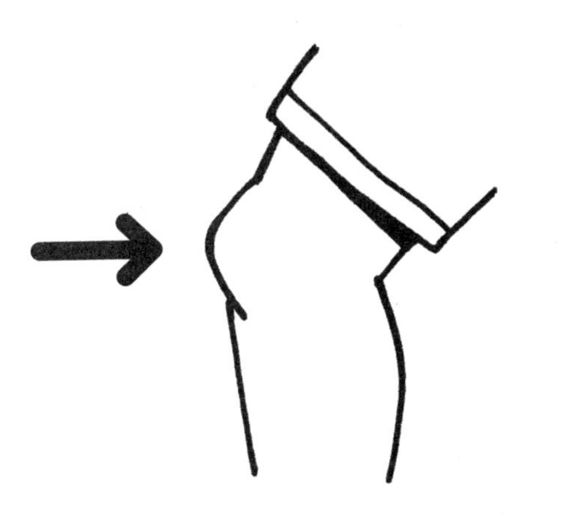

Picture words (L–R): mow, knee, she, zoo, shoe, moo

Words With 2 Phonemes

Start With Stop Sounds (CV)

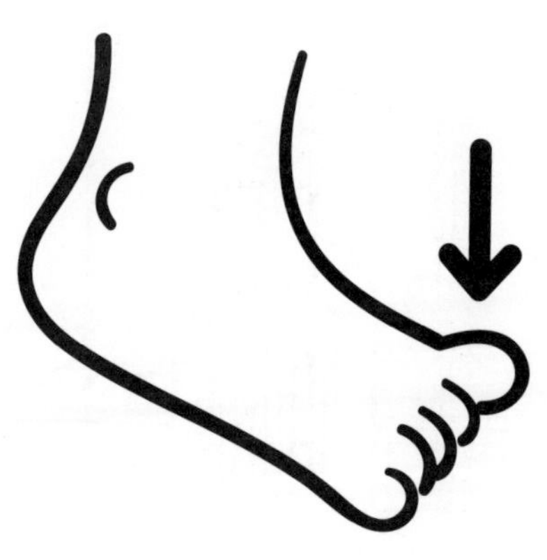

Picture words (L–R): pie, key, toe, bow, tea, boy

Words With 2 Phonemes

(VC Sounds)

Picture words (L–R): ice, eat, on, off, ape, app

Words With 3 Phonemes

Start With Continuous Sounds

Picture words (L–R): fish, five, nose, ship, moon, thumb

Words With 3 Phonemes

Start With Continuous or Stop Sounds

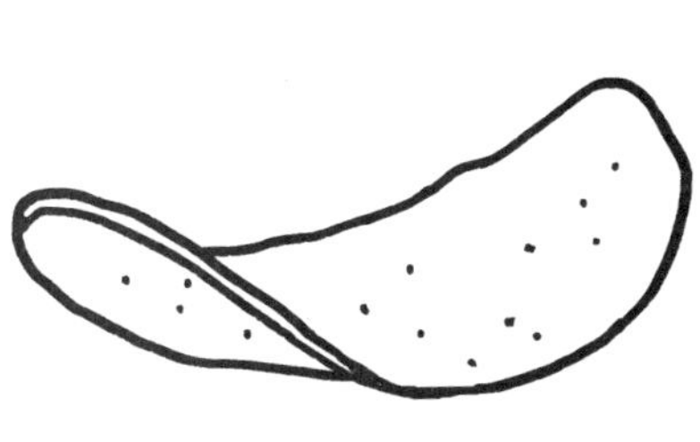

Picture words (L–R): leaf, cake, home, juice, chip, bike

CVC Words

Start With Continuous Sounds

log

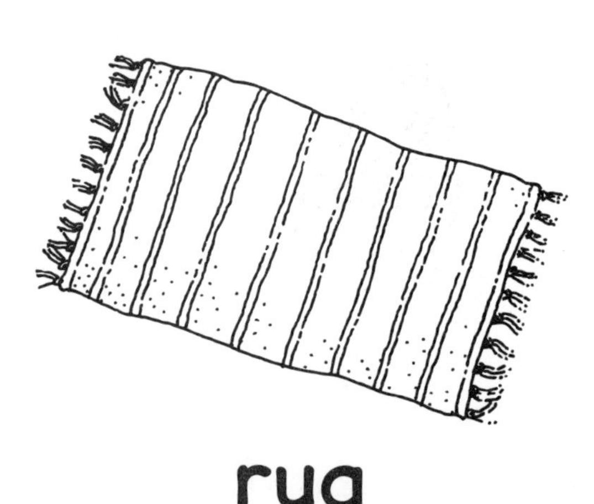

rug

van

hat

zip

mud

CVC Words

Start With Continuous Sounds

net

map

rat

fin

fog

lip

CVC Words

Start With Stop Sounds

pan

dog

jet

can

bed

pot

CVC Words

Start With Stop Sounds

top

wet

bug

jog

cat

kid

Multisyllabic Words

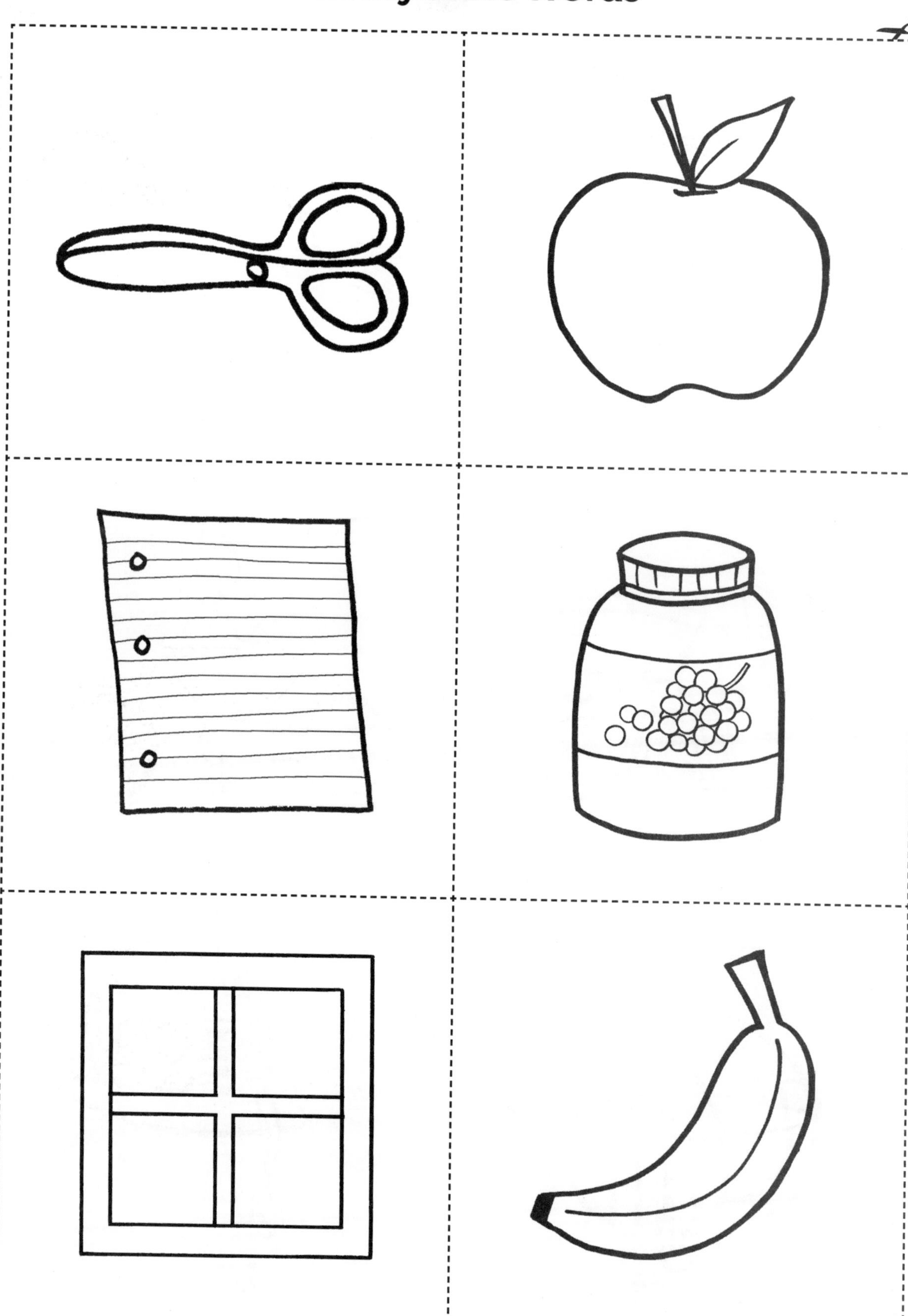

Picture words (L–R): scissors, apple, paper, jelly, window, banana

Multisyllabic Words

Picture words (L–R): lemonade, dinosaur, elephant, bicycle, umbrella, spaghetti

Multisyllabic Words

Picture words (L–R): hamburger, computer, potato, motorcycle, helicopter, calculator

Compound Words

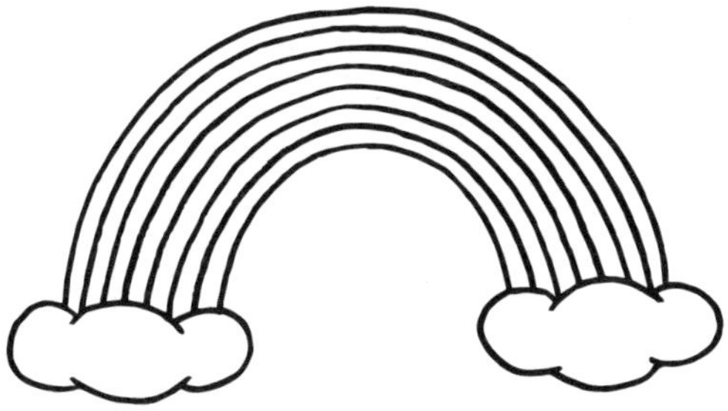

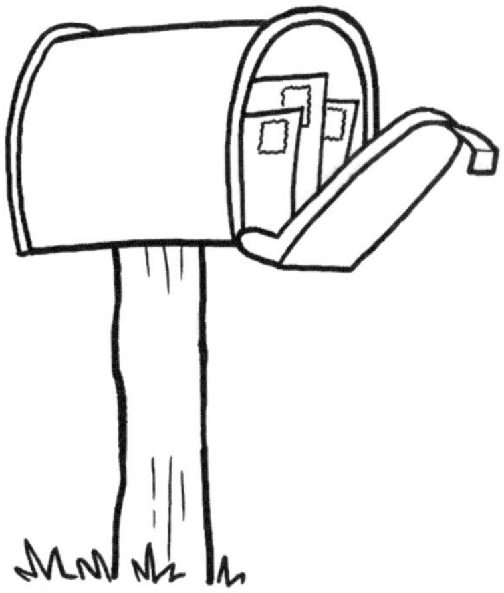

Picture words (L–R): butterfly, sidewalk, ladybug, popcorn, rainbow, mailbox

Compound Words

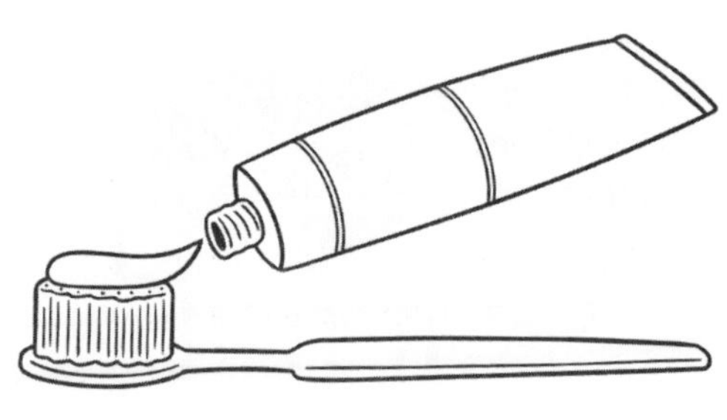

Picture words (L–R): snowman, pancakes, wheelchair, toothpaste, spaceship, sunflower

Word Chains for Decoding and Encoding

Word chains are a great way to build phonemic awareness and phonics skills at the same time! Give students a word and ask them to change only one phoneme or grapheme at a time to create a new word. Use a dry-erase board or make photocopies of the Magic Word Chain worksheet (pages 53–54). You can have students write directly on the paper or use magnetic letters, or you can laminate the sheet for students to write on with dry-erase markers.

Use for: Children who need practice with phonemic awareness and spelling

Length of Activity: 3–5 minutes

Materials:

- Teacher: Word Chain Lists (pages 45–52)
- Students: dry-erase boards and markers or magnetic letters, Magic Word Chain blank worksheets (pages 53–54)

Directions

Tell students they will be magicians who will magically turn the first word into the final word. For example, if the first word of a chain is *fox* and the last word is *pig*, tell students that they will be turning a fox into a pig!

Make "Magic Chains"

Choose a Word Chain List. Say the first word and have students spell the word on their dry-erase sheet or on the first line of the Magic Word Chain worksheet. (Make sure they say the sounds as they write.) After checking that everyone spelled the word correctly, say: "Now, change the word ____ to ____." Monitor students' spelling again and then say: "Now, change the word ____ to ____." Repeat for the remaining words on the chain. For example:

> "Write the word *man*. Now, change *man* to *fan*. Change *fan* to *fin*. Now, change *fin* to *fig*."

Word Chain Lists

CVC Words

Turn a fox into a pig!	Turn a cat into a dog!	Turn a rat into a dog!	Turn a pig into a bat!	Turn a dog into a cat!	Turn a dog into a fox!
fox	cat	rat	pig	dog	dog
fix	sat	rot	pin	dig	hog
fit	hat	cot	pen	dug	hot
fat	hit	cut	pet	hug	pot
sat	hid	cup	pat	hut	pit
sag	lid	cub	sat	hub	hit
bag	lit	hub	sad	cub	sit
wag	lot	hug	had	cut	six
wig	dot	hog	hat	cot	fix
pig	dog	dog	bat	cat	fox

Turn a bat into a hen!	Turn a bat into a bug!	Turn a hen into a bat!	Turn a bug into a rat!	Turn an ox into a cat!	Turn a dog into a hen!
bat	bat	hen	bug	ox	dog
bit	bet	den	rug	fox	dig
fit	bit	pen	rag	fix	did
sit	hit	pin	ran	fit	lid
sat	hat	fin	run	bit	led
fat	had	fit	bun	big	bed
fan	tad	pit	bin	bug	bet
pan	tag	sit	bit	bag	pet
pen	tug	sat	bat	bat	pen
hen	bug	bat	rat	cat	hen

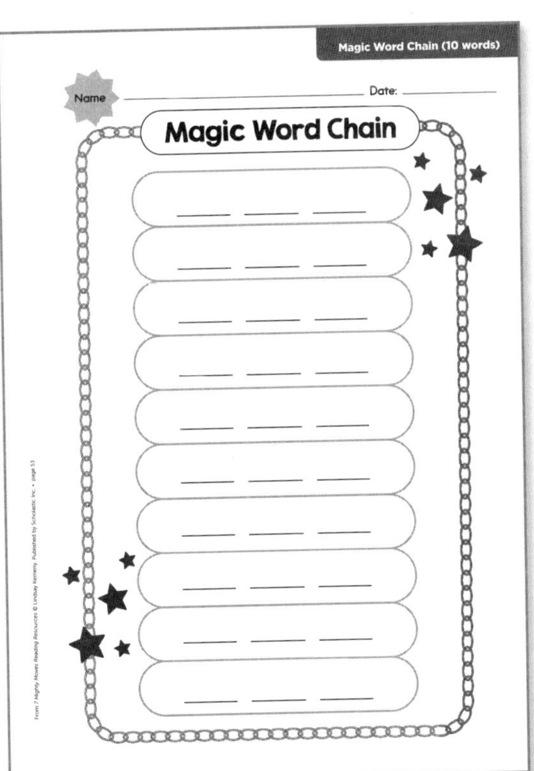

Variation: Another option is to tell students the exact letter to change instead of the phoneme. For example:

> "Write the word *man*. Now, change the *m* to *f*. What's the new word?" (*fan*)
> "Now, change the *a* to *i*. What's the new word?" (*fin*)

You can switch between these two tasks as you see fit. I spend more time on the original activity because it is a more difficult phonemic awareness task. In this activity, students need to segment the phonemes, isolate the one that changed, substitute the new phoneme, write the correct spelling, and then blend them back together. The variation is a bit easier but is also valuable because it turns the task into more of a decoding activity. In the variation, you give the specific letters to change, not the full word. Students must then blend the sounds to decode the word.

Differentiation Tips

If students have difficulty, consider the following scaffolds.

- Use words with fewer phonemes.
- Use sound boxes (page 55).
- Say the word slowly and point to the letters for the child. Emphasize the sound that changed as you point to it. For example, say: "Listen to the word *sip*. *Sssiiiipp*." (Point to the letters as you say them.) "I want you to change *siiiip* to *saaaaaap*." (Point to the letters again as you emphasize the /a/ sound.) "Which sound changed? Yes, that's right. We need to change the middle letter. What letter says /a/? Yes, the *a*. Erase that *i* and put the *a*. Nice job!"
- Have students use magnetic letters instead of writing the word.

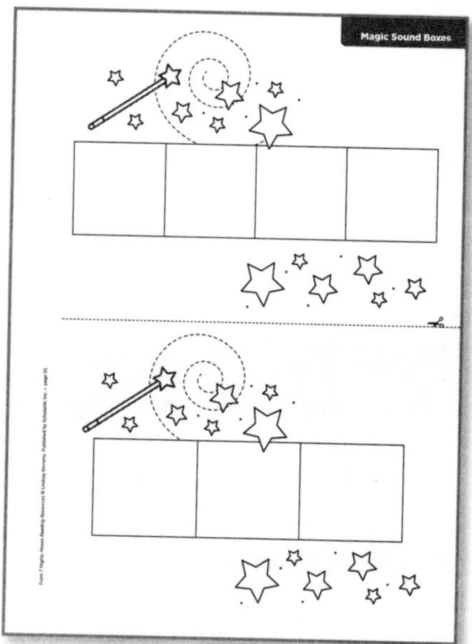

To make the activity more challenging, try these.

- Use words with more phonemes.
- Use words with consonant clusters.
- Have students write the words rather than use magnetic letters.
- Use words with more complex spelling patterns.

CVC Words

Turn a fox into a pig!	Turn a cat into a dog!	Turn a rat into a dog!	Turn a pig into a bat!	Turn a dog into a cat!	Turn a dog into a fox!
fox	cat	rat	pig	dog	dog
fix	sat	rot	pin	dig	hog
fit	hat	cot	pen	dug	hot
fat	hit	cut	pet	hug	pot
sat	hid	cup	pat	hut	pit
sag	lid	cub	sat	hub	hit
bag	lit	hub	sad	cub	sit
wag	lot	hug	had	cut	six
wig	dot	hog	hat	cot	fix
pig	dog	dog	bat	cat	fox

Turn a bat into a hen!	Turn a bat into a bug!	Turn a hen into a bat!	Turn a bug into a rat!	Turn an ox into a cat!	Turn a dog into a hen!
bat	bat	hen	bug	ox	dog
bit	bet	den	rug	fox	dig
fit	bit	pen	rag	fix	did
sit	hit	pin	ran	fit	lid
sat	hat	fin	run	bit	led
fat	had	fit	bun	big	bed
fan	tad	pit	bin	bug	bet
pan	tag	sit	bit	bag	pet
pen	tug	sat	bat	bat	pen
hen	bug	bat	rat	cat	hen

CVC Words			Digraphs		
Turn a hen into a pig!	Turn a hog into a cat!	Turn a pig into a cod!	Turn a fish into cash!	Turn a fish into a ship!	Turn a chip into a bed!
hen	hog	pig	fish	fish	chip
pen	dog	big	dish	fin	chop
pet	dig	beg	dig	fun	hop
bet	big	bet	big	fan	hip
bed	bin	bit	fig	pan	sip
red	fin	hit	fit	pat	sit
rid	fan	hot	fat	pot	set
rig	fat	not	cat	pop	net
big	sat	cot	cap	shop	bet
pig	cat	cod	cash	ship	bed

Digraphs					
Turn a chip into a hog!	Turn a moth into a cat!	Turn a moth into a rat!	Turn a fish into a pig!	Turn a fish into a bug!	Turn a ship into a hen!
chip	moth	moth	fish	fish	ship
chop	math	math	fin	dish	shin
chap	mad	path	tin	dash	chin
sap	map	pad	tip	mash	chip
sat	mop	dad	ship	mush	sip
chat	hop	did	shin	much	sit
pat	top	rid	win	such	pit
hat	tap	red	with	sun	pin
hot	cap	rad	wig	bun	pen
hog	cat	rat	pig	bug	hen

Blends

Turn a flag into a rat!	Turn a frog into a pig!	Turn a slug into a rag!	Turn trash into a crab!	Turn a crab into a ham!	Turn a nest into a sloth!
flag	frog	slug	trash	crab	nest
flap	fog	slush	rash	crash	rest
flop	hog	slash	sash	clash	best
flip	hot	lash	stash	lash	bet
lip	lot	bash	mash	lush	pet
sip	plot	trash	mush	mush	pit
rip	pot	rash	rush	much	spit
trip	spot	rush	brush	such	spot
trap	spit	rug	crush	sum	slot
rap	pit	rag	crash	hum	sloth
rat	pig		crab	ham	

Turn a tent into a pig!	Turn a clam into a pig!	Turn a clam into a fox!	Turn a raft into a dish!	Turn a flag into a ship!	Turn a ship into a flag!
tent	clam	clam	raft	flag	ship
rent	clap	clap	rat	flap	sip
rant	clop	clip	brat	lap	slip
ant	cop	slip	brag	tap	slap
pant	cap	flip	rag	tip	slam
plant	lap	flop	rug	top	slim
plan	lag	flap	run	stop	slid
pan	log	lap	rush	slop	lid
pin	hog	lag	rash	sop	lad
pig	fog	log	dash	hop	lash
	fig	fog	dish	hip	flash
	pig	fox		ship	flag

ng/nk					
Turn a ring into a fang!	Turn a king into a swing!	Turn a king into a ring!	Turn a sink into a skunk	Turn a skunk into a tank!	Turn a tank into a ring!
ring	king	king	sink	skunk	tank
thing	thing	ping	rink	sunk	thank
ding	ring	pong	brink	sank	rank
dung	rung	long	blink	bank	drank
rung	hung	lung	blank	bang	drink
run	sung	rung	bank	rang	rink
pun	song	flung	bunk	ring	brink
bun	sing	slung	junk	rink	blink
sun	wing	sling	sunk	rank	slink
sung	swing	sing	skunk	tank	sling
sang		ring			sing
fang					ring

CVCe (a_e)			CVCe (i_e)		
Turn a bat into a rat!	Turn a plate into mud!	Turn a vase into tape!	Turn a bike into a kite!	Turn a bride into a dime!	Turn a pipe into a bike!
bat	plate	vase	bike	bride	pipe
cat	slate	case	hike	ride	ripe
cap	late	cake	hide	rid	rip
cape	fate	came	hid	rip	rim
came	fat	cape	hip	ripe	rid
same	mat	cap	tip	rise	ride
game	mate	lap	lip	wise	wide
tame	made	map	lit	wide	hide
tape	mad	tap	sit	tide	hike
tap	mud	tape	kit	time	like
rap			kite	dime	bike
rat					

CVCe (o_e)			CVCe (u_e and mixed)		
Turn a rope into a note!	Turn a rose into a stone!	Turn a home into a cod!	Turn a cube into a dude!	Turn a mule into a cub!	Turn a bike into a bride!
rope	rose	home	cube	mule	bike
nope	pose	hose	cute	rule	hike
mope	chose	hope	cut	ruse	hid
mop	choke	hop	cub	fuse	had
hop	poke	mop	tub	use	mad
shop	spoke	mope	tube	muse	made
shot	smoke	mole	tune	mute	mode
pot	stoke	mode	dune	cute	rode
not	stove	code	duke	cut	rod
note	stone	cod	dude	cub	rid
					ride
					bride

CVCe (mixed)					
Turn a stone into a cat!	Turn a robe into a plate!	Turn a kite into a home!	Turn a rope into a cup!	Turn a sled into a chip!	Turn a dime into a cape!
stone	robe	kite	rope	sled	dime
stove	rode	kit	hope	slid	lime
stoke	code	hit	hop	slide	slime
smoke	cod	hive	top	side	slim
spoke	rod	hide	tap	wide	slam
spike	rot	hid	tape	tide	slap
pike	rat	had	shape	time	sap
pile	rate	hat	cape	dime	tap
pale	late	hot	cap	dim	tape
pal	plate	hop	cup	dip	cape
pat		hope		chip	
cat		home			

r-Controlled Vowels					
Turn a shark into a pot!	Turn a pot into a hat!	Turn a farm into a star!	Turn a fork into a horn!	Turn a store into a fort!	Turn a car into a fork!
shark	pot	farm	fork	store	car
hark	pat	far	for	score	card
bark	part	car	fort	sore	cart
barn	park	cart	sort	chore	cat
yarn	shark	chart	port	core	mat
yard	mark	mart	pore	more	mart
card	mart	tart	tore	shore	mark
cod	dart	start	torn	short	shark
pod	art	stark	corn	sort	park
pot	at	star	horn	fort	pork
	hat				fork

r-Controlled Vowels			Vowel Teams		
Turn a corn into a fork!	Turn a star into a shirt!	Turn a shirt into a ship!	Turn rain into a snail!	Turn a brain into a tray!	Turn clay into hay!
corn	star	shirt	rain	brain	clay
thorn	tar	short	brain	rain	lay
horn	tart	port	braid	pain	ray
born	part	part	raid	pen	gray
bore	port	park	paid	ten	tray
shore	fort	spark	pail	hen	pray
tore	sport	shark	mail	he	play
store	sort	sharp	tail	hay	lay
sore	short	shop	nail	say	way
sort	shirt	ship	snail	stay	sway
fort				stray	say
fork				tray	hay

Vowel Teams					
Turn feet into a seed!	**Turn a bee into a sheep!**	**Turn a seal into a tree!**	**Turn a goat into a toad!**	**Turn a toad into a boat!**	**Turn a pie into snow!**
feet	bee	seal	goat	toad	pie
sheet	beep	seat	moat	road	tie
sheep	beet	meat	coat	rod	lie
shop	bet	meal	coach	rid	low
hop	beg	mean	roach	ride	flow
hot	bog	men	rich	hide	blow
not	bop	me	rip	hid	bow
net	shop	see	lip	had	show
wet	hop	tee	lid	hat	tow
wed	hip	tree	led	mat	stow
weed	ship		load	moat	slow
seed	sheep		toad	boat	snow

Vowel Teams			Long and short oo		
Turn snow into a bow!	**Turn soap into a meal!**	**Turn feet into toast!**	**Turn a book into wood!**	**Turn a spoon into a roof!**	**Turn a stool into a moon!**
snow	soap	feet	book	spoon	stool
stow	sip	fight	nook	soon	tool
slow	ship	might	took	toon	fool
low	shop	meat	look	tool	pool
glow	sharp	beat	cook	pool	pal
flow	harp	bat	rook	pal	pad
flown	heap	boat	hook	pat	pod
blown	heal	coat	hood	rat	mod
blow	heat	coast	good	root	mood
bow	meat	roast	wood	room	moon
	meal	toast		roof	

Variant Vowels

Turn a claw into a paw!	Turn a fawn into a pan!	Turn a coin into a bat!
claw	fawn	coin
flaw	lawn	join
draw	pawn	joint
raw	pan	point
row	pin	paint
grow	pine	pant
glow	shine	pan
low	shin	pat
law	thin	cat
paw	tin	bat
	tan	
	pan	

Turn a coin into a goat!	Turn a clown into a pig!	Turn an owl into a boy!
coin	clown	owl
can	crown	ow
cash	drown	cow
dash	drain	wow
lash	rain	how
flash	ran	pow
flat	an	pay
float	at	say
gloat	out	soy
goat	pout	toy
	pit	boy
	pig	

Name ______________________ Date: ______________

Magic Word Chain

______ ______ ______

______ ______ ______

______ ______ ______

______ ______ ______

______ ______ ______

______ ______ ______

______ ______ ______

______ ______ ______

______ ______ ______

______ ______ ______

Name ______________________________ Date: ____________

Magic Word Chain

_____ _____ _____ _____

_____ _____ _____ _____

_____ _____ _____ _____

_____ _____ _____ _____

_____ _____ _____ _____

_____ _____ _____ _____

_____ _____ _____ _____

_____ _____ _____ _____

_____ _____ _____ _____

_____ _____ _____ _____

_____ _____ _____ _____

_____ _____ _____ _____

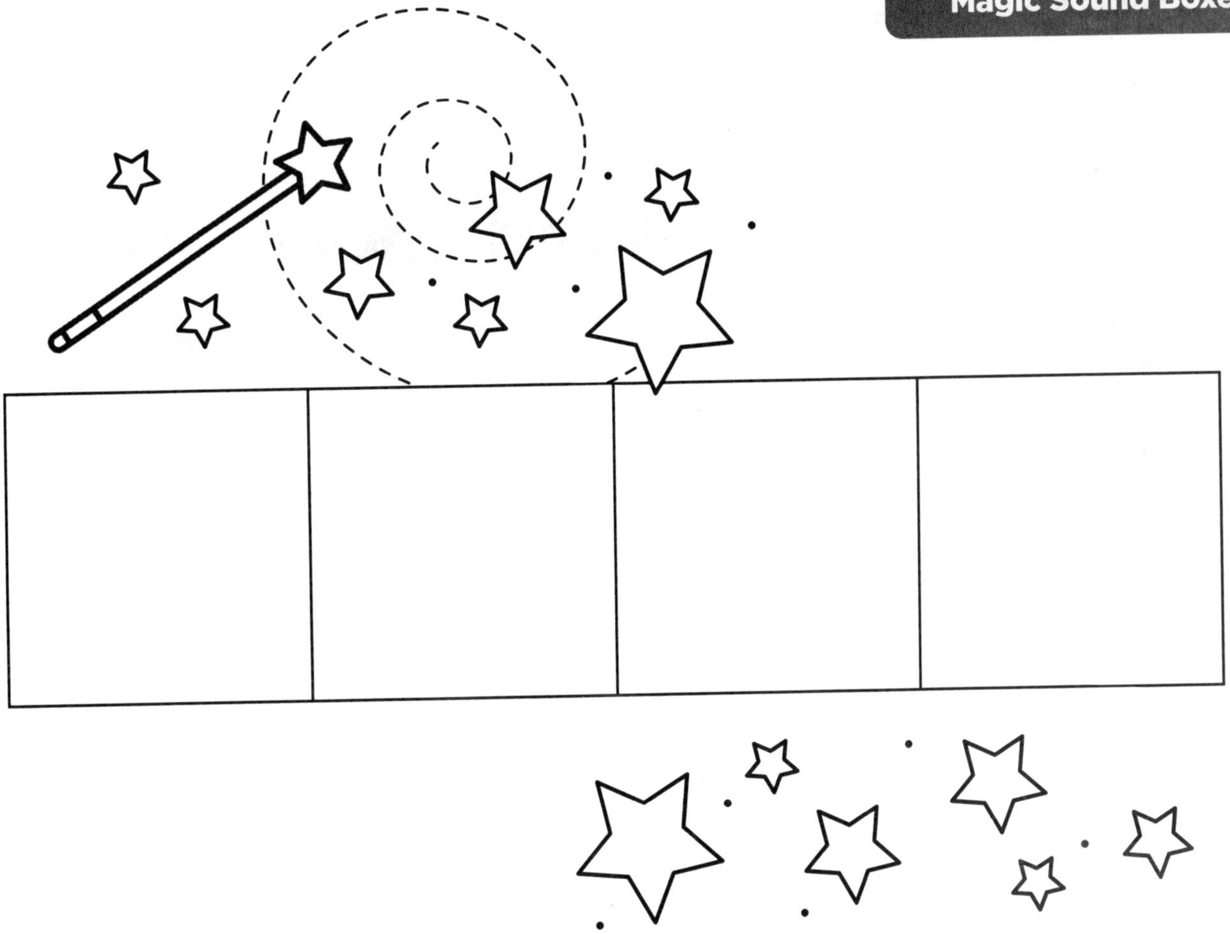

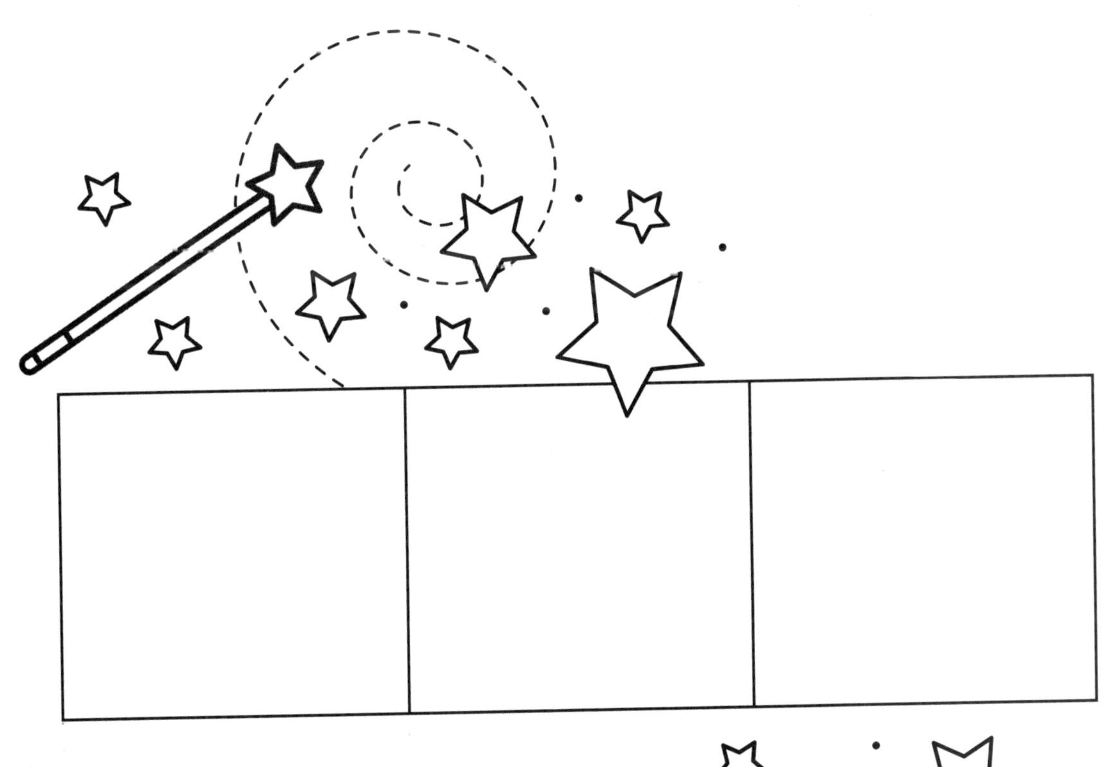

MOVE 2

Teach Phonics Explicitly and Systematically

Move 2 downloadables are available here.

In my early years as a teacher, I thought I was teaching phonics well. But the truth is I didn't understand what good phonics instruction looked like. I was facilitating phonics activities rather than actually teaching my students the code of the English language. Now I know that I need to follow a scope and sequence of phonics skills so students don't have holes in their knowledge. I also know that research strongly supports the use of explicit and systematic methods. In addition, I've increased opportunities for students to respond in my phonics lessons to boost engagement and learning. Students' responses can be verbal, such as saying the sound a grapheme represents in unison; written, such as writing a word that you dictate; or physical, such as making a gesture or pointing to a word.

Phonics instruction should include:

- explicit lessons in phoneme-grapheme correspondences
- explicit instruction in blending phonemes to read words and segmenting phonemes to spell words
- substantial practice opportunities to apply those skills

Let's review key points about Move 2.

- Research strongly supports explicit and systematic phonics.
- Using an incidental approach to phonics can leave students with gaping holes in their phonics knowledge.
- Systematic phonics relies on a clear and organized scope and sequence that progresses from simple to complex skills.
- Explicit instruction means precise directions and step-by-step procedures.
- Phonics lessons should follow an "I Do, We Do, You Do" approach.
- Allowing students to respond frequently during lessons keeps them engaged and enhances learning. It also reduces disruptive behavior.
- The sounds in English can be represented with one to four letters. Explicit instruction in those sounds and their spellings is essential to cracking the code.
- Teachers who have a deep understanding of the code are more effective in helping their students learn to read and spell.
- Phonics can be "drill and thrill"!

MOVE 2: Routines and Resources

RESOURCE		PAGE
2.A	Phonics Lesson Plan Template	58
2.B	Alphabet Practice Pages	62
2.C	Word Lists by Phonics Skills	89
2.D	Dictation Sheets for Spelling Words and Writing Sentences	99
2.E	"Show What You Know" Assessments	106
2.F	Vowel Tents and Vowel Intensive Exercise	110
2.G	Word Sorts to Build Spelling Skills	116
2.H	Secret Password to Review Phonics Skills	124

KEEP Facilitating *effective* word work activities for practice of previously taught skills.

STOP  Using an incidental, haphazard approach to phonics.

START  Teaching phonics in a systematic and explicit way.

Habits of Teachers Who Practice Explicit and Systematic Phonics Instruction

What they do:

- Follow a clear sequence of phonics skills, progressing from simple to complex.
- Leave nothing to chance.
- Use a program that connects and unifies skills.
- Establish routines.
- Follow a step-by-step procedure.
- Gradually release responsibility using the "I Do, We Do, You Do" approach.
- Break down critical content into manageable chunks.
- Teach interactively, giving students frequent opportunities to respond.
- Give students meaningful and judicious practice opportunities.

What they don't do:

- Teach concepts only as they come up.
- Expect students to discover basic phonics concepts on their own.
- Work without a reliable scope and sequence.
- Work without established routines.
- Give phonics activities instead of providing solid instruction.

2.A Phonics Lesson Plan Template

Use for: Students who are learning to read and/or spell accurately

Length of Activity: 30 minutes

Materials:

- Teacher: Phonics Lesson Plan Template (pages 60–61)
- Students: dry-erase boards and markers or Dictation Sheets (pages 101–102), Phonics Word Lists (pages 90–98), decodable passage

Teaching phonics explicitly and systematically transformed my classroom. Phonics instruction should teach phoneme-grapheme correspondences—blending those phonemes and graphemes to read words, segmenting them to write words—and offer plenty of practice time for students to apply those skills. Providing students with lots of opportunities to respond during these lessons means not only are they engaged, but they're also actively learning and decoding words with confidence. Ensuring purposeful practice helps students develop automaticity with the skills you're teaching. If you don't have a phonics program or need to boost your current one, these reproducibles are here to help.

Directions

The two versions of the Phonics Lesson Plan Template can be used for small- and whole-group instruction. Remember: Covering all components is critical, but the order can be flexible. Choose the plan you like best and arrange the components to fit your needs.

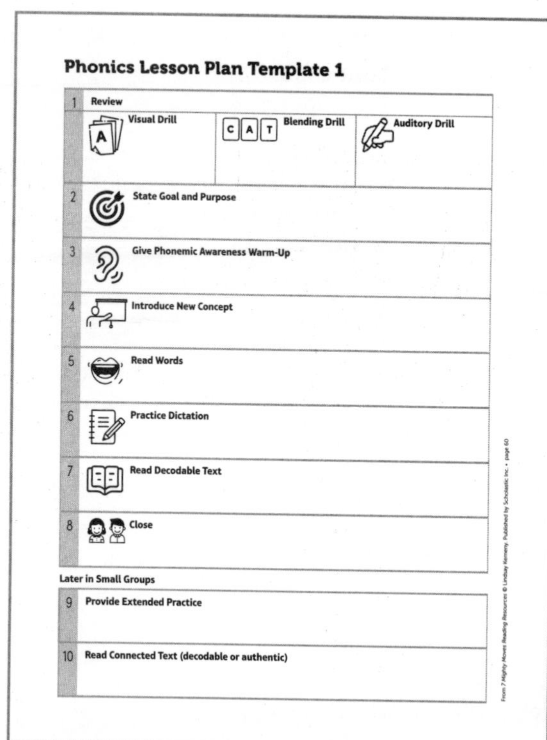

Phonics Lesson Plan Template 1

1 Review
- Visual Drill
- Blending Drill
- Auditory Drill

2 State Goal and Purpose

3 Give Phonemic Awareness Warm-Up

4 Introduce New Concept

5 Read Words

6 Practice Dictation

7 Read Decodable Text

8 Close

Later in Small Groups

9 Provide Extended Practice

10 Read Connected Text (decodable or authentic)

From 7 Mighty Moves Reading Resources © Lindsay Kemeny. Published by Scholastic Inc. • page 60

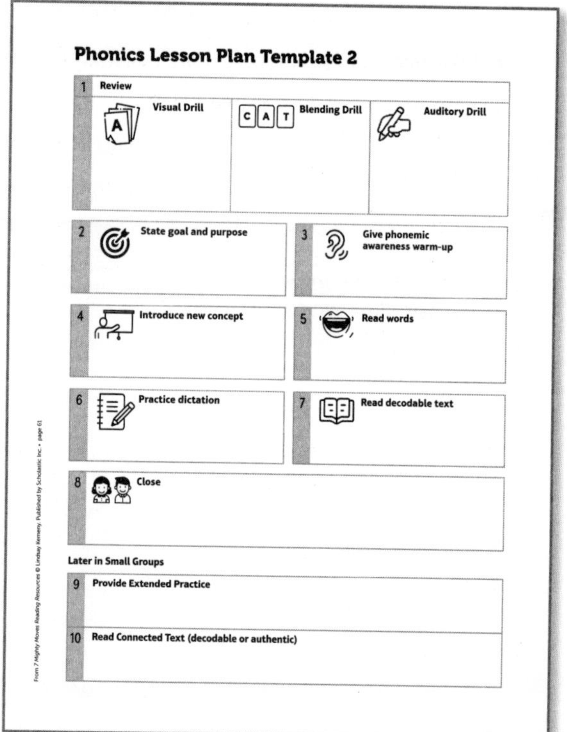

Phonics Lesson Plan Template 2

1 Review
- Visual Drill
- Blending Drill
- Auditory Drill

2 State goal and purpose

3 Give phonemic awareness warm-up

4 Introduce new concept

5 Read words

6 Practice dictation

7 Read decodable text

8 Close

Later in Small Groups

9 Provide Extended Practice

10 Read Connected Text (decodable or authentic)

From 7 Mighty Moves Reading Resources © Lindsay Kemeny. Published by Scholastic Inc. • page 61

Differentiation Tips

If students have difficulty, consider the following scaffolds.

- Provide additional practice opportunities in small groups or one-on-one.
- Use words with fewer phonemes (e.g., *far* instead of *smart*).
- Provide an alphabet strip when encoding.
- Sit them close to the teacher or a positive peer.
- Use magnetic letters instead of having students write the letters.
- Try successive blending, in which students blend the first two sounds together before adding on the last sound (e.g., *sat* is read /s/ /a/, /sa/ /t/, /sat/).
- When decoding a word list, have students point to and repeat the new sound-spelling before reading the word (e.g., /or/ *fort*; /or/ *corn*; /or/ *sport*).
- Use shorter decodable texts so students can read it several times in the allocated time.
- Use books with a higher percentage of decodable words.
- Use simpler sentences for sentence dictation; consider providing the spelling for any high-frequency words.
- Review, review, review.

To make the activity more challenging, try these.

- Use words with more phonemes (e.g., *stamp* instead of *sat*).
- Use words with more than one syllable (e.g., *garden* instead of *farm*).
- Use longer decodable texts.
- Use books/passages with a lower percentage of decodable words.
- For sentence dictation, use a longer and more sophisticated sentence that includes previously taught irregular high-frequency words.
- Have students compose their own sentence or paragraph using as many target skill words as possible.

Phonics Lesson Plan Template 1

1	**Review**
	Visual Drill / **Blending Drill** (C A T) / **Auditory Drill**
2	**State Goal and Purpose**
3	**Give Phonemic Awareness Warm-Up**
4	**Introduce New Concept**
5	**Read Words**
6	**Practice Dictation**
7	**Read Decodable Text**
8	**Close**

Later in Small Groups

9	**Provide Extended Practice**
10	**Read Connected Text (decodable or authentic)**

Phonics Lesson Plan Template 2

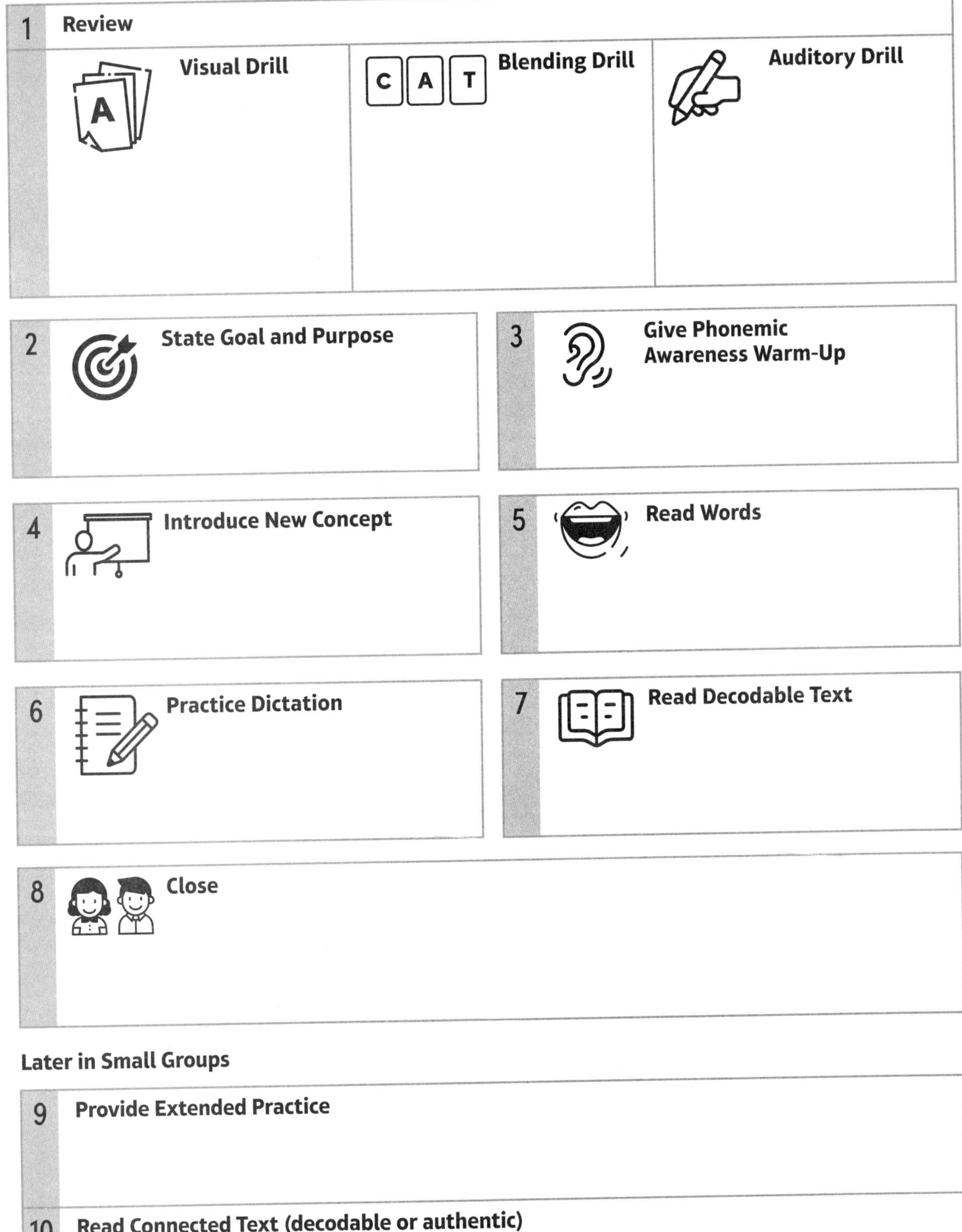

Later in Small Groups

9	Provide Extended Practice
10	Read Connected Text (decodable or authentic)

2.B Alphabet Practice Pages

Use for: Students who are learning to form and identify the letters of the alphabet

Length of Activity: 10 minutes

Materials:

- Students: Alphabet Letter of the Day practice (pages 63–88), pencils

Teaching correct letter formation is an important part of early literacy instruction. Becoming familiar with the critical features of letters helps students better recognize them (Reutzel et al., 2019). I decided to create my own alphabet handwriting pages exactly the way I wanted them.

I model how to form a letter and then have students write that letter three or four times. As they write, I walk around to ensure everyone is forming their letters correctly and following the lines on the page. I'd much rather see three or four nicely formed letters than a page full of sloppy or incorrect ones.

Directions

After introducing the sound and name of the letter, tell students they will now get to write it.

1. Point out the mouth picture on the paper and have students produce the sound.
2. Model the correct formation of the uppercase letter for students using simple language to describe the writing strokes.
3. Model again, but this time invite students to trace the letter with their finger on the paper.
4. Ask students to pick up their pencil and write the letter along with you.
5. After walking around to ensure they wrote the letter correctly, encourage them to write three more letters and circle their best one. Have them say the name and sound of the letter as they write.
6. Repeat these steps with the lowercase letter.
7. Finally, have students say the word that matches each of the pictures and circle the ones that start with the targeted letter.

Differentiation Tips

If students have difficulty, consider the following scaffolds.

- Have them use a pencil grip.
- Use a marker to place a dot at each place students should begin when they form the letter.
- Trace the baseline with a bold marker.
- Write the letter for them with a highlighter and have them trace it.

To make the activity more challenging, try this.

- Have students write a word that includes the targeted letter, ensuring all letters in the word are formed correctly.

Name

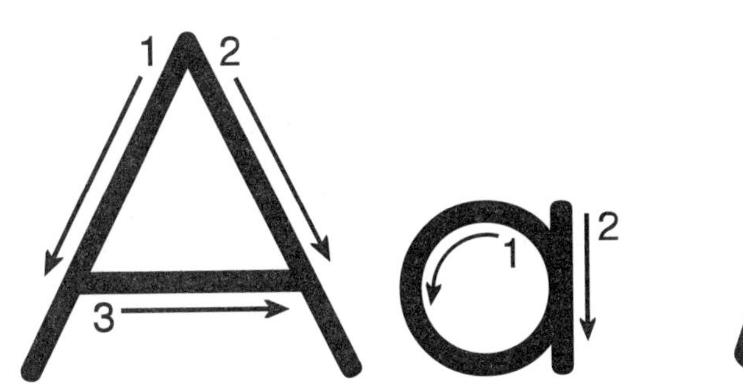

Write it

Say it

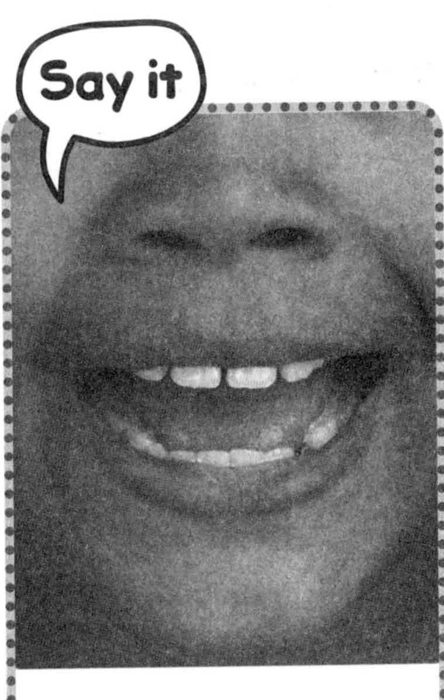

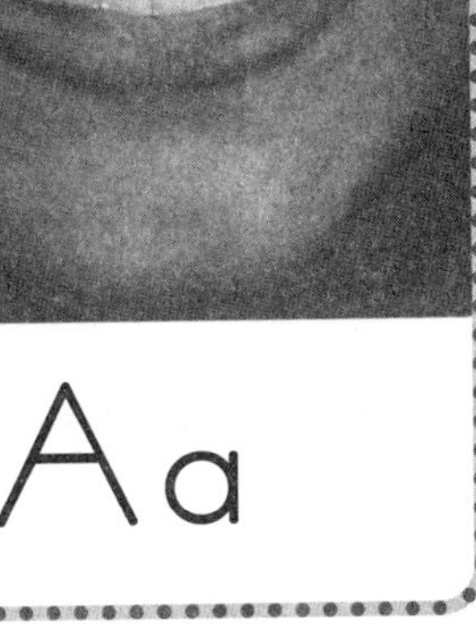

Circle it

Name

B

b

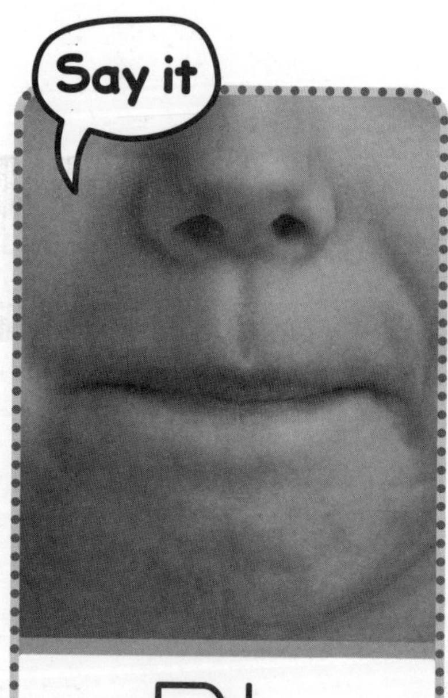

Name

C c

C

c

Say it

C c

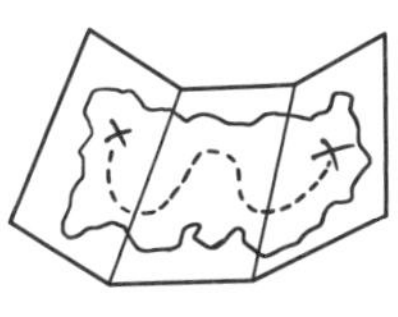

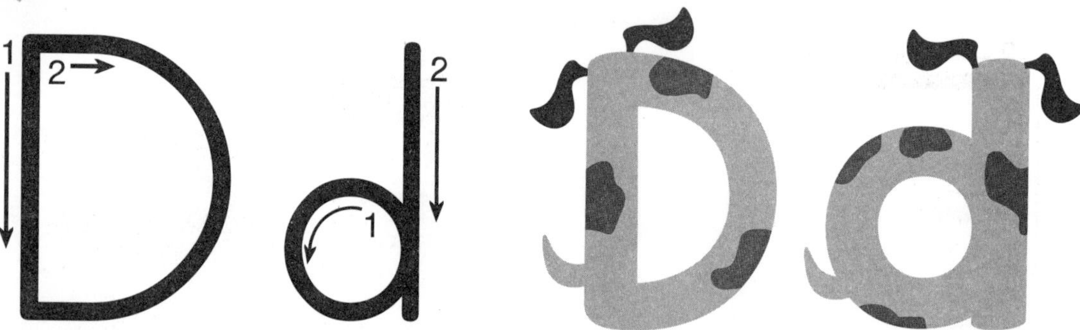

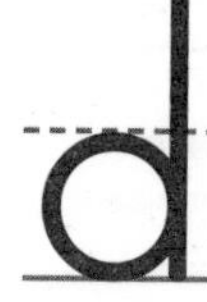

d

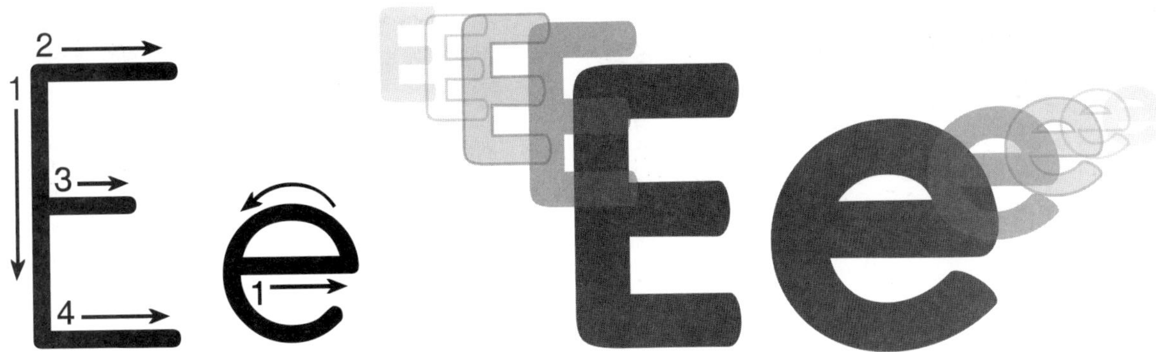

E

e

Circle it

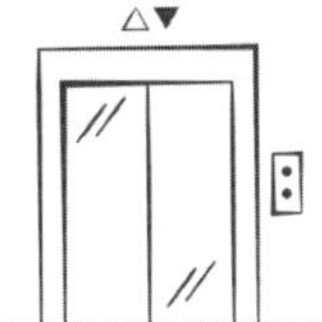

Name

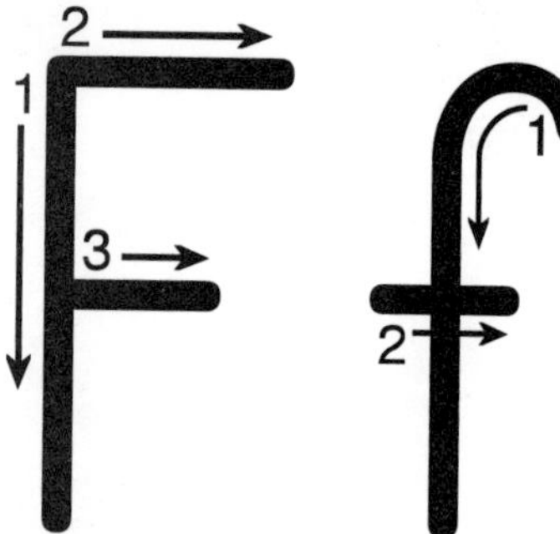

F

f

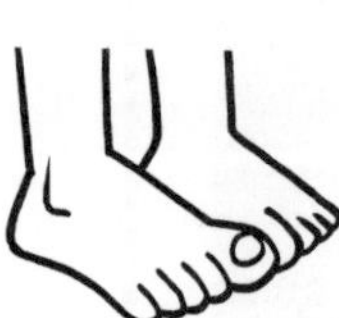

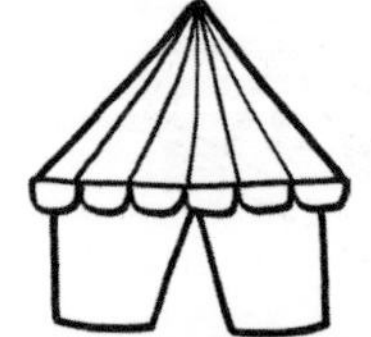

 •

Name

Write it

G

g

Say it

Gg

Circle it

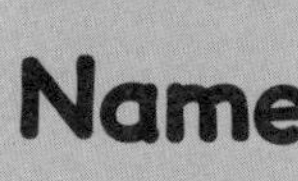
Name

1
2
3
1
2

Write it

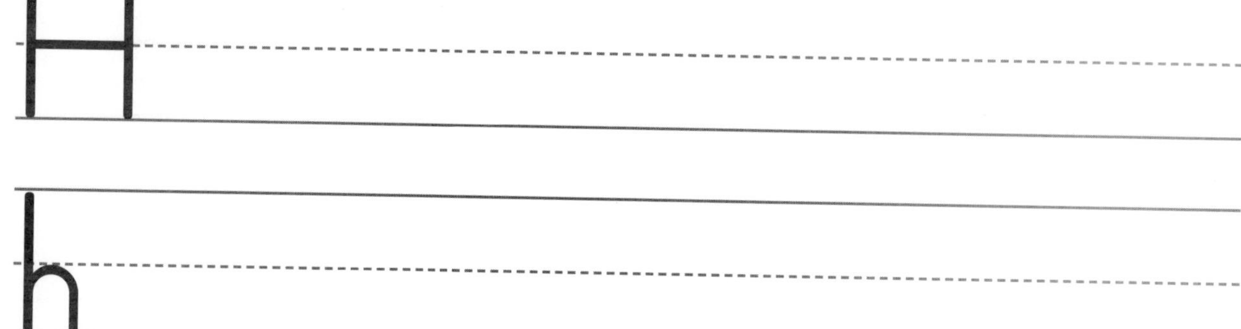
H
h

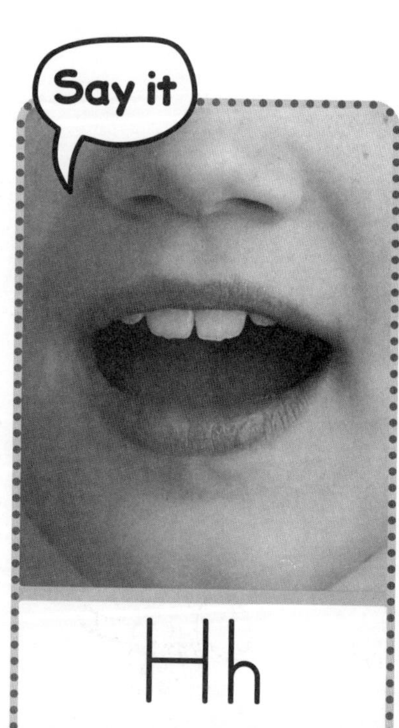
Say it
Hh

Circle it

Name

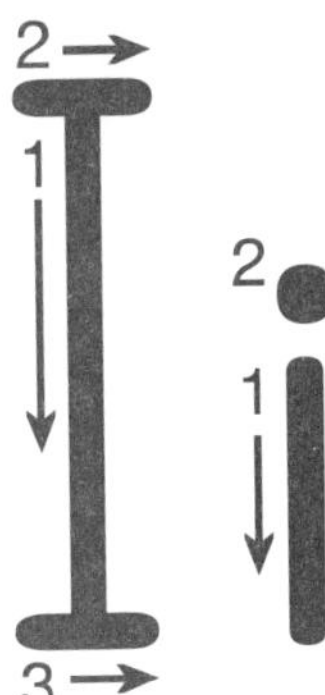

Write it

I

i

Say it

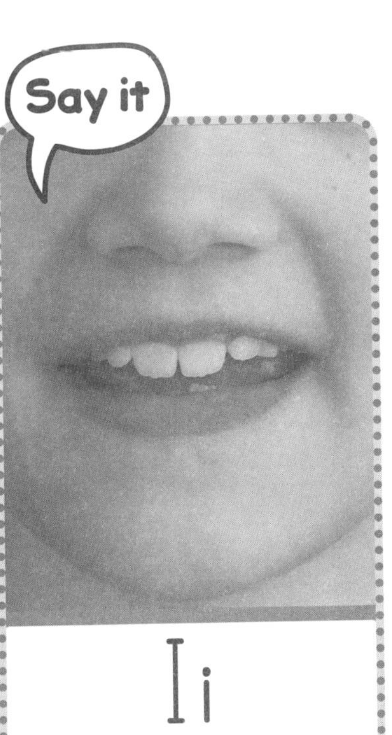

Circle it

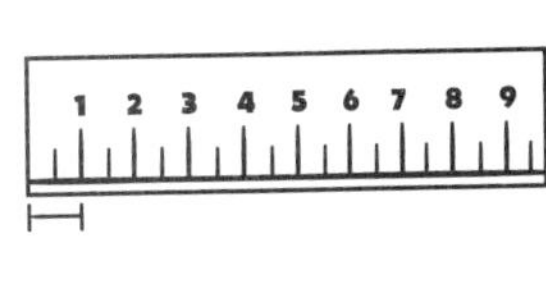

Name

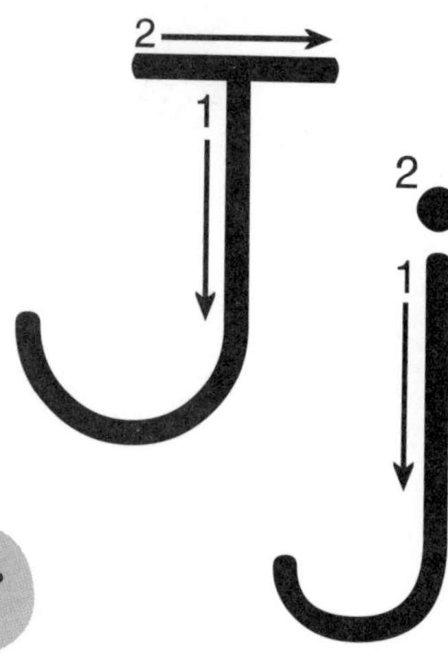

Write it

J

j

Say it

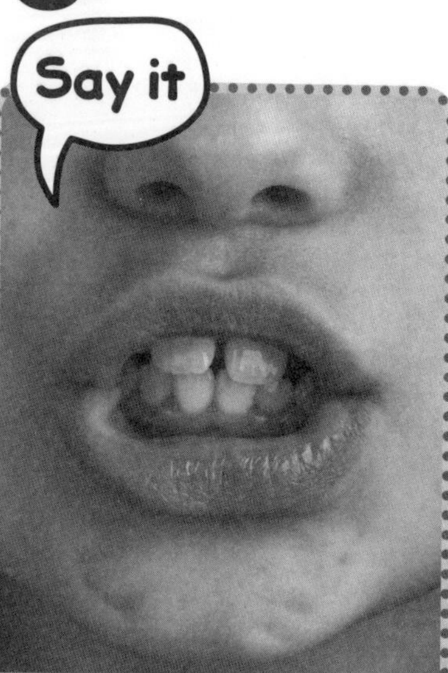

Circle it

Name

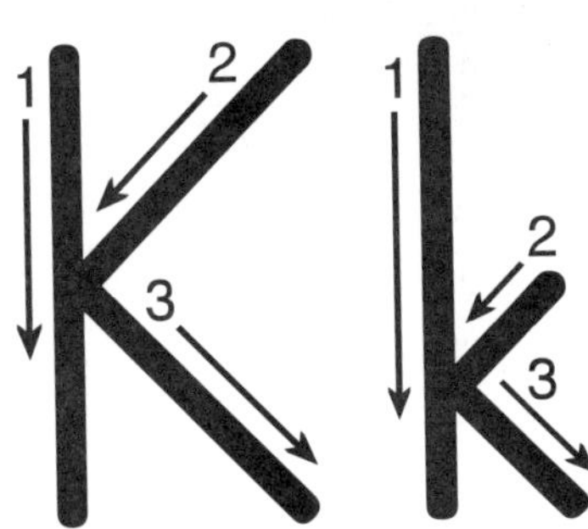

Write it

Say it

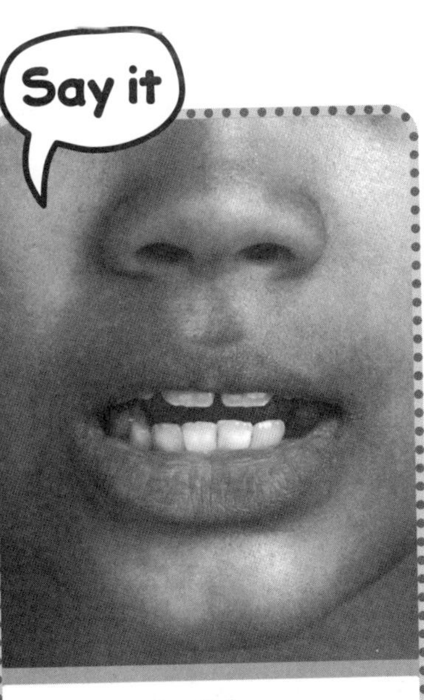

Kk

Circle it

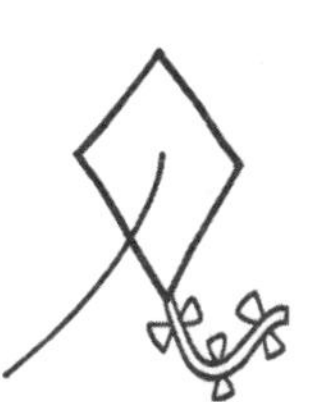

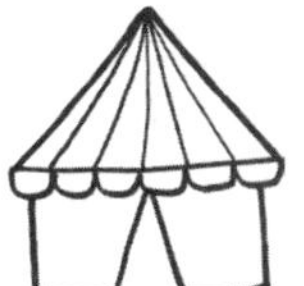

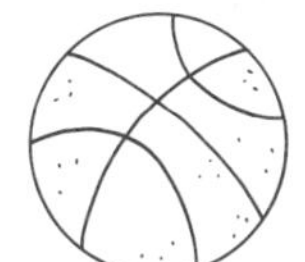

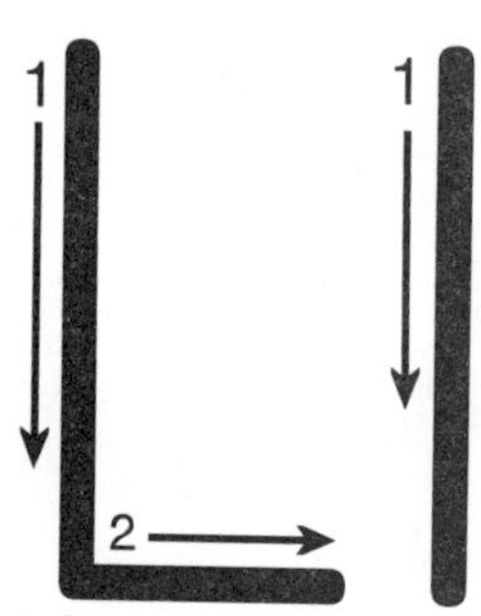

L

l

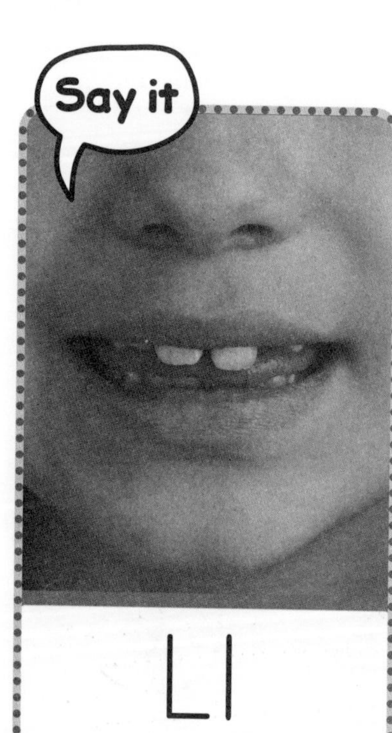

Name

M m Mm

M

m

Say it

Circle it

Name

N

n

Name

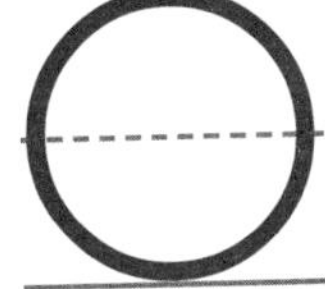

Say it

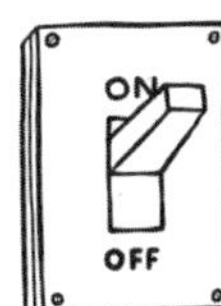

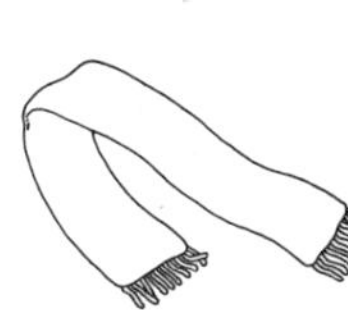

Name

Write it

P

p

Say it

Pp

Circle it

Name

Write it

Qu

qu

Say it

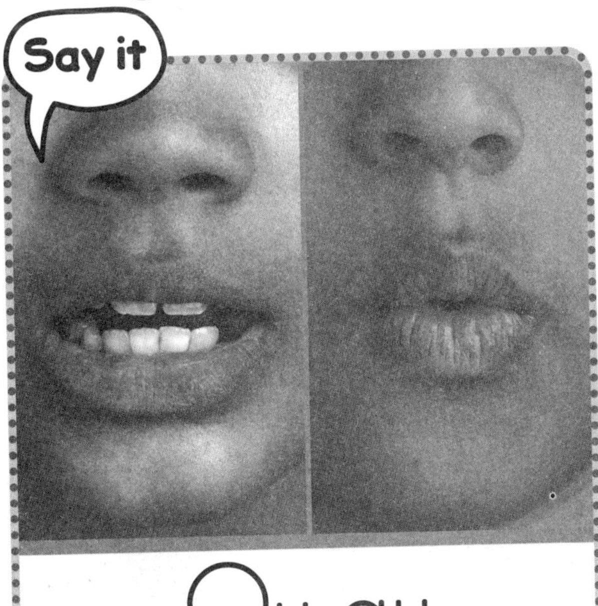

Qu qu

Circle it

Name

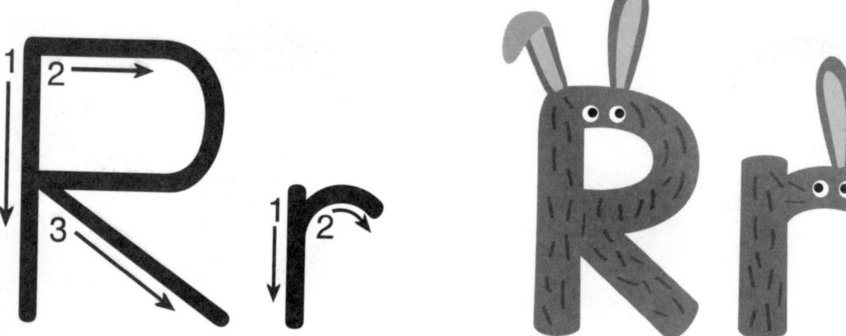

R

r

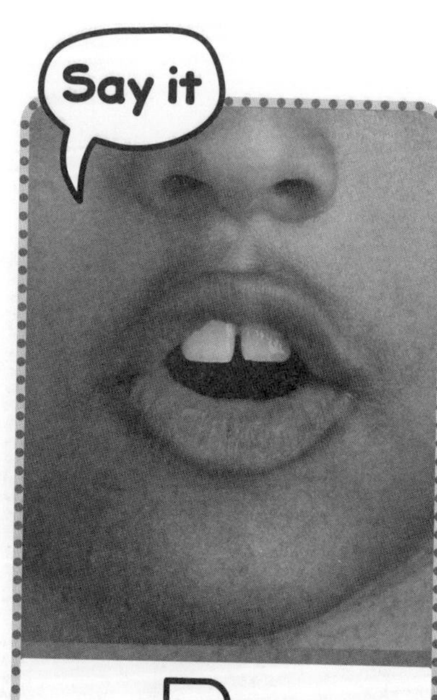

Name

Ss

Write it

S

s

Say it

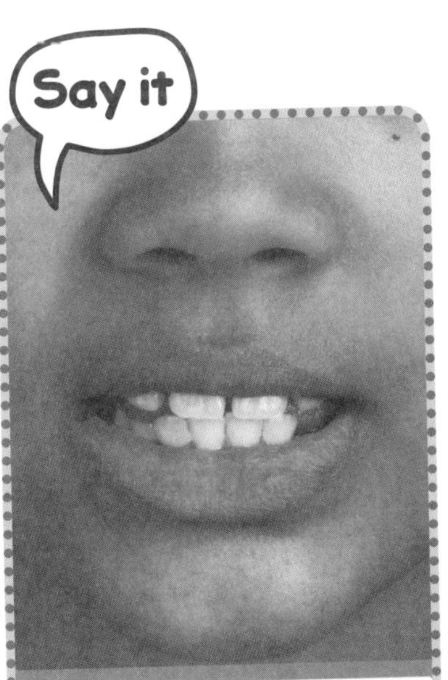

Ss

Circle it

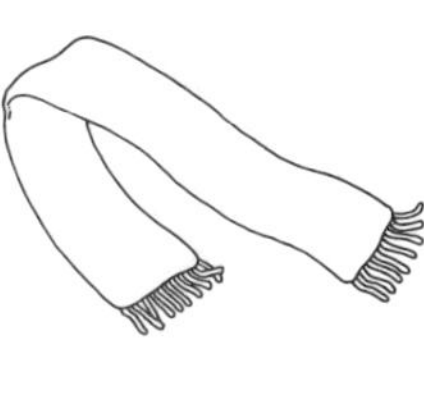

Name

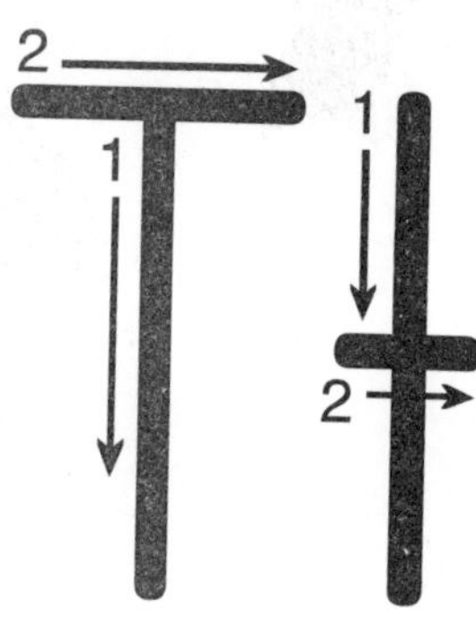

Write it

T

t

Say it

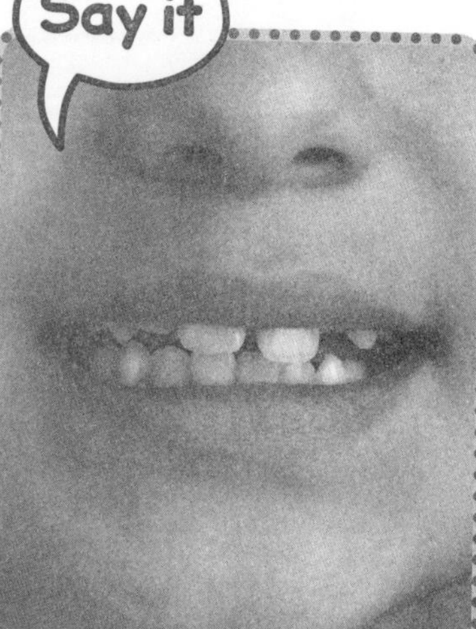

Tt

Circle it

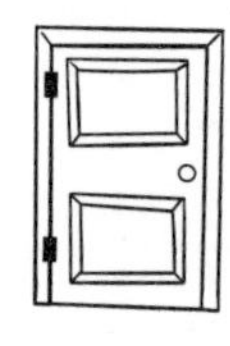
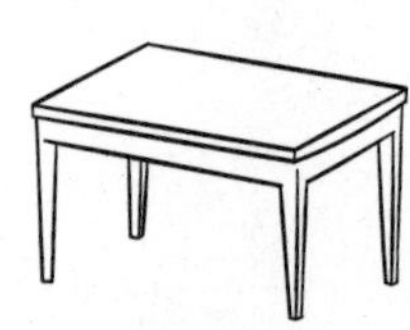
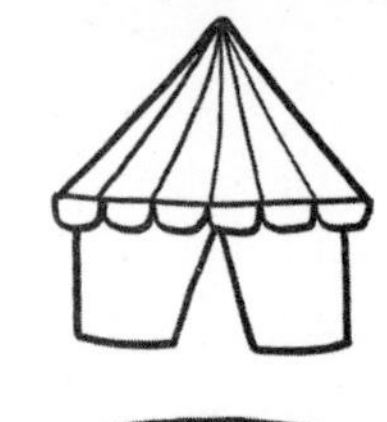
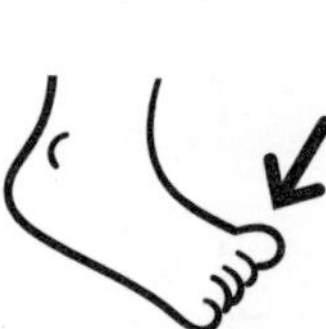

Name

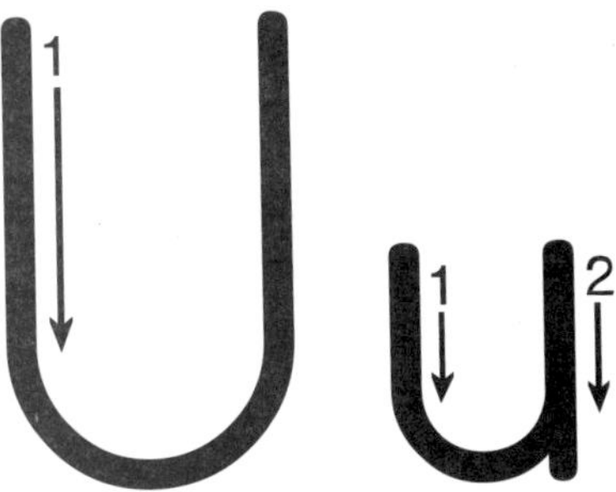

U

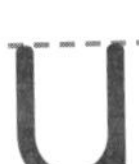

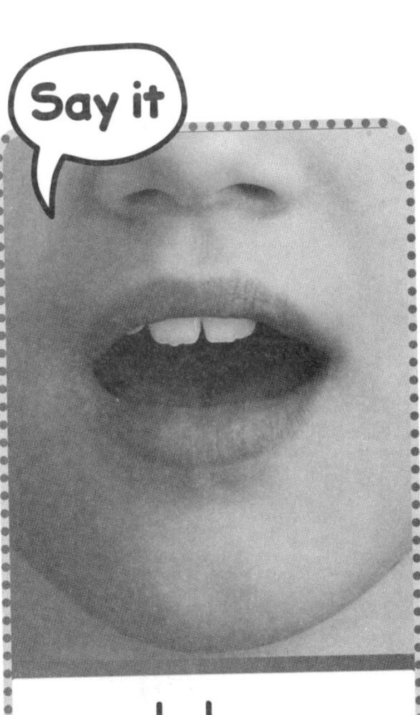

Name

Write it

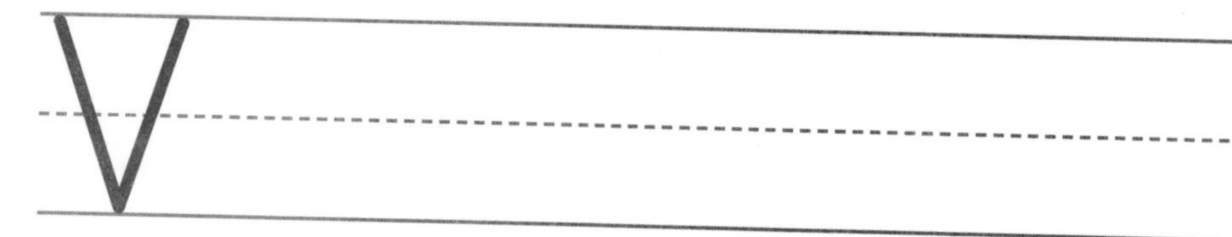

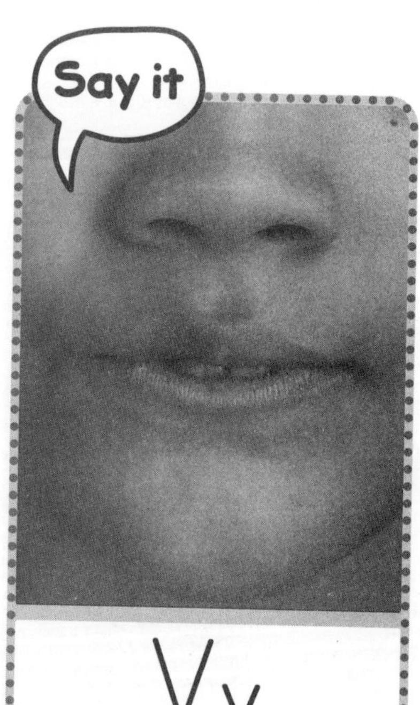

Name

1 2 3 4

W w

Ww

W

w

Name

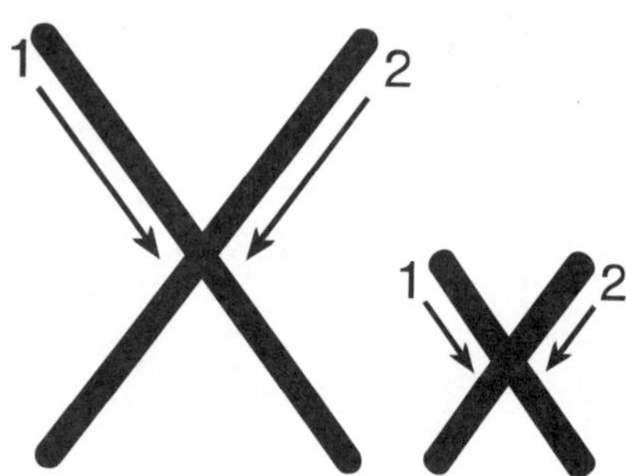

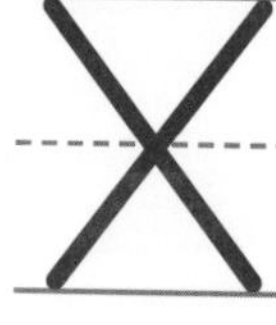

Say it

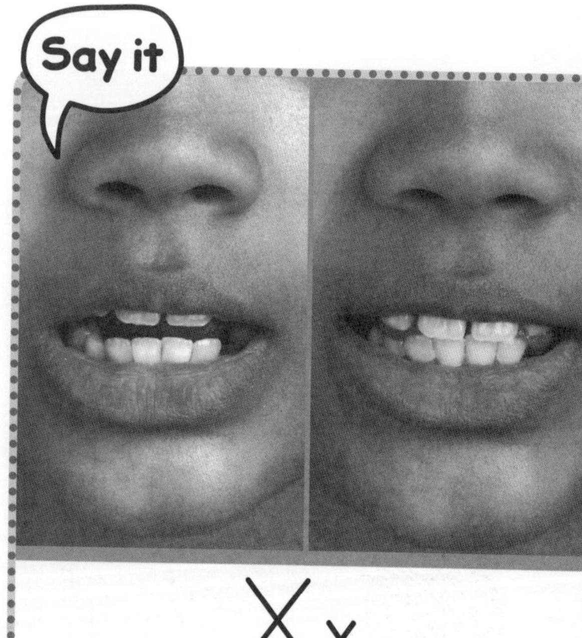

Circle it
(last letter)

Name

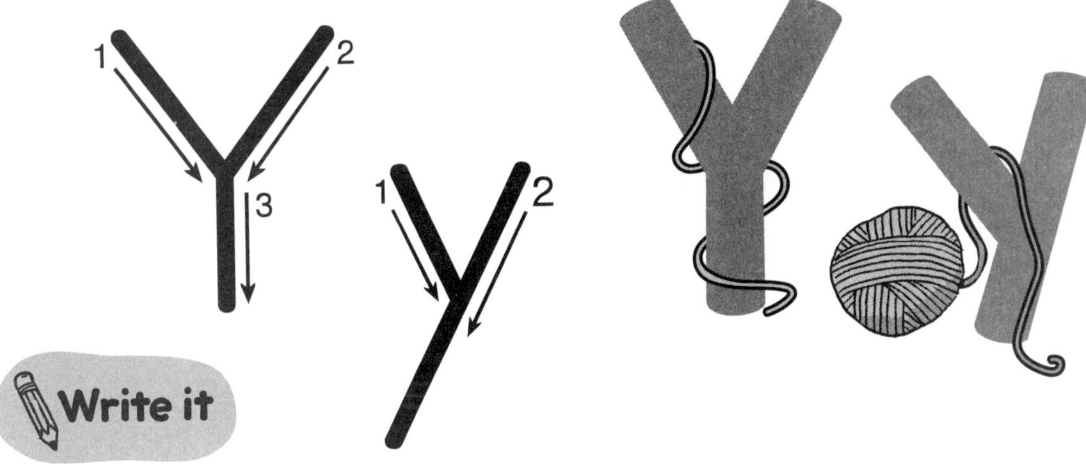

Write it

Y

y

Say it

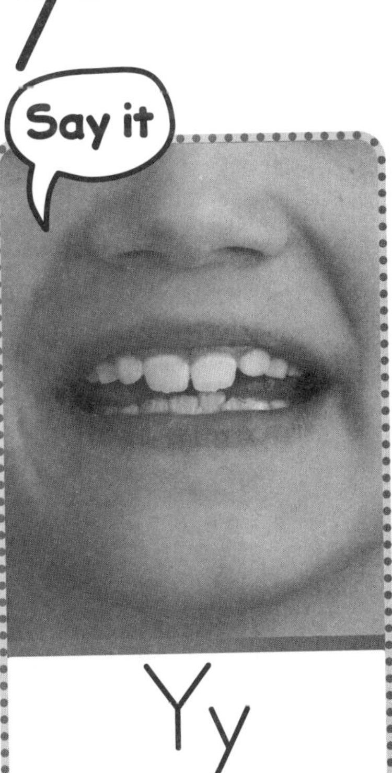
Yy

Circle it

Name

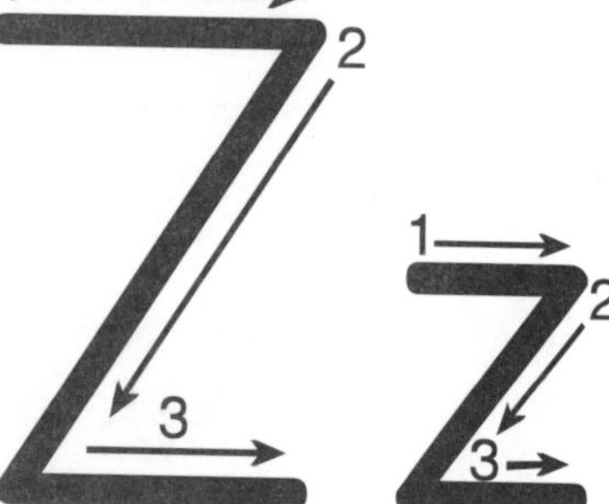

Write it

Z

z

Say it

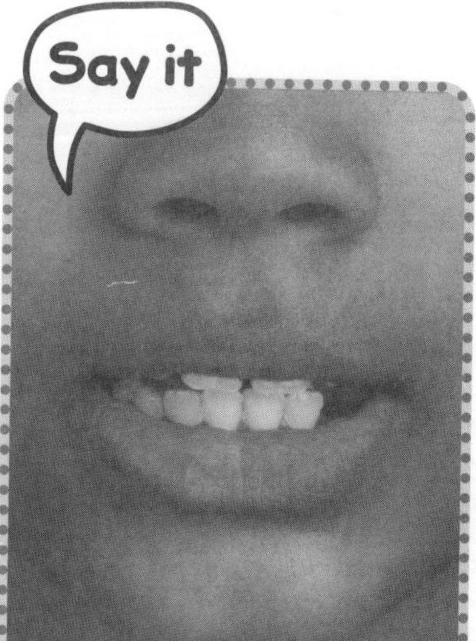

Circle it

Word Lists by Phonics Skills

Students need plenty of exposure to and practice in phonics skills to develop automaticity. I've created word lists that follow the graphemes students are learning in our phonics lessons. During these lessons, students read those lists with a partner.

I pair up students to read the word lists and ensure there is a stronger reader in each partnership. I walk around to monitor and provide help as needed. After both partners have read the list once, I have them repeat the process until I say to stop. We spend a few minutes reading word lists and then continue with our lesson.

Use for: Students who are learning to read accurately and with automaticity

Length of Activity: 2–4 minutes

Materials:

- Students: Word Lists (pages 90–98), Tic-Tac-Toe Writing Grid (optional, pages 104–105)

Directions

Choose a word list (pages 90–98) based on your target phonics skill and provide each child with a copy. Have Partner A (the stronger reader) read the list first, while Partner B follows along with a finger. Then have them switch roles so that Partner B reads the words and Partner A follows along with a finger. When Partner B finishes, Partner A takes another turn, and they repeat the procedure until you say "stop."

Variations: Here are other ways to use the phonics word lists.

- Send the lists home with students to practice with a caregiver.
- Use the activity in small-group lessons before reading a decodable text.
- Use the lists for dictation with partners. Partner A reads a word from the list, and Partner B spells the word. Then children can switch. Use the Tic-Tac-Toe Writing Grid (pages 104–105) for a fun variation.

Differentiation Tips

If students have difficulty, consider the following scaffolds.

- Use words with fewer phonemes.
- Use words with only one syllable.
- Encourage successive blending, in which students blend the first two sounds together before adding on the last sound (e.g., *sat* is read /s/ /a/, /sa/ /t/, /sat/).
- Have students underline and say the target skill in each word before reading the word.
- Provide more practice opportunities with a teacher or paraprofessional.

To make the activity more challenging, try these.

- Use words with more phonemes.
- Use words with more than one syllable.
- Encourage students to compose a sentence using as many of the words on the list as they can.

Short *a*	Short *e*	Short *i*	Short *o*	Short *u*
sat	fed	sip	sob	sun
map	men	sit	fog	mud
fat	net	fit	mop	nut
nap	hen	mix	nod	sum
ham	leg	hit	log	run
van	red	lid	hop	hug
yam	web	win	hot	hut
cat	yes	wig	cot	bus
bag	bed	dip	box	bug
can	pen	hid	top	cut
wag	ten	tin	job	cup
tap	jet	pig	pot	gum

l-Blends	r-Blends	s-Blends	Digraph ck	Digraph sh
sled	frog	smug	sock	shed
slim	grip	snap	neck	shin
slot	grin	slip	rock	shop
slid	prep	slid	duck	shut
flag	drip	slop	back	shell
fled	drum	stop	snack	ship
plus	drop	spot	stuck	wish
plan	crib	spin	block	rush
club	crab	skin	click	lash
clip	trip	skit	clock	dish
glad	trap	scan	trick	flash
glob	brag	swim	truck	crush

Digraph *ch*	Digraph *th* (unvoiced)	Digraph *th* (voiced)	Digraph Review	*-tch*
much	thin	than	shut	itch
such	thud	that	chop	fetch
rich	thick	them	bath	hutch
chin	math	then	with	pitch
chip	moth	this	chin	ditch
chop	with	thus	that	latch
chat	path	they	check	match
check	bath	their	shop	switch
chick	sloth	these	them	sketch
chest	cloth	those	chest	stitch
brunch	thump	thy	smash	snatch
ranch	tenth	the	crunch	crutch

-dge	-ing	-ng	-nk	a_e
edge	sing	sang	sank	save
fudge	ring	song	sink	same
judge	king	thing	sunk	shade
ledge	ding	lung	rink	shake
lodge	wing	long	honk	made
ridge	zing	rung	junk	bake
badge	swing	ring	chunk	tape
bridge	sting	hang	stink	gave
fridge	thing	hung	think	plate
pledge	fling	bang	thank	grade
smudge	bring	ding	blank	brake
sludge	cling	gong	drink	snake

i_e	*o_e*	*u_e*	VCe Review	*-ce*
side	rode	mule	tap	ice
ripe	rose	mute	tape	mice
ride	rope	rude	rid	nice
line	vote	rule	rode	lace
fine	home	fume	note	face
mine	joke	cube	not	rice
dime	globe	cute	rate	race
bike	froze	use	rat	pace
shine	broke	tube	cut	place
slide	spoke	tune	cute	price
spike	stone	June	dim	trace
quite	throne	flute	dime	twice

y as Long i	ar	or	er	ir
my	art	for	her	bird
by	far	fork	herd	girl
fly	car	sort	per	shirt
spy	march	porch	perk	birth
sly	card	torn	verb	fir
sky	barn	worn	term	firm
why	shark	horse	serve	chirp
try	park	short	stern	dirt
fry	dark	north	perch	first
cry	chart	force	swerve	skirt
dry	smart	shore	under	thirst
pry	start	more	winter	squirt

ur	r-Controlled Vowel Review	ai	ay	ee
fur	fort	rain	say	see
burn	card	wait	may	bee
hurt	first	sail	way	seed
turn	girl	chain	day	feet
purse	curb	mail	stay	week
curve	herd	paid	sway	sheep
blur	north	paint	play	teeth
spur	sharp	stain	clay	cheese
burst	sport	brain	gray	sleep
turtle	smart	snail	spray	sweet
further	garden	train	stray	speech
murmur	number	braid	maybe	green

ea	*oa*	*ow*	*igh*	**Short *oo***
sea	oat	row	sigh	nook
eat	soap	bow	high	shook
beach	soak	tow	thigh	foot
heat	load	show	light	look
leaf	loaf	flow	sight	wood
mean	boat	blow	right	hook
cheat	coat	grow	tight	hood
teach	goat	slow	flight	book
dream	toad	snow	fright	cook
steam	float	grown	bright	took
sneak	toast	bowl	sunlight	stood
please	throat	blown	tonight	brook

Long oo	aw/au	oi/oy	ou	ow
moon	saw	soil	out	now
food	paw	soy	ouch	how
soon	thaw	join	shout	cow
zoo	hawk	boy	south	town
too	haul	toy	couch	down
roof	pause	coin	cloud	frown
tooth	draw	ploy	sprout	growl
pool	claw	spoil	count	crowd
smooth	crawl	point	found	clown
spoon	yawn	moist	ground	crown
gloom	launch	joint	house	brown
bloom	straw	voice	round	scowl

Dictation Sheets for Spelling Words and Writing Sentences

2.D

Use for: Students who are learning to read and/or spell accurately

Length of Activity: 5–10 minutes

Materials:

- Teacher: lists of words and sentences for dictation (You can use the Phonics Word Lists on pages 90–98.)
- Students: dry-erase boards and markers, Dictation Sheet (pages 101–102 and online), Letter-Sound Mapping Sheet (page 103), Tic-Tac-Toe Writing Grid (pages 104–105)

Dictation is a powerful part of my phonics instruction. It helps students solidify new skills while reviewing past concepts. I constantly walk around and monitor my students as they write, providing immediate feedback. Dictation also offers a great opportunity to reinforce good handwriting by reminding students to use correct letter formation and spacing.

I love using dry-erase boards during this part of our phonics lesson because it's easy for me to see student responses and super simple for students to correct any mistakes they make. Paper and pencil work as well and are a great alternative if you don't have dry-erase boards. It's also nice to have records of students' writing to compare at a later time.

Directions

A routine for dictation ensures students feel successful as they practice applying phonics concepts to their writing. With a routine, you'll spend less time on transitions and more time on what's really important: learning.

Word Dictation Routine

Depending on your class, choose 6 to 12 words to dictate. Provide students with dry-erase boards and markers or the appropriate dictation paper. Then follow this step-by-step routine for dictating words.

1. Say to students: "The word is *ship...ship*."
2. Have students repeat the word: *ship...ship*.
3. Have students tap each sound with their thumb and fingers: /sh/ /i/ /p/
4. Use the word in a sentence: "I saw a *ship* in the ocean."
5. Say: "Now, say as you write the sounds in *ship*."
6. Have students spell the word while saying each sound. For example, for *ship*, they would say /sh/ while writing the letters *s* and *h*, /i/ as they write *i*, and /p/ as they write *p*.
7. Circulate to give students specific feedback as they write to ensure each one has spelled the word correctly. Then choose one child to write the word on the board. This motivates students and allows time for you to monitor responses.

Variations:

- For students who need more scaffolding, use the Letter-Sound Mapping Sheet (page 103). After tapping each sound with their thumb and finger, students should write the sound in each sound box, then write the whole word.
- Have students write their words on the Tic-Tac-Toe Writing Grid (pages 104–105). Afterward, they can play a quick game of tic-tac-toe with a partner. Make sure they read the word in the space they choose to put their X or O.

Sentence Dictation Routine

Follow this step-by-step routine for dictating sentences.

1. Say to students: "The sentence is: 'The ship has a red flag.'"
2. Have students repeat the sentence: "The ship has a red flag."
3. Say: "Let's say it again and count the words."
4. Repeat the sentence and hold up a finger for each word.
5. Ask students: "How many words?" (6)
6. Have students write the sentence while you walk around to assist. Repeat the sentence as many times as students need.
7. When they are finished, have students raise their hand for you to check. Once you've checked their sentence, they can draw a picture to match.

Differentiation Tips

If students have difficulty, consider the following scaffolds.

- Encourage children to say the sounds aloud as they write the word.
- Use words with fewer phonemes.
- Use one-syllable words.
- Use shorter, simpler sentences.
- Review high-frequency words immediately before students write the sentence.
- Provide a word card with the high-frequency word for them to copy.
- Provide an alphabet strip.
- Draw lines to represent each word in the sentence.
- Give students extra help by walking them through segmenting and spelling each word.
- Sit them close to the teacher or a positive peer.
- Provide a fill-in-the-blank sentence.

To make the activity more challenging, try these.

- Use words with more phonemes.
- Use words with more than one syllable.
- Use longer, more complex sentences.
- Use sentences that contain multisyllabic words.
- Use sentences with more irregular high-frequency words.
- Have students compose their own sentence or paragraph using as many target skill words as possible.

Name

Listen to the sounds!

1.

2.

3.

4.

5.

6.

Sentence:

Name

Listen to the sounds!

1.

2.

3.

4.

5.

6.

7.

8.

Sentences:

1.

2.

Name

Listen to the sounds!

Letter-Sound Mapping

How many sounds?

Write and read the word

Tic-Tac-Toe

Tic-Tac-Toe

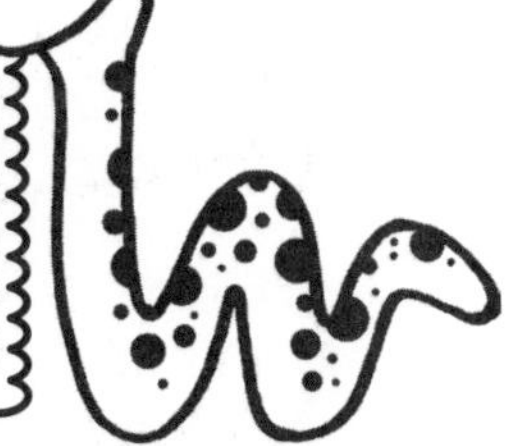

2.E "Show What You Know" Assessments

Use for: All students to build phonics skills

Length of Activity: 5–10 minutes

Materials:

- Teacher: list of words and sentences for assessment (based on your phonics curriculum)
- Students: "Show What You Know" assessment sheets (pages 107–109 and online), pencils

One way to assess students' phonics skills is by analyzing their writing. Administering an end-of-week "Show What You Know" spelling assessment can help you monitor students' knowledge, as well as their ability to apply the phonics concepts you have taught. This is not your typical spelling test, in which students memorize a list of words. In fact, you won't be giving students the words ahead of time. But you can let them know what phonics skill they will be asked to apply (for example, words with *-ng*). Do not give them a word with a spelling pattern you haven't taught. I also challenge students with one or two high-frequency (or "heart") words we've been working on to see if they can spell them correctly and identify any words where additional instruction may be needed.

If students miss something, it tells me the skills to work on with those students in small-group instruction. If a large majority of my students struggle with a skill, it tells me I need to address it again during the whole-class instruction.

Directions

Choose 5 to 12 words, depending on your students and the focus phonics skill. Pass out copies of the appropriate "Show What You Know" page. State each word and use it in the sentence. State the word again and allow time for students to write the word. Walk around to monitor students as they write, but do not immediately correct responses since it is an assessment.

Name

Show What You Know

1.
2.
3.
4.
5.
♥

Sentence:

Differentiation Tips

If students have difficulty, consider the following scaffolds.

- Encourage students to say the sounds as they write the word.
- Use words with fewer phonemes.
- Use words with one syllable.
- Allow more time to write the word.
- Encourage students to segment the word orally first.
- Assess fewer words.
- Provide lines for each word in the sentence.
- Reassure students that you just want to see what they know. I say, "It's okay if you don't know something. It just lets me know what I need to teach you."

To make the activity more challenging, try these.

- Use words with more phonemes (e.g., *blast* instead of *bat*).
- Use words with more than one syllable (e.g., *report* instead of *corn*).
- Use longer and more sophisticated sentences.
- Use sentences with more irregular high-frequency words.

Name

Show What You Know

1.

2.

3.

4.

5.

♥

Sentence:

Name

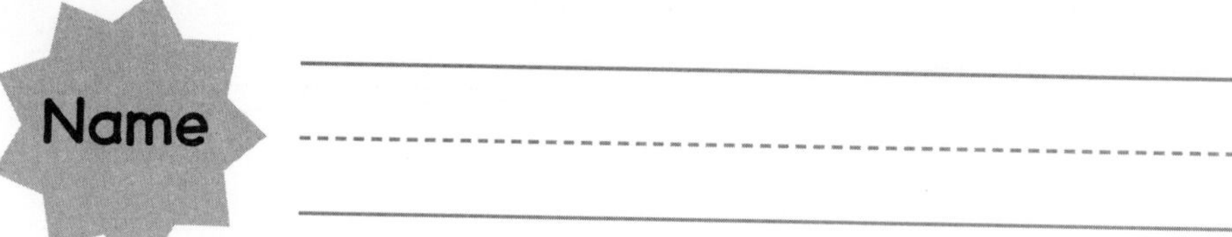

Show What You Know

1.

2.

3.

4.

5.

6.

7.

8.

♥

♥

Sentence:

Name ______________________

Show What You Know

1. ______________________
2. ______________________
3. ______________________
4. ______________________
5. ______________________
6. ______________________
7. ______________________
8. ______________________
9. ______________________
10. ______________________

♥ ______________________

♥ ______________________

Sentences:

1. ______________________

____

2. ______________________

____

2.F Vowel Tents and Vowel Intensive Exercise

Use for: Students who have difficulty with short-vowel sounds

Length of Activity: 3–5 minutes

Materials:

- Teacher: Vowel Intensive Word Lists (pages 111–113)
- Students: Vowel Tents (pages 114–115)

For students who need extra support with short-vowel sounds, I implement a vowel intensive exercise that I learned from the Institute for Multi-Sensory Education. This is a great activity to carry out in small groups so you can provide immediate feedback and support.

This activity helps students tune into individual vowel sounds and vowel sounds within words. I always start at the individual-sound level and see how students are doing before moving on to the more challenging syllable and word levels.

Directions

To create Vowel Tents for each child, make photocopies of pages 114–115 on cardstock and cut the cards apart. Fold each card so that each side of the tent has the same vowel. Provide each child with a set of five Vowel Tents. Have students place the tents in front of them in alphabetical order: *a, e, i, o, u*.

I always start at the sound level to warm up. First, say a sound and then have students determine the vowel and hold up the corresponding Vowel Tent. Then, move to the syllable level, saying the sound and having students hold up the appropriate Vowel Tent. If students are successful after a few syllables, move to the word level and stay there for the remaining time in the session. Below are some examples of how this exercise goes.

Differentiation Tips

If students have difficulty, consider the following scaffolds.

- Use only two or three vowel tents.
- Give more repetitions at the sound and syllable levels before moving on to the word level.
- At the word level, say the word slowly while you emphasize the vowel sound.
- Focus on the articulation. Point to your mouth.
- Have students use mirrors as they say the sounds. Discuss the difference in articulation between the sounds.

To make the activity more challenging, try these.

- Use words with more phonemes (e.g., *slip* instead of *sip*).
- Once the task is easy, students no longer need this activity.

Sound Level

TEACHER: The sound is /ĕ/.

STUDENTS: /e/. *e* spells /e/. (Students hold up the letter *e* tent.)

TEACHER: The sound is /ĭ/.

STUDENTS: /i/. *i* spells /i/. (Students hold up the letter *i* tent.)

Syllable Level

TEACHER: The syllable is /ack/.

STUDENTS: /ack/. *a* spells /a/. (Students hold up the letter *a* tent.)

TEACHER: The syllable is /op/.

STUDENTS: /op/. *o* spells /o/. (Students hold up the letter *o* tent.)

Word Level

TEACHER: The word is *fun*.

STUDENTS: *Fun*. *u* spells /u/. (Students hold up the letter *u* tent.)

TEACHER: The word is *sip*.

STUDENTS: *Sip*. *i* spells /i/. (Students hold up the letter *i* tent.)

Words With Short Vowels				
a	e	i	o	u
back	bed	big	Bob	bud
bag	beg	bin	bot	bug
bath	bell	bit	chop	bun
cab	bet	chick	cob	bus
can	Beth	chin	cod	chum
cat	check	chip	cog	cub
catch	deck	did	cop	cup
chat	den	dig	cot	cut
dad	fed	dip	dock	duck
fat	fell	dish	dog	dug
gap	get	fill	doll	fudge
gas	hedge	fin	dot	fun
had	hem	fish	fog	fuss
ham	hen	fit	got	gum
has	jet	hid	hog	gut
hat	Ken	hip	hop	hub
jam	led	hit	hot	huff
lad	ledge	jig	job	hug
mad	less	kick	jog	hum
man	let	kid	jot	hush
map	men	lick	lock	hut
mat	mess	lid	log	judge
nag	met	lip	lot	jug
nap	neck	pick	mom	jut
pad	net	pig	mop	luck

Words With Short Vowels (continued)				
a	e	i	o	u
pan	peck	pin	moss	lug
pat	peg	pit	nod	much
patch	pen	rich	not	mug
path	pet	rim	pod	nut
rag	red	rip	pop	pug
ram	sell	ship	pot	pup
ran	set	sick	rob	rug
rap	shed	sip	rock	run
rat	shell	sit	rod	rush
sack	Ted	thick	rot	rut
sad	tell	thin	shock	such
sap	ten	tin	shop	sum
sat	them	tip	sob	sun
tag	then	wig	sock	thud
tap	wed	win	sod	thumb
van	wet	wish	top	tub
wag	yes	zip	tot	tug

Words With Consonant Clusters				
a	e	i	o	u
black	bench	brick	blob	brush
clam	bend	bridge	block	bunch
clap	bent	chips	blog	club
class	best	click	broth	crumb
crab	bled	cliff	clock	drum
crack	chest	crib	clot	fluff
cram	felt	flip	cloth	glum
crash	fetch	fridge	cost	gust
drag	fled	gift	crop	husk
fact	melt	grin	cross	jump
fast	nest	grip	drop	just
flag	pest	inch	flop	lump
flap	rent	lift	fond	lunch
flat	rest	lips	frog	must
gasp	send	skin	frost	pluck
glass	shred	skip	glob	plug
hand	sled	slid	lost	plum
lamp	speck	slip	plop	plus
mask	sped	snip	plot	pump
pant	step	spin	pond	runt
sand	tend	spit	slot	scuff
slam	tent	stick	sloth	shrub
smash	test	stiff	smog	slug
snack	text	still	soft	smug
snap	theft	switch	spot	stuck
swam	vest	trick	stock	stuff
trap	went	trip	stop	truck
trash	west	wind	trot	tusk

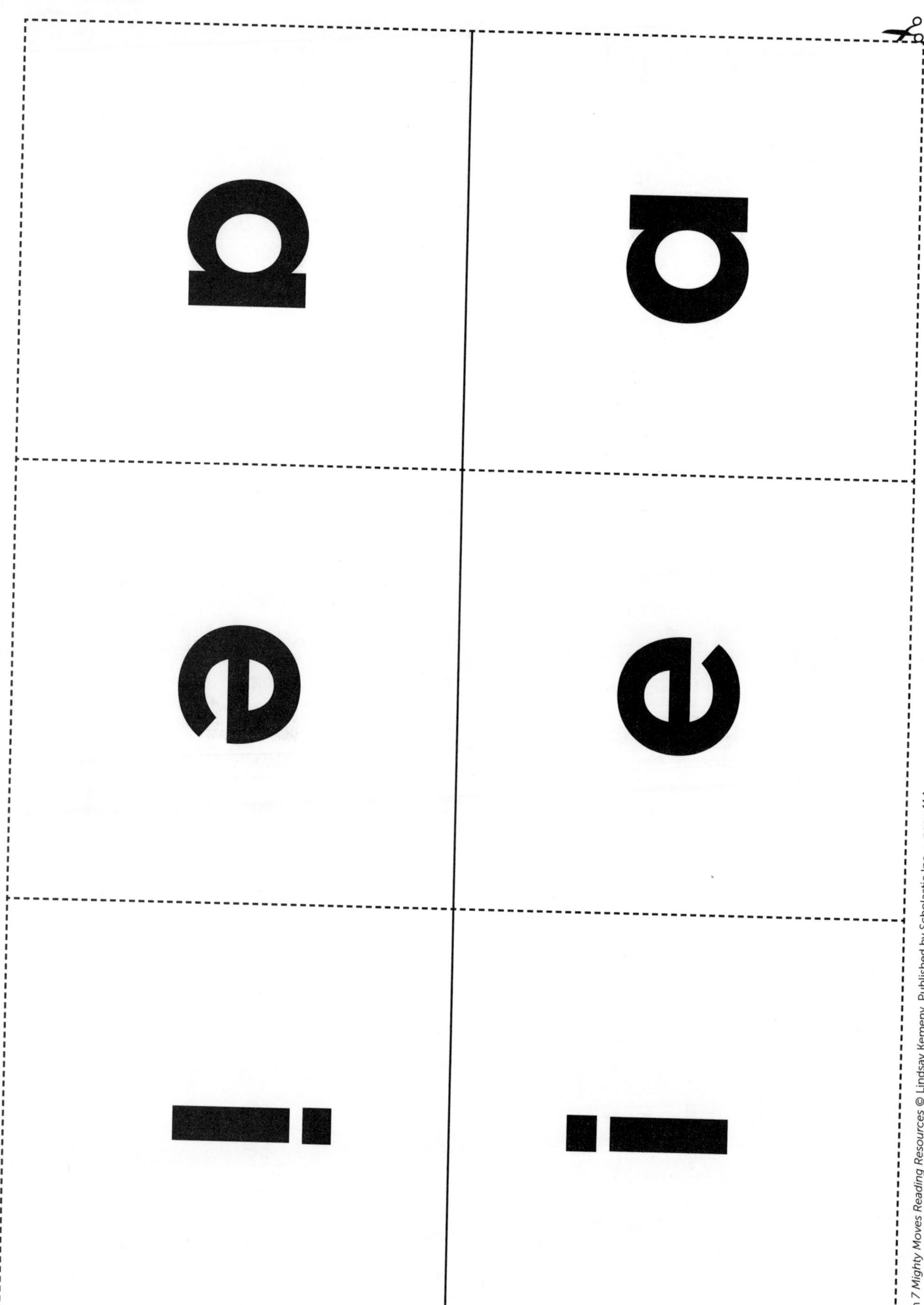

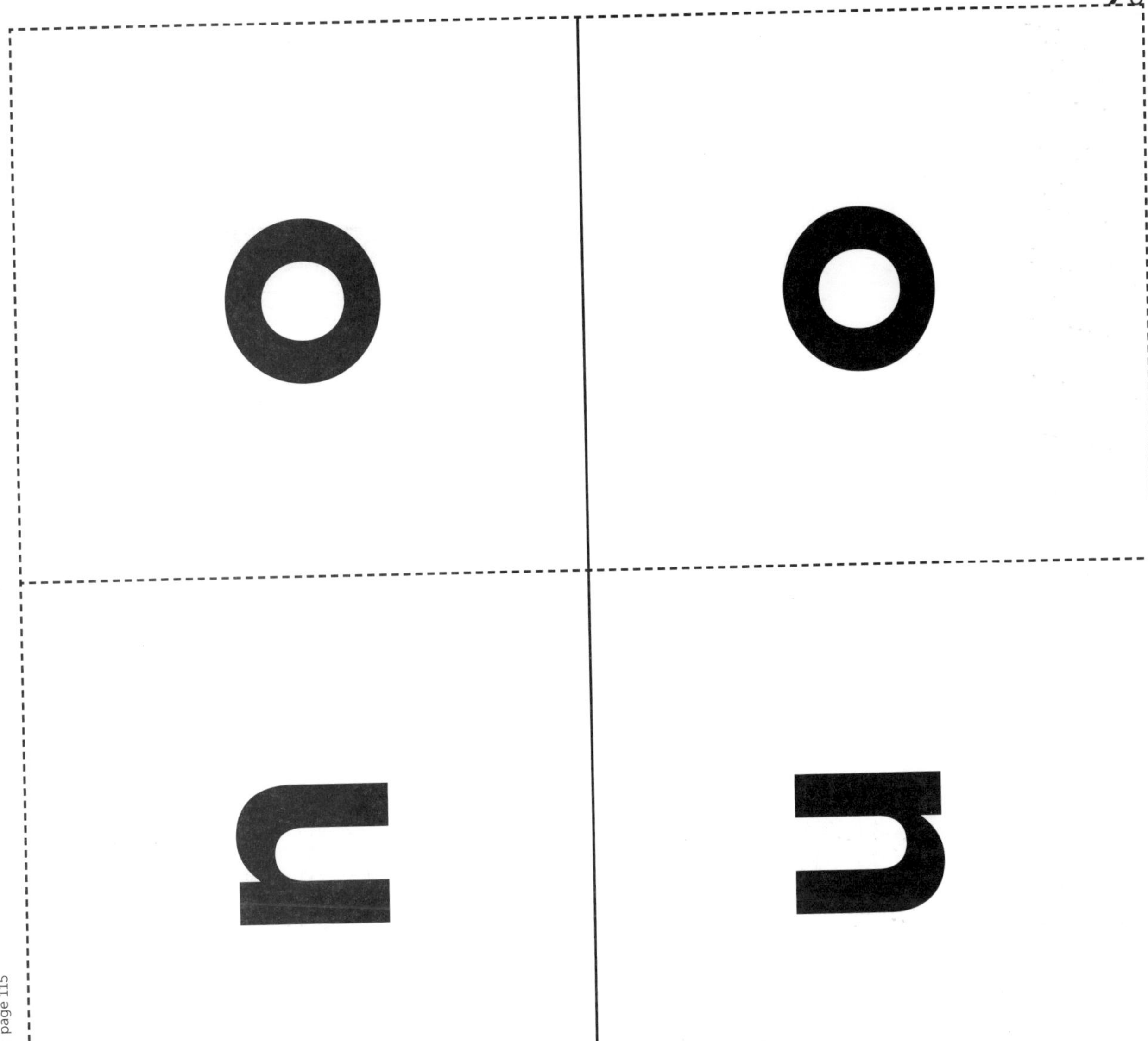
o
o
u
u

2.G Word Sorts to Build Spelling Skills

Use for: Students who need practice reading and spelling words with certain phonics patterns

Length of Activity: 10 minutes

Materials:

- Teacher: Word Lists for Word Sorts (pages 118–119)
- Students: Word Sorting Sheet (pages 120–123) and pencil, or dry-erase board and marker

Word sorts are a great way to review and solidify phonics skills. I love that they give students an opportunity to analyze and focus on spelling patterns. Remember, students need to become familiar with the details of words. They also need plenty of opportunities to apply the phonics skills they've learned. Word sorts are a fun way to provide purposeful, targeted phonics practice *and* build spelling skills. I learned a better way to implement word sorts from Nora Chahbazi, founder of the Evidence-Based Literacy Instruction (EBLI) program.

Directions

Choose a phonics pattern that your students need to practice (pages 118–119). Copy the practice sheet (pages 120–123) with the appropriate number of columns, depending on how many target skills students will sort. Then follow the steps below. (You can use this activity in place of the "dictation" step in your phonics program or as part of your small-group instruction.)

1. Have students write the target phonics pattern at the top of each column on the practice sheet. (For example, students may write *oa* in column 1 and *ow* in column 2 at the top of the two-column practice page.)
2. Say a word that contains one of the targeted spellings and have students repeat.

   TEACHER: The word is *low.* What word?

   STUDENTS: *Low.*

3. Have students hold up the number of fingers that match the column the word should go in.

   TEACHER: In which column should the word *low* go?

   STUDENTS: (Hold up two fingers.)

4. Confirm the correct column and have students say the word as they write it.

   TEACHER: Yes, the word *low* belongs in column 2 because it is spelled with *ow.* Write the word *low* in column 2.

   STUDENTS: (Write the word.)

5. Repeat steps 2 to 4 until students have written three to five words in each column.
6. Have students read the words in each column.

   TEACHER: Now read your words while I walk around to listen.

7. Discuss the patterns you notice and any relevant spelling tendencies.

   TEACHER: What patterns do you notice? Is *oa* at the end of any of the words? (No) The spelling *oa* is usually at the beginning and middle of words. It is not at the end of the words. Where do we see the *ow* spelling? (At the end) Yes, we often see *ow* at the end of words.

Differentiation Tips

If students have difficulty, consider the following scaffolds.

- Use only two different spellings for students to sort (for example, sort words with short *e* and *i*, instead of using all the short vowels).
- Show the word for students to sort rather than just saying it. Then have students decide which column it goes into.
- Provide cards with the words printed on them for students to sort rather than have them spell the words themselves.
- Use words with one syllable.
- Use words with fewer phonemes (e.g., *boat* instead of *float*).
- Sort less-complex phonics patterns.

To make the activity more challenging, try these.

- Use multisyllabic words.
- Use words with more phonemes (e.g., *storm* instead of *for*).
- Use more spellings for students to sort (for example, sort *ing, ang, ung, ong* instead of only *ing* and *ung*).
- Sort more-complex phonics patterns.

Phonics Skill	Possible Words
Short Vowels (Choose two to five short vowels to sort.)	***a*** – cab, hat, sad, pal, bag, fan ***e*** – bed, hen, pen, pet, fed, red ***i*** – sit, tip, hid, tin, lit, sip ***o*** – hop, fog, hot, top, dog, dot ***u*** – run, cut, fun, hug, mud, bug
Digraphs (Choose two or three digraphs to sort.)	***ch*** – chin, much, chip, chest, chop, chat ***sh*** – shed, shut, ship, shop, fish, wish ***th*** – thin, bath, math, with, thud, moth
Voiced/Unvoiced *th*	**Voiced *th*** – than, that, them, then, this **Unvoiced *th*** – thud, thin, bath, moth, math, sloth
ng (Choose two to four spellings to sort.)	***ang*** – bang, sang, hang, rang, fang ***ing*** – sing, ring, thing, bring, wing, king ***ong*** – long, song, gong ***ung*** – sung, hung, flung, stung, swung
a or ***a_e***	***a*** – hat, sat, bath, rag, dad, bat ***a_e*** – made, cape, shade, name, date, came
i or ***i_e***	***i*** – wish, sit, did, bin, win, slip ***i_e*** – bite, mine, hide, kite, drive, shine
o or ***o_e***	***o*** – pot, dog, hot, moth, fox, log ***o_e*** – bone, home, drove, chose, close, smoke
u or ***u_e***	***u*** – cup, mud, shut, thud, gum, sun ***u_e*** – flute, cute, use, cube, tune, dude
c or ***k*** I teach my students the rhyme: "*K* takes *i* and *e*; *C* takes the other three (*a*, *o*, *u*)."	***c*** – cat, cup, cod, scuff, cut, can ***k*** – kite, kick, kit, kiss, skip, skit
ch or ***-tch***	***ch*** – chest, chin, inch, bench, lunch, chug ***tch*** – patch, catch, witch, itch, ditch, match
j or ***-dge***	***j*** – jam, just, jump, jet, jog, job ***-dge*** – fudge, bridge, dodge, pledge, smudge, ledge
Which sound for *y*?	**Long *i*** – shy, sky, dry, fly, my, try **Long *e*** – happy, bunny, bumpy, mommy, muddy, daddy
Three sounds of *-ed*	**/t/** – jumped, crashed, locked, wished, tricked, bumped **/d/** – filled, called, pulled, rolled, stormed, yelled **/ə/** – blasted, landed, lifted, twisted, wanted, rested
ai or ***ay***	***ai*** – brain, sail, stain, wait, train, chain ***ay*** – say, clay, day, play, stay, way

Phonics Skill	Possible Words
oa or ***ow***	***oa*** – goat, road, soap, throat, toast, coach ***ow*** – slow, bow, grow, snow, throw, show
Which sound for *oo*?	**Long /oo/** – cool, bloom, moon, food, gloom, spoon **Short /oo/** – book, look, took, foot, good, wood
ar or ***or***	***ar*** – car, far, charm, hard, farm, shark ***or*** – born, sport, thorn, torch, worn, fort
or or ***ore***	***or*** – porch, sort, fork, storm, north, short ***ore*** – core, more, score, shore, snore, store
ar, or, or ***er***	***ar*** – barn, chart, harsh, arm, smart, sharp ***or*** – sort, porch, corn, dorm, horn, torn ***er*** – her, fern, herd, perch, stern, verb
oi or ***oy***	***oi*** – boil, coin, moist, spoil, join, point ***oy*** – boy, joy, soy, toy, coy, ploy
ou or ***ow***	***ou*** – loud, shout, south, round, cloud, found ***ow*** – cow, wow, how, now, howl, frown
Ways to spell /k/ at the end of a word	***k*** – milk, desk, beak, speak, dusk, week ***ck*** – sick, stuck, rock, snack, truck, clock ***ke*** – like, cake, take, snake, bike, poke
Spelling rules for adding the suffix *-ing*	**Just add *-ing*** – jumping, dusting, frosting, dumping, planting, blocking **Doubling rule** – clapping, swimming, skipping, winning, shopping, running **Drop the *e*** – hoping, making, fading, shaking, diving, waving
Spelling rules for adding the suffix *-ed*	**Just add *-ed*** – jumped, landed, melted, asked, bumped, crushed, pinched **Doubling rule** – trimmed, napped, slammed, nodded, slipped, stopped **Drop the *e*** – baked, smiled, joked, biked, piled, hiked
Adding the suffix *-ing*: Long vowel or short vowel	**Short vowel** – tapping, hopping, mopping, scrapping, tilling **Long vowel** – taping, hoping, moping, scraping, tiling
Prefix or Suffix	**Prefix** – refill, return, redo, preheat, prepay, prewash **Suffix** – longer, softer, slowest, oldest, quickly, gladly

Name: ______________________ Date: ____________

1

2

Name: ______________________ Date: ____________

1	2	3

Name: ______________________ Date: ____________

1	2	3	4

Name: ______________________ Date: ____________

1

2

3

4

5

2.H Secret Password to Review Phonics Skills

Use for: Students who need to learn or master a particular phonics skill

Length of Activity: Less than one minute

Materials:

- Teacher: Secret Password Template (page 125 and online), sticky note or dry-erase marker

After I introduce a phonics skill, I provide reinforcement with a "secret password."

Directions

I write the new grapheme (spelling) on a sticky note and place it on the doorway of our classroom. Every time students enter or exit the room, they touch the grapheme and say the sound—or secret password!

Print out and laminate the Secret Password template. You can also find a version of this template online that you can use to hang on a door. You can write the grapheme (e.g., *sh*) you'd like students to review on a sticky note and place it on the template or use a dry-erase marker to write it on the template itself. Place the Secret Password template near the entrance to your classroom. Encourage students to touch the template and say the sound or sounds the grapheme represents (e.g., /sh/) each time they enter or exit the room.

Differentiation Tips

If students have difficulty, consider the following scaffold.

- Say the sound and have them repeat it.

To make the activity more challenging, try these.

- Have students say all the sounds for the spelling that they've learned so far.
- Have students say a word that contains that grapheme.

PASSWORD of the DAY

MOVE 3

Teach Decoding Strategies, Not Cueing Strategies

Move 3 downloadables are available here.

One of the most impactful teaching moves I've made is to abandon the use of the three-cueing system. "Three cueing" refers to the idea that readers use various cues to figure out words as they are reading: semantics (Does it make sense?), syntax (Does it sound right?), and visual (Does it look right?).

For years I encouraged my students to guess words by using context or pictures, but research does not support this. We use context and pictures to help us understand the *meanings* of words and to *support* comprehension, but we don't want to use these cues to figure out what the word is. Instead, we want students to become familiar with the details of the words. Cognitive scientist Mark Seidenberg said, "The best 'cue' to a word is the word itself." We want students to connect the sounds they hear with the letters they see and attach them to meaning in a process known as *orthographic mapping*. To help facilitate this, we need to move from teaching "guessing" strategies to teaching decoding strategies.

It can be hard to realize that something we have taught and relied on for years is not best for students and is not backed by research. I felt so many emotions: shock, guilt, anger, discouragement...but then determination. Try not to look back but look forward instead. When we know better, we do better.

MOVE 3: Routines and Resources		
RESOURCE		**PAGE**
3.A	Error-Correction Procedure	128
3.B	Decoding Dragon Chart and Certificate	130
3.C	Eye-Spy Words Chart and Certificate	139
3.D	Look-Alike Words	147

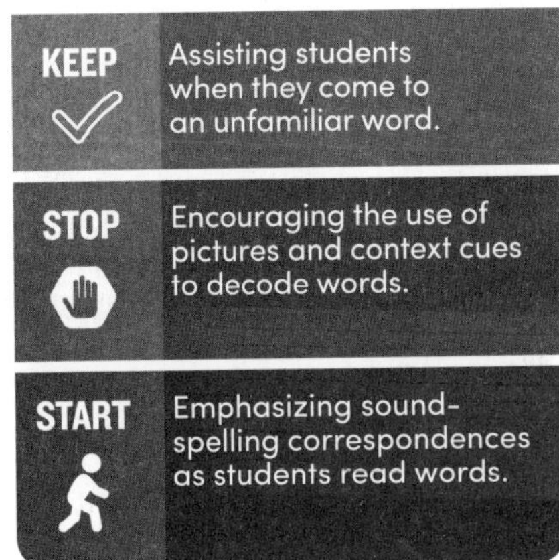

Let's review key points about Move 3.

- When we teach cueing strategies, students can develop guessing habits that are difficult to break.
- The three-cueing system can create an appearance of reading, so look closely to see if students are actually decoding the words.
- When students take their eyes off the words and guess, it inhibits the processes necessary to store words in their memories.
- Orthographic mapping is the mental process we use to permanently store words for immediate, effortless retrieval (Kilpatrick, 2016).
- Students need to match the sounds they hear to the letters on the page to facilitate orthographic mapping.
- Students need to resist the urge to guess, keep their eyes on the words, and point to the words as they read.
- We can help students as they read by encouraging them to blend words continuously and break multisyllabic words into syllables, and by providing unknown sounds.
- We can use a blending board, look-alike words, and encoding practice to build students' decoding skills, as well as explicit phonics and phonemic awareness instruction.

3.A Error-Correction Procedure

Use for: Students who misread a word

Length of Activity: 1 minute

Materials:

- Teacher: Error-Correction Procedure Reference Card (page 129)
- Students: word list, text passage, or book to read

When students encounter a word they don't know, lead them through the decoding process, not the three-cueing strategies. Direct their attention to each part of the word and encourage them to identify the sounds and blend them.

Directions

This is the procedure I like to follow.

1. **Pointing Prompt:** Point to the part of the word the child missed and allow time for him or her to state the correct sound.
2. **Verbal Prompt:** If the child can't recall the sound, provide it for him or her.
3. **Blending Prompt:** Encourage the student to blend the sounds. If the child is unable to blend the sounds, model how to do it (and prioritize instruction to strengthen his or her phonemic awareness).

Let's walk through the steps if a student misreads the word *noise*.

1. **Pointing Prompt:** Point to the word again and give the child time to self-correct.
2. **Verbal Prompt:** If the child doesn't correctly identify the word, point to *oi* and say: "These letters spell /oi/. What sound?" (/oi/) The child repeats the sound /oi/.
3. **Blending Prompt:** Say: "Yes. Now say and blend the sounds." The child blends the sounds and correctly reads "noise."

This procedure gives students an opportunity to connect the letters they see with the sounds they hear. If I just told them the entire word, I would be doing the work for them. This procedure gives students targeted practice and helps them master phonics and phonemic awareness skills.

Correcting Reading Mistakes

Photocopy the Error-Correction Procedure Reference Card on cardstock. This serves as a quick reminder for teachers on the steps to take students through when they read a word incorrectly. You may also want to print a card for any paraprofessionals or volunteers who work in your classroom.

Differentiation Tips

If students have difficulty, consider the following scaffolds.

- Provide additional practice opportunities.
- Provide the unknown sound for students and have them repeat it.
- Use words with continuous sounds.
- Use text with fewer irregular words.
- Try successive blending, in which students blend the first two sounds together before adding on the last sound (e.g., *sat* is read /s/ /a/, /sa/ /t/, /sat/).
- If students struggle to blend, use words with fewer phonemes.
- Model blending and have children repeat.

To make the activity more challenging, try these.

- Use words with more phonemes (e.g., *stamp* instead of *sat*).
- Use words with more than one syllable.
- Use more difficult texts.

Error-Correction Procedure

1 

Pointing Prompt
Point to the part of the word the child missed and allow time for him or her to state the correct sound.

2 

Verbal Prompt
If the child can't recall the sound, provide it for him or her.

3 

Blending Prompt
Encourage the child to blend the sounds. If the child is unable to blend the sounds, model how to do it and have him or her repeat.

Error-Correction Procedure

1 

Pointing Prompt
Point to the part of the word the child missed and allow time for him or her to state the correct sound.

2 

Verbal Prompt
If the child can't recall the sound, provide it for him or her.

3 

Blending Prompt
Encourage the child to blend the sounds. If the child is unable to blend the sounds, model how to do it and have him or her repeat.

3.B Decoding Dragon Chart and Certificate

Use for: Students who tend to guess words instead of decoding them

Length of Activity: 10+ minutes

Materials:

- Students: Decoding Dragon Templates (page 132), Decoding Dragon Bookmarks (page 133), My Decoding Dragon Chart (page 134), Decoding Dragon Stickers (page 135 and online), Decoding Dragon S/T Chart (page 136), Decoding Dragon Badges (page 137), Decoding Dragon Certificate (page 138), books or text passages to read

It can be difficult for students to break the habit of guessing the words from pictures or context instead of decoding them. Remember, we want students to become familiar with the details of the words. We don't want them to skip the critical step of solidifying their knowledge of sound-symbol correspondences. They need to match the phonemes and graphemes.

Directions

Discourage guessing with the Decoding Dragon, a character that was brought to life by author and linguist Lyn Stone. The Decoding Dragon chases the Guessing Monster away. Use the chart and stickers to help reward and motivate students when they carefully decode a word instead of glancing at the first letter and guessing the rest.

Decoding Dragon Reminders

Print the Decoding Dragon templates on cardstock and fold it in half so it stands upright. Place it in front of students as a fun reminder to decode instead of guess. Print the bookmarks for students to use as they read.

Decoding Dragon Point Game

Photocopy the Dragon S/T Chart to use when reading with a student. Each time the student guesses a word while reading, put a point under the T (teacher) column. After he or she reads a certain length of the text (e.g., a sentence, paragraph, or page) without guessing, put a point under the S (student) column. Keep the game positive by giving the student lots of chances to earn points. At the end of the reading session, if the child has earned more points than the teacher, fill in a square on the Decoding Dragon Chart. Once the child has filled in all the squares on the Decoding Dragon Chart, he or she can earn a prize, badge, or sticker.

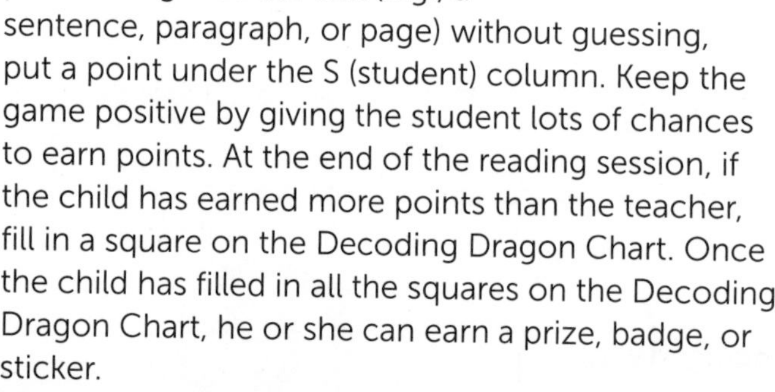

Alternative: Print and laminate the Decoding Dragon Chart. After the student reads a certain length of text without guessing, fill in a box right on the chart. Once the chart is full, the student can earn a prize, badge, or sticker.

Decoding Dragon Snowman Game

Each time a student guesses a word while reading, draw a part of a snowman on a sheet of paper (Stone, 2018). The student's goal is to prevent you from completing your snowman by decoding words rather than guessing them. If the student successfully prevents you from completing your snowman at the end of the book or session, she or he gets to fill in a square on the Decoding Dragon Chart.

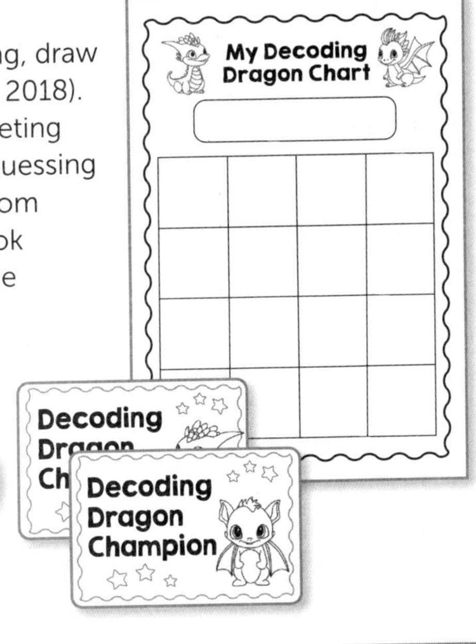

Decoding Dragon Stickers and Badges

Print the stickers and badges on sticker paper. You can purchase precut stickers from Premium Label Supply (Template Code PLS312 for the stickers on page 135 and Template Code PLS504 for the badges on page 137) or you can print them on your own cardstock and cut them out. Give them to students as a reminder not to guess or as a reward for decoding and not guessing.

Decoding Dragon Certificate

When you feel students have successfully scared the Guessing Monster away, award them the Decoding Dragon Certificate.

Differentiation Tips

If students have difficulty, consider the following scaffolds.

- Use decodable texts that are appropriate for the students. Make sure they have been taught the phonics skills contained in the book.
- Consider using an easier decodable text, with skills that have been taught earlier in your scope and sequence.
- If you notice a child who continually attempts to guess from the pictures, use a decodable passage without pictures or cover the picture until after the child reads the text on the page.

To make the activity more challenging, try this.

- Use more complex decodable texts or authentic texts.

Read, don't guess!

Read, don't guess!

Read, don't guess!

Read, don't guess!

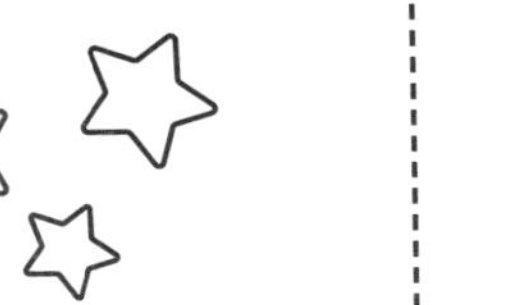

Read, don't guess!

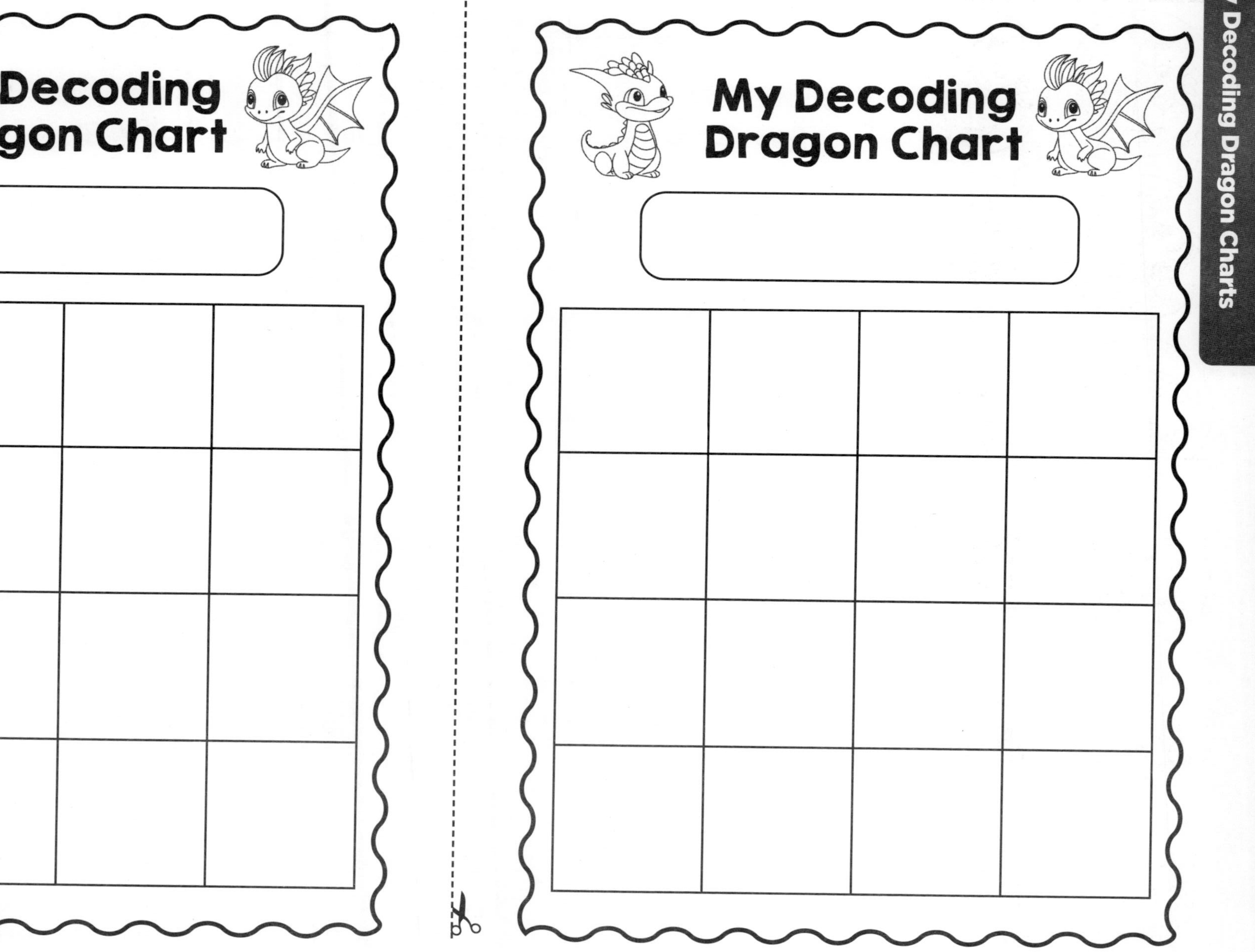
My Decoding Dragon Chart
My Decoding Dragon Chart

Decoding Dragon Stickers

S	T

S	T

S	T

S	T

Decoding
Dragon
Champion

Decoding
Dragon
Champion

Decoding
Dragon
Champion

Decoding
Dragon
Champion

Decoding
Dragon
Champion

Decoding
Dragon
Champion

Decoding
Dragon
Champion

Decoding
Dragon
Champion

Decoding
Dragon
Champion

Decoding
Dragon
Champion

Decoding Dragon Champion

This certificate is presented to

______________________________,

for becoming a Decoding Dragon Champion,
who has successfully chased
the Guessing Monster away.

Eye-Spy Words Chart and Certificate

One of the most common behaviors of struggling readers is not keeping their eyes on the words. They will look to us for approval or help, look at the ceiling, look at the picture for a clue, or look at almost anything else to avoid the words themselves. We want students to develop the habit of keeping their eyes on the words the entire time they are reading. After all, how can they map those phonemes to graphemes if they don't look at the words? Encourage students to look at the pictures *after* they read the words on the page. Pictures are wonderful supports to the meaning of the story, but we don't want students using them to guess the words.

Use for: Students who often take their eyes off the words as they read

Length of Activity: 10+ minutes

Materials:

- Students: Eye-Spy Words Bookmarks (page 141), My Eye-Spy Words Chart (page 142), Eye-Spy Words Stickers (page 143 and online), Eye-Spy Words S/T Chart (page 144), Eye-Spy Words Badges (page 145), Eye-Spy Words Certificate (page 146), dry-erase markers or pencils, books or text passages to read

Directions

The following resources can help you motivate and reward students to keep their eyes on the words.

Eye-Spy Words Point Game

Photocopy the Eye-Spy S/T (Student/Teacher) Chart to use when reading with a child. Award a point to the child each time she keeps her eyes on the words as she reads. (Print the bookmarks for students to use as they read.) If she takes her eyes off a word while she says it, put a point under the T (teacher) column. Keep the game fun by giving the child lots of opportunities to beat you, while reinforcing the desired behavior. If the child earns more points than you after reading a book, fill in a square on the Eye-Spy Words Chart. Once the chart is full, the child can earn a prize, sticker, badge, or certificate.

Alternative: Print and laminate the Eye-Spy Words Chart. When a child keeps his or her eyes on the words for an entire sentence, paragraph, or page, fill in a box on the chart. Use a dry-erase marker so you can reuse the chart. Once it's full, the child can earn a prize, badge, or sticker.

Eye-Spy Words Stickers and Badges

Print the stickers and badges on sticker paper. You can purchase precut stickers from Premium Label Supply (Template Code PLS312 for the stickers on page 143 and Template Code PLS504 for the badges on page 145) or you can print them on your own cardstock and cut them out. Give them to students as a reminder to keep their eyes on words as they read or as a reward.

Eye-Spy Words Certificate

When you feel students have mastered keeping their eyes on the words, award them the Eye-Spy Words Champion Certificate.

Eye-Spy Words Certificate

Eye-Spy Words Champion

This certificate is presented to

__________________________,

for becoming an Eye-Spy Words Champion, who has successfully kept both eyes on the words while reading.

Differentiation Tips

If students have difficulty, consider the following scaffolds.

- Encourage the child to point to the words as she reads them. Make sure the child's finger is under the word being read and not lagging behind or jumping ahead.
- Use your pencil to point above the words while the child points below them to assist her in keeping pace with you and keeping her finger exactly on the words being read.
- Frequently remind students to keep their eyes and fingers on the words.
- Use decodable texts that are appropriate for students. Make sure they know the phonics skills contained in the book.

To make the activity more challenging, try this.

- Use more complex decodable texts or authentic texts.

I can keep my eyes on the words.

I can keep my eyes on the words.

I can keep my eyes on the words.

I can keep my eyes on the words.

I can keep my eyes on the words.

My Eye-Spy Words Chart

My Eye-Spy Words Chart

Eye-Spy Words Stickers

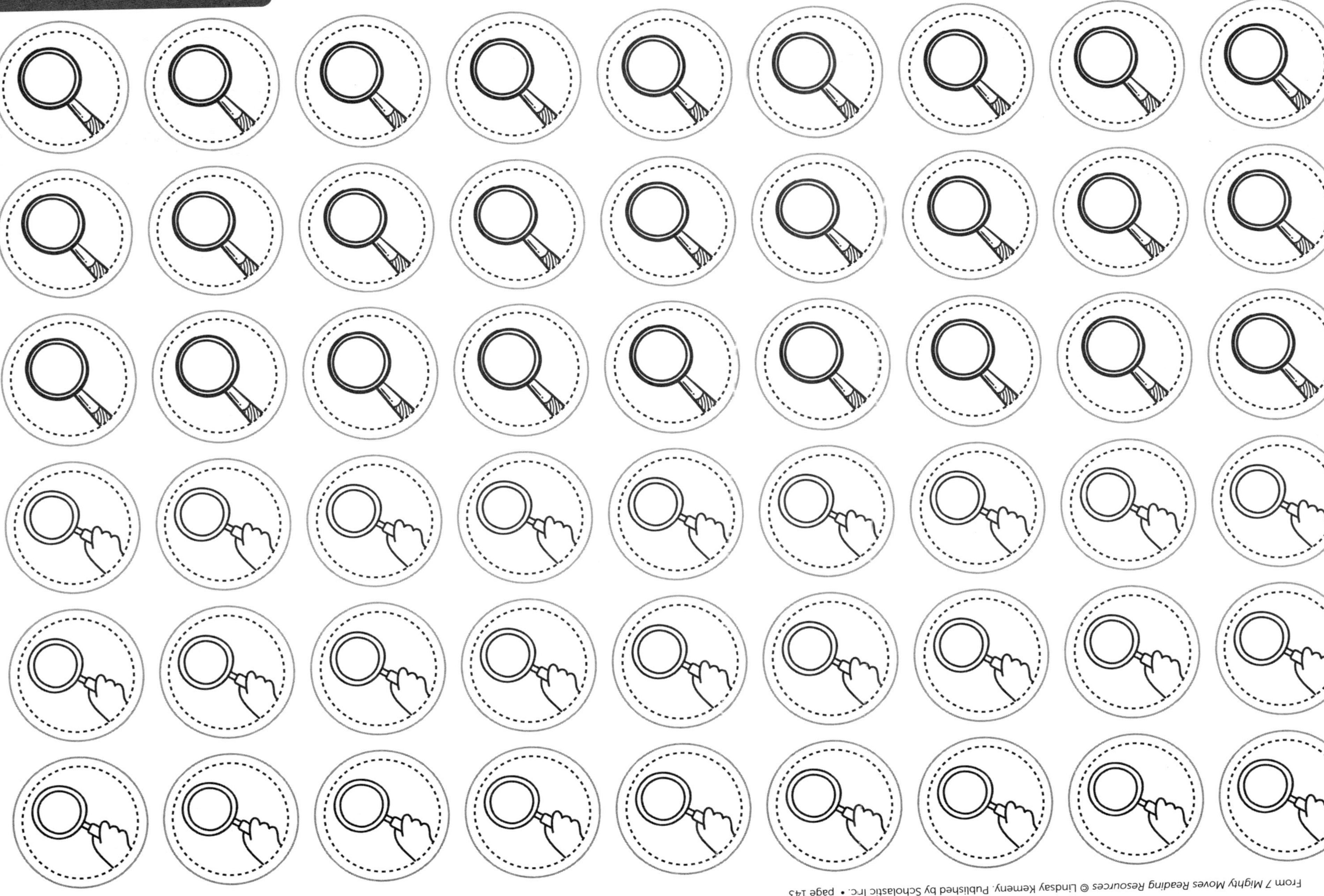

S
T

S
T

S
T

S
T

Eye-Spy
Words
Champion

Eye-Spy
Words
Champion

Eye-Spy
Words
Champion

Eye-Spy
Words
Champion

Eye-Spy
Words
Champion

Eye-Spy
Words
Champion

Eye-Spy
Words
Champion

Eye-Spy
Words
Champion

Eye-Spy
Words
Champion

Eye-Spy
Words
Champion

Eye-Spy Words Champion

This certificate is presented to

______________________________,

for becoming an Eye-Spy Words Champion, who has successfully kept both eyes on the words while reading.

Look-Alike Words

3.D

Help students develop the mental habit of attending to every letter within a word by presenting them with words that look similar. Using look-alike words for a variety of activities forces students to look carefully at the internal units of the word. Cueing strategies will not work with this type of task.

Try these games and activities to give students practice in reading words carefully. Make sure you have taught the phonics skills necessary to read the words on the boards and grids.

Use for: Students who don't look carefully at all the letters in the word

Length of Activity:
5–10 minutes

Materials:

- Students: Look-Alike Words Grids (pages 148–167), Tic-Tac-Toe Writing Grid (pages 104–105), Blank Bingo Boards (pages 168–169), Look-Alike Bingo Boards (online), bingo chips, interlocking cubes, or other manipulatives

Directions

You can use the pre-made grids and boards or create your own tailored to your students' needs and phonics scope and sequence. For example, if a child frequently mixes up the words *what* and *that*, print out a Blank Bingo Board and write those two words several times on the sheet. Fill in the extra spaces with other words that are similar but are easier for the child, such as *this, thin, wag*.

Look-Alike Words Grids

Distribute copies of Look-Alike Words Grids (inspired by Heidi Jane from the Droppin' Knowledge with Heidi website) to students. Have them read the words and circle the one that matches the picture in the first column. This activity is perfect for independent work or small groups.

Look-Alike Word Tic-Tac-Toe

Have students play tic-tac-toe with a partner. Fill in a blank Tic-Tac-Toe Writing Grid (pages 104–105) with words the students often mix up, then make a copy for each player. Provide two different colors of cubes (or other manipulatives to use as markers), one color for each player. To play, students take turns reading a word on the grid. If correct, they place their chip in the space. If they read the word incorrectly, they must go to a different spot. The first player to get three in a row wins.

Look-Alike Word Bingo

This game works well with small groups. Distribute a Look-Alike Word Bingo Board to each child. Have students read all the words on their boards. Then call out a word and have students search for that word on their board and cover it with a chip. When a child has covered three (or four) words in a row, he or she yells, "Bingo!" Have the child uncover and read each word to you to ensure he or she chose the correct words and to provide practice reading.

Alternative: Dictate the look-alike words and have students write them randomly on the blank bingo template. Make sure they spell them correctly. Then play bingo!

Differentiation Tips

If students have difficulty, consider the following scaffolds.

- Ensure you've taught the phonics skills necessary to read the look-alike words you've chosen.
- Use a bank of words with simpler phonics concepts.
- Use the 3 x 3 Bingo Board.
- Customize the board with a limited set of words repeated for multiple exposures.

To make the activity more challenging, try these.

- Use a bank of words with more advanced phonics concepts.
- Use the 4 x 4 Bingo Board.
- Have students spell the words on the blank bingo template before playing the game.

Name: ______________________________ Date: ______________

LOOk-Alike Words

Look at the picture. Read each word. Circle the word that matches the picture.

1.	fix	fox	box	mix
2.	peg	pin	pig	pit
3.	dug	dad	dig	dog
4.	sun	sum	sap	set
5.	fat	fan	fit	fun
6.	peg	pet	pad	pop
7.	did	den	dip	dig
8.	set	sad	sit	sip

Name: ______________________ Date: __________

LOOk-Alike Words

Look at the picture. Read each word. Circle the word that matches the picture.

1.	sit	six	tax	fax
2.	peg	pan	tin	pen
3.	gas	gap	sag	gag
4.	cap	cup	cab	can
5.	bid	big	bed	bud
6.	hat	hit	had	hut
7.	wed	wet	wig	web
8.	lug	lit	log	leg

Name: ______________________________ Date: ______________

LOOK-Alike Words

Look at the picture. Read each word. Circle the word that matches the picture.

1.	cap	cog	cab	can
2.	lap	leg	lip	lid
3.	mud	mad	map	mug
4.	jet	jot	jog	job
5.	cod	cot	cut	cat
6.	ram	run	rim	rag
7.	mum	mud	mug	mop
8.	not	net	nip	nap

Name: ______________________ Date: ____________

LOOk-Alike Words

Look at the picture. Read each word. Circle the word that matches the picture.

1.	frog	fog	flop	fled
2.	sap	slap	slab	sled
3.	flat	flip	flag	flap
4.	pots	stop	spot	snip
5.	crib	cram	crab	cab
6.	drip	drum	brim	drag
7.	clam	clip	clap	club
8.	bet	felt	melt	belt

Name: ______________________________ Date: ______________

LOOK-Alike Words

Look at the picture. Read each word. Circle the word that matches the picture.

1.	black	back	blab	block
2.	plot	plant	pant	plop
3.	clap	clip	cram	clam
4.	step	spot	stop	pats
5.	slam	slim	swim	slap
6.	twist	wig	wilt	twig
7.	vast	vest	vent	west
8.	lamp	lump	limp	land

Name: ______________________ Date: ____________

LOOK-Alike Words

Look at the picture. Read each word. Circle the word that matches the picture.

1.	crab	crib	clip	cram
2.	grass	grit	grin	grab
3.	plug	plum	plan	plot
4.	skim	skin	skid	skip
5.	drum	brim	dip	drip
6.	pets	pots	pats	spot
7.	felt	met	help	melt
8.	lift	lit	left	last

Name: ______________________ Date: ______________

LOOK-Alike Words

Look at the picture. Read each word. Circle the word that matches the picture.

1.	branch	bunch	bench	pinch
2.	shell	shed	shift	shin
3.	dish	dash	fish	flash
4.	crush	brush	blush	crash
5.	chip	chin	chop	chick
6.	bunch	munch	hunch	lunch
7.	shop	shot	shut	ship
8.	crash	cash	clash	dish

Name: ______________________ Date: ______________

LOOk-Alike Words

Look at the picture. Read each word. Circle the word that matches the picture.

1.	cape	cane	cake	case
2.	duke	duck	dune	drove
3.	slide	side	slid	shade
4.	cake	came	chase	cave
5.	drive	dime	dome	dive
6.	robe	rode	rose	ride
7.	cute	cube	cub	cut
8.	kit	cute	cake	kite

Name: ______________________________ Date: ______________

LOOk-Alike Words

Look at the picture. Read each word. Circle the word that matches the picture.

1.	bake	back	bite	bike
2.	cap	cape	cake	cave
3.	dim	dive	dime	dune
4.	rose	rode	ride	robe
5.	hose	nope	nose	home
6.	tap	tape	take	tide
7.	line	like	lime	life
8.	hide	hike	have	hive

Name: ______________________ Date: ____________

LOOK-Alike Words

Look at the picture. Read each word. Circle the word that matches the picture.

1.	note	not	hope	hole
2.	tub	tune	ton	tube
3.	hope	home	hose	nope
4.	mute	muse	mole	mule
5.	shake	skate	shade	shape
6.	wake	whale	while	white
7.	flute	flake	flame	fluke
8.	late	plane	plate	lap

Name: ______________________ Date: __________

LOOK-Alike Words

Look at the picture. Read each word. Circle the word that matches the picture.

1.	bang	brink	bank	drank
2.	long	sing	sink	sting
3.	brink	bring	rink	drink
4.	sing	sling	swing	sting
5.	think	thing	thin	brink
6.	rang	bring	bang	ring
7.	sang	sink	rink	sting
8.	black	block	blink	blast

Name: ____________________ Date: ____________

LOOk-Alike Words

Look at the picture. Read each word. Circle the word that matches the picture.

1.	card	cart	car	scar
2.	bran	barn	bark	burn
3.	scarf	sharp	smart	shark
4.	arm	ram	arch	ark
5.	form	fork	fort	first
6.	hard	horse	horn	hark
7.	start	tart	strap	star
8.	frog	fort	fir	fire

Name: ______________________________ Date: ______________

LOOk-Alike Words

Look at the picture. Read each word. Circle the word that matches the picture.

1.	birth	bird	brag	brick
2.	card	cart	car	chart
3.	shore	sport	start	snore
4.	hark	hard	harp	had
5.	shark	scarf	sharp	scar
6.	grill	gill	girl	grin
7.	art	rat	scar	ark
8.	skirt	swirl	squirt	shirt

Name: ____________________ Date: ____________

LOOk-Alike Words

Look at the picture. Read each word. Circle the word that matches the picture.

1.	core	chore	cord	corn
2.	shirt	skirt	skip	swirl
3.	cart	chart	card	dart
4.	firm	first	farm	fern
5.	snore	stork	score	shore
6.	bark	dark	drag	brag
7.	horn	hard	horse	harsh
8.	pork	porch	port	prop

Name: ______________________ Date: ____________

LOOk-Alike Words

Look at the picture. Read each word. Circle the word that matches the picture.

1.	boast	beat	boat	boot
2.	feel	feet	feed	flee
3.	seat	steal	steam	seal
4.	pain	pant	paint	plant
5.	three	trip	trap	tree
6.	sleep	sheep	sheet	speech
7.	pay	say	spray	stay
8.	tail	train	trail	tram

Name: ______________________ Date: ____________

LOOk-Alike Words

Look at the picture. Read each word. Circle the word that matches the picture.

1.	blow	bowl	blown	boat
2.	cheek	cheap	cheese	creep
3.	load	float	loaf	leaf
4.	snail	sail	stain	tail
5.	east	seam	seat	eat
6.	tree	three	trip	trap
7.	boom	boot	bloom	broom
8.	seat	sea	east	seed

Name: ______________________ Date: ____________

LOOk-Alike Words

Look at the picture. Read each word. Circle the word that matches the picture.

1.	shop	soak	slow	soap
2.	boom	boo	doom	boot
3.	loaf	leaf	leap	lean
4.	brain	bait	braid	brag
5.	sleep	sheep	street	sweep
6.	sail	stain	snail	strain
7.	steam	team	stream	tea
8.	show	slow	sow	snow

Name: ______________________ Date: ____________

LOOk-Alike Words

Look at the picture. Read each word. Circle the word that matches the picture.

1.	scoop	stool	soon	stoop
2.	paid	pal	tail	pail
3.	thaw	jaw	yawn	yarn
4.	sweep	sleep	steel	street
5.	sea	see	seal	seat
6.	jaw	paw	pawn	pal
7.	sneak	speak	scream	seek
8.	toad	throat	toast	float

Name: ______________________ Date: ____________

LOOK-Alike Words

Look at the picture. Read each word. Circle the word that matches the picture.

1.	boy	boil	toy	blow
2.	coil	choice	coin	count
3.	most	moist	mount	mouse
4.	spoil	soy	soil	say
5.	couch	cloud	loud	out
6.	paint	ploy	play	point
7.	shot	shout	spot	scout
8.	cloud	crow	clown	crown

Name: ______________________ Date: ____________

LOOK-Alike Words

Look at the picture. Read each word. Circle the word that matches the picture.

1.	the	three	there	where
2.	from	for	frog	of
3.	this	that	thin	the
4.	said	sad	it	sit
5.	once	lone	one	bone
6.	may	man	many	mat
7.	other	mother	moth	father
8.	bath	both	with	that

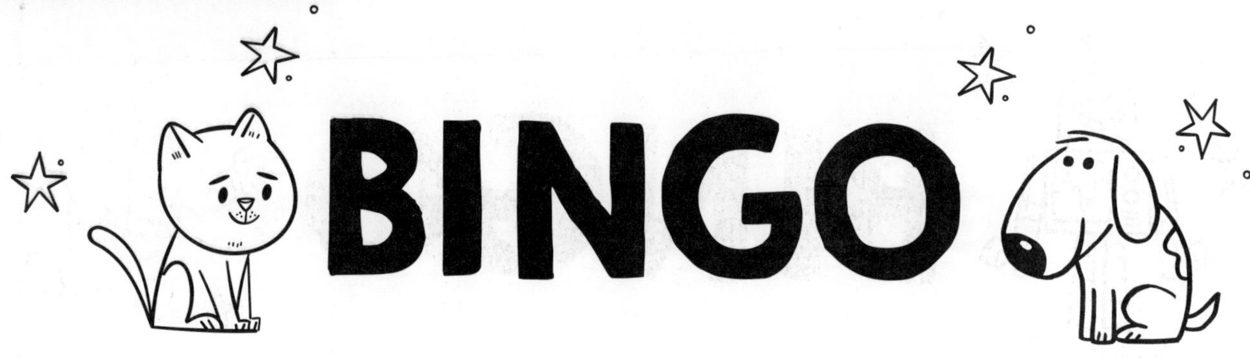
BINGO

BINGO

________	________	________	________
________	________	________	________
________	________	________	________
________	________	________	________

MOVE 4

Use Decodable Texts Instead of Predictable Texts With Beginning Readers

One of the most critical moves I've made in my instruction is providing my beginning readers with decodable texts instead of predictable, repetitive texts. The only way for beginning readers to "read" predictable texts is by memorizing the patterns or using the three-cueing strategies I discouraged in Move 3. This is not reading! It is memorizing and guessing. Students may sound like they are reading, but they are skipping an important step—decoding words. We want students to sound out the words initially because they need this practice to solidify the sound-symbol correspondences we teach in our phonics lessons.

Decodable texts are like training wheels: Kids need them for only a short amount of time. The goal is to transition away from them as soon as students are ready. Once students have a strong phonics base and no guessing habit, move them into authentic texts (i.e., trade books).

Three Purposes of Decodable Texts

1. Support readers in word identification.
2. Allow readers to apply what they've learned from your phonics lessons.
3. Direct readers to the letters and sounds.

(Mesmer, 2001)

Also, decodable books should not be the only books students are exposed to. Our students can read to learn at the same time they are learning to read. Decodable texts give them practice in transferring phonics skills to connected text. Grade-level and read-aloud texts expose them to more advanced concepts, genres, and vocabulary as well as build background knowledge.

Types of Texts to Use

- **Decodable Texts:** Students apply their phonics skills to connected text.
- **Authentic Grade-Level Texts:** Students read complex text, with teacher support and scaffolding.
- **Read-Aloud Texts:** Teachers read books that students are not able to read themselves.

MOVE 4: Routines and Resources

	RESOURCE	PAGE
4.A	Small-Group Decodable Text Routine	172
4.B	Whole-Group Decodable Text Routine	177
4.C	Take-Home Book System	179
4.D	My Favorite Decodable Book Sets	184

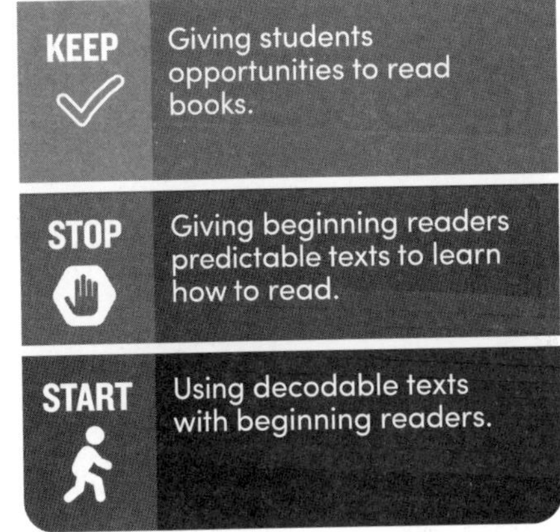

Let's review key points about Move 4.

- Beginning readers typically "read" predictable, repetitive texts by memorizing the pattern or guessing words from the context and pictures.
- Predictable, repetitive texts create an illusion of reading and, unless you look closely, the student's inability to read is hidden from view.
- Decodable texts are a tool that allows targeted, purposeful practice of the phonics skills you are teaching.
- Decodable texts are only decodable if you have taught the phonics skills featured in them.
- Align your decodable book collection to your phonics scope and sequence.
- Decodables should be used for a limited time, similar to training wheels. You should transition students out of them as soon as they are ready.
- Decodable texts should never be the only type of books students experience. You should support students in grade-level texts and read aloud more complex, authentic texts to them.
- The more you understand about phonics concepts, the better you'll understand decodable texts.

4.A Small-Group Decodable Text Routine

Use for: Students who are applying phonics skills to connected text

Length of Activity: 10–30 minutes

Materials:

- Teacher: Small-Group Lesson Plan Template (page 174), Small-Group Lesson Reference Card (page 175), Small-Group Reading Notes (page 176), dry-erase board and marker
- Students: phonics word lists and decodable books

My favorite part of the day is working with my students in small groups, using decodable texts. I love giving them time to practice applying the phonics skills I teach in our phonics lessons. In first grade, almost all my students are using decodable texts at the beginning of the year. As their reading skills progress, I can transition them from books that are highly decodable to books that are less decodable, and then to regular trade books. I have found that most of my students are ready to start transitioning in the middle of first grade. Second- and third-grade teachers might have only a few students who still use decodable texts in small groups, while other students can read regular trade books successfully. Use this small-group routine for any type of text.

You should spend the majority of your small-group time having students read the text aloud. Keep a quick pace in your before-reading activities so you can get to this critical part of the routine.

Directions

Planning

Use the Small-Group Lesson Plan Template to help you plan your lesson beforehand. Or simply use the reference card to help you as you teach the lesson. Take a moment to review any student observations you've recorded on the Small-Group Reading Notes template so you can be best prepared to target your students' needs.

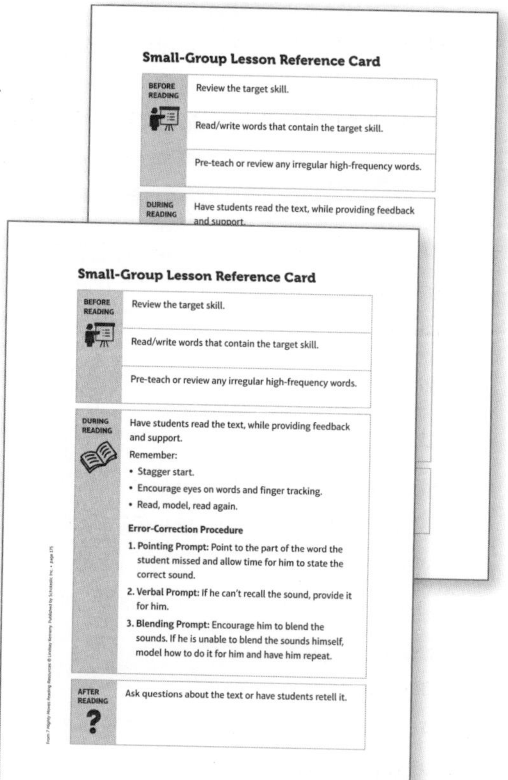

Small-Group Lesson Reference Card

BEFORE READING	Review the target skill.
	Read/write words that contain the target skill.
	Pre-teach or review any irregular high-frequency words.
DURING READING	Have students read the text, while providing feedback and support. Remember: • Stagger start. • Encourage eyes on words and finger tracking. • Read, model, read again. **Error-Correction Procedure** 1. **Pointing Prompt:** Point to the part of the word the student missed and allow time for him to state the correct sound. 2. **Verbal Prompt:** If he can't recall the sound, provide it for him. 3. **Blending Prompt:** Encourage him to blend the sounds. If he is unable to blend the sounds himself, model how to do it for him and have him repeat.
AFTER READING ?	Ask questions about the text or have students retell it.

Before Reading

Briefly review the target phonics skill and have students read or write words containing this skill. I like to choose words right from the decodable text we are going to read. Be sure to pre-teach or review any irregular words that students may struggle with. This is also the time to teach any relevant background knowledge or vocabulary words students need to know to understand the text.

During Reading

Stagger-start students so they are each reading the text aloud without echoing what their neighbor says. Lean in to give students feedback and support as they read. Record observations on the Small-Group Reading Notes template. I like to take note of any words or concepts students struggle with, so I remember to review them in future lessons. I also record the book we read and student behaviors or any goals we discuss together.

Remember, this step is where you should spend the majority of your small-group time. Students need many minutes of reading practice. For example, if I have 15 minutes to meet with a group, I'll allot 10 minutes on this step. If I have 20 minutes to meet, I might spend 12–15 minutes on it.

After Reading

Ask comprehension questions or have students retell the story to monitor their understanding of the text. Responses can be verbal or, if you have more time, written.

Differentiation Tips

If students have difficulty, consider the following scaffolds.

- Provide more attention and support while they're reading.
- Use the Error-Correction Procedure (page 129).
- Make sure to preview difficult words or concepts before students read.
- Use shorter decodable books so students can read it several times within the allotted time.
- Use books with a higher percentage of decodable words.
- Use books with fewer irregular words.
- Use books that contain more previously mastered phonics skills.
- Try successive blending, in which students blend the first two sounds together before adding on the last sound (e.g., *sat* is read /s/ /a/, /sa/ /t/, /sat/).

To make the activity more challenging, try these.

- Use longer decodable texts.
- Use books/passages with a lower percentage of decodable words.
- Use books with more irregular high-frequency words and sophisticated vocabulary terms.
- Transition students out of decodable texts and into authentic texts.
- Encourage students to use an appropriate rate and good expression and phrasing as they read.
- After reading, have students write a summary about the text or their response to a prompt.

Small-Group Lesson Plan Template

	Lesson Steps	Lesson Plan
BEFORE READING	Review the target skill.	
	Read/write words that contain the target skill.	
	Pre-teach or review any irregular high-frequency words.	
DURING READING	Have students read the text, while providing feedback and support. Remember: • Stagger start. • Encourage eyes on words and finger tracking. • Read, model, read again. **Error-Correction Procedure** 1. **Pointing Prompt:** Point to the part of the word the student missed and allow time for him to state the correct sound. 2. **Verbal Prompt:** If he can't recall the sound, provide it for him. 3. **Blending Prompt:** Encourage him to blend the sounds. If he is unable to blend the sounds himself, model how to do it for him and have him repeat.	
AFTER READING ?	Ask questions about the text or have students retell it.	

Small-Group Lesson Reference Card

BEFORE READING

- Review the target skill.
- Read/write words that contain the target skill.
- Pre-teach or review any irregular high-frequency words.

DURING READING

Have students read the text, while providing feedback and support.

Remember:

- Stagger start.
- Encourage eyes on words and finger tracking.
- Read, model, read again.

Error-Correction Procedure

1. **Pointing Prompt:** Point to the part of the word the student missed and allow time for him to state the correct sound.
2. **Verbal Prompt:** If he can't recall the sound, provide it for him.
3. **Blending Prompt:** Encourage him to blend the sounds. If he is unable to blend the sounds himself, model how to do it for him and have him repeat.

AFTER READING

Ask questions about the text or have students retell it.

Small-Group Reading Notes 

DATE	BOOK	LESSON	NOTES

Whole-Group Decodable Text Routine

Give students plenty of opportunities to practice the phonics skills you are teaching in your whole-group lessons. Specifically, give them opportunities to transfer isolated skills to connected text. That way, they get meaningful practice decoding words that contain the targeted skill.

If you teach second or third grade, you may find that most of your students no longer need decodable texts. If that is the case, you may want to forego this whole-group routine and use it only in small groups for students who need it. Alternatively, you may find it valuable to adapt the routine for the advanced concepts you are teaching in your spelling and morphology lessons. Use a more advanced passage with many words that contain the targeted skill.

Use for: Students who are applying phonics skills to connected text

Length of Activity: 10–15 minutes

Materials:

- Teacher; Whole-Group Lesson Reference Card (page 178)
- Students: decodable text passages, highlighters or yellow crayons

Directions

Follow this routine for reading decodables with your whole class.

1. Provide each student with a copy of the decodable text.
2. Give students one to two minutes to highlight the target-skill words in the text. If they finish before the time is up, have them whisper-read the highlighted words.
3. Have students read the highlighted words as a class, individually, or with a partner.
4. Choral-read the entire passage together as a class or have students partner-read it with a classmate.
5. Ask questions about the passage or have students retell it to a partner.

Differentiation Tips

If students have difficulty, consider the following scaffolds.

- Provide more practice and support in small groups (use Error-Correction Procedure, page 129). Consider using the passage in small groups before or after you use it in the whole class.
- Preview difficult words or concepts before students read.
- Model the passage first by reading it aloud. Read the first paragraph, then have students choral-read the first paragraph; read the second paragraph, then have students choral-read the second paragraph; and so on.
- Use shorter passages so students can read it several times within the allotted time.
- Use passages with a higher percentage of decodable words.
- Use passages with fewer irregular words.
- Encourage successive blending in which students blend the first two sounds together before adding on the last sound (e.g., *sat* is read /s/ /a/, /sa/ /t/, /sat/).

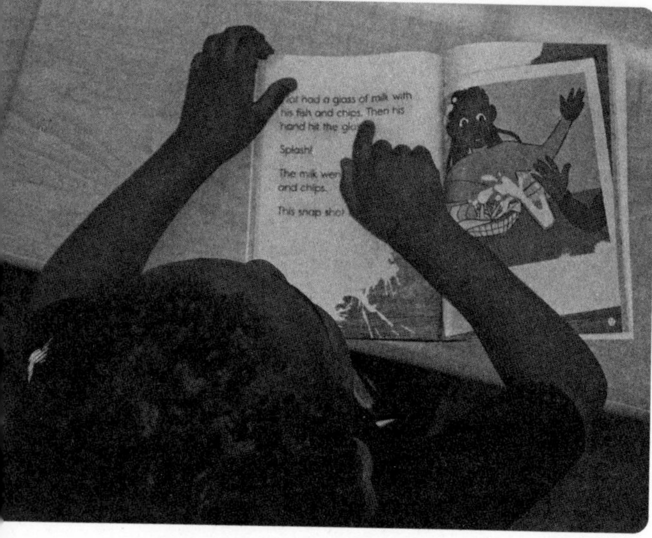

To make the activity more challenging, try these.

- Use longer passages.
- Use passages with a lower percentage of decodable words.
- Use passages with more irregular high-frequency words and sophisticated vocabulary terms.
- Encourage students to use an appropriate rate and good expression and phrasing as they read.
- After reading, have students write a summary about the text or their response to a prompt.

Whole-Group Lesson Reference Card

BEFORE READING	Give students 1–2 minutes to highlight target-skill words in the text.
	Have students read highlighted words as a class, with a partner, or independently.
DURING READING	Invite students to choral-read the text as a class or with partners.
AFTER READING	Have student retell the story and answer questions about the text.

Take-Home Book System

I want students to apply the phonics skills they learned at school to reading they do at home, but not many public or home libraries contain decodable books. So I have set up a system for students to check out decodable texts from my classroom. My first graders take home three decodable books on Mondays and return them on Fridays. I encourage them to read each book at least three times to a caregiver to strengthen their decoding skills. I make sure to provide reading tips for family members, so they know how best to support their beginning reader.

Use for: Students who need practice applying phonics skills in connected text

Length of Activity: 15–20 minutes

Materials:

- Teacher: decodable books or passages to send home
- Students: decodable books or passages, a bag or folder to tote them to and from school
- Caregivers: Book Bag Buddies (page 180), or Tips for Families Sheet (page 181), Book Bag Buddies Contract (page 182), Error-Correction Procedure Bookmarks (page 183)

Directions

Assign students extra reading practice at home. Here's how.

1. Kick things off by sending home the Book Bag Buddies contract for caregivers and students to review and sign. This clarifies expectations for reading routines and book care.
2. Dive into your decodable library and select books that are appropriate for each student. Dedicate time to assembling the Book Bags or recruit a parent volunteer.
3. Consider including some helpful resources for parents in the Book Bags. See the Book Bag Buddies sheet with simple directions, caregiver tips, and the Error-Correction Procedure bookmarks.
4. Fridays are for book swaps! Have students return their Book Bags. Then curate fresh selections for the following week. You can do this on your own or with the help of a dedicated volunteer.

Remember:

- Consistency is key! Maintain a regular schedule for book check-in and check-out to ensure a smooth program flow.
- Celebrate milestones! Acknowledge students' reading progress and encourage them to share their favorite Book Buddies with the class.

Differentiation Tips

If students have difficulty, consider the following scaffolds.

- Make sure the decodable is a good fit. Use books with a higher or lower percentage of decodable words, depending on the student's needs.
- Remind students and parents to return the books.
- If students frequently forget to return the books, send home printable passages instead.

To make the activity more challenging, try these.

- Send home four or five decodable texts instead of three.
- Send home books with a lower percentage of decodable words.
- Send home regular, authentic texts.
- Graduate students from the Book Bag Buddies program and encourage them to read trade books from their home/public library.

BOOK BAG BUDDIES

DIRECTIONS:

Three new books will be sent home each week on **Monday**. Please **listen** to your child read the books **nightly**, and then return the books on **Friday**. Place a tally mark on the recording sheet each time your child reads a book. Each book should be read at least three times. This repetition helps your child master sound-symbol correspondences and **improves** decoding fluency.

Read Aloud: After your child reads to you, choose some favorite books to read to her or him.

Special Care

These books are from my personal library. Please encourage your child to treat them and the bag respectfully and keep them in a safe space.

This time is very special
for our growing readers.
Be patient and enjoy every minute.
Make it a special part of the day.

Tips for Families

1. **Find a consistent time to read.**
2. **Sit next to your child and give your undivided attention.**
3. **Use a pencil to point to the words.** You can point above the words while your child uses a finger to point below them.
4. **If your child struggles to read a word, point to the part she or he missed and say the sound.** Then have your child re-blend the word.

   EXAMPLE: Child misses the word *join.* Point to the *oi* and say, "These letters spell *oi.* What sound?" (oi). "Good. Now sound out the word." Point to the letters as they blend /j/ /oi/ /n/.

5. **"Read, Model, Read Again"** After your child has read a short section of text (a sentence, paragraph, or page), read aloud the same section yourself, modeling appropriate pacing and expression, while your child follows along with a finger. Then have your child read the same section a second time.

Tips for Families

1. Find a consistent time to read.
2. Sit next to your child and give your undivided attention.
3. Use a pencil to point to the words. You can point above the words while your child uses a finger to point below them.
4. If your child struggles to read a word, point to the part she or he missed and say the sound. Then have your child re-blend the word.

   EXAMPLE: Child misses the word join. Point to the oi and say, "These letters spell oi. What sound?" (oi). "Good. Now sound out the word." Point to the letters as they blend /j/ /oi/ /n/.

5. "Read, Model, Read Again" After your child has read a short section of text (a sentence, paragraph, or page), read aloud the same section yourself, modeling appropriate pacing and expression, while your child follows along with a finger. Then have your child read the same section a second time.

BOOK BAG BUDDIES:

A Fun Way to Build Reading Skills

Welcome to our exciting Book Bag Buddies program! This program is designed to be a fun and engaging way for your child to strengthen his or her reading skills outside of the classroom. By participating, you and your child become a team, working together to explore new books and spark a love for reading.

Our Book Bag Buddies use decodable books. These books focus on the letter-sounds we're learning in class, so children can sound out words themselves instead of relying on pictures or guessing from context. By helping your child read these books, you'll be supporting your child's phonics skills and building a strong foundation for reading success!

Here's how we can all be Book Bag Buddies:

- **Book Bag Buddies:** Your child will get to bring home two or three new books each Monday in a special Book Bag. Your child will become Book Bag Buddies with these books, reading them throughout the week and returning them on Friday.
- **Nightly Reading Adventures:** Each night, set aside some special time to snuggle up and listen to your child read his or her books. This is a fantastic opportunity to bond and practice reading skills!
- **Reading Champions:** Aim for at least three readings of each book—the more your child reads, the more confident he or she will become! We suggest reading for 15–20 minutes each night. After your child reads these books, create special memories by reading some of your child's favorite books to him or her.
- **Book Care Buddies:** We want our Book Bag Buddies to stay happy and healthy! Please help your child treat the bag and books with care. If a book or bag is accidentally damaged or lost, we kindly ask for a replacement cost to keep our Book Bag Buddies program thriving.

We're so excited to embark on this reading journey with you and your child! If you have any questions, please don't hesitate to ask.

Let's sign below to show we're ready to be Book Bag Buddies!

STUDENT PROMISE: I promise to be a good Book Bag Buddy! I will read my books carefully, take care of the bag, and return them on time each Friday.

____

(Student Signature)

PARENT/GUARDIAN PROMISE: I have read the Book Bag Buddies information and promise to assist my child in reading, taking care of, and returning the books each week. We're excited to embark on this reading adventure together!

____

(Parent/Guardian Signature)

Error-Correction Procedure

Pointing Prompt: Point to the part of the word your child missed and allow time for him or her to state the correct sound.

Verbal Prompt: If your child can't recall the sound, provide it.

Blending Prompt: Encourage your child to blend the sounds. If he or she is unable to blend the sounds, model how to do it. For example, stretch out the sounds /m/ /a/ /p/ slowly at first; then repeat them more quickly /ma/ /p/. See if your child can say the word, *map*. If not, say the word for them and have them repeat.

Error-Correction Procedure

Pointing Prompt: Point to the part of the word your child missed and allow time for him or her to state the correct sound.

Verbal Prompt: If your child can't recall the sound, provide it.

Blending Prompt: Encourage your child to blend the sounds. If he or she is unable to blend the sounds, model how to do it. For example, stretch out the sounds /m/ /a/ /p/ slowly at first; then repeat them more quickly /ma/ /p/. See if your child can say the word, *map*. If not, say the word for them and have them repeat.

Error-Correction Procedure

Pointing Prompt: Point to the part of the word your child missed and allow time for him or her to state the correct sound.

Verbal Prompt: If your child can't recall the sound, provide it.

Blending Prompt: Encourage your child to blend the sounds. If he or she is unable to blend the sounds, model how to do it. For example, stretch out the sounds /m/ /a/ /p/ slowly at first; then repeat them more quickly /ma/ /p/. See if your child can say the word, *map*. If not, say the word for them and have them repeat.

Error-Correction Procedure

Pointing Prompt: Point to the part of the word your child missed and allow time for him or her to state the correct sound.

Verbal Prompt: If your child can't recall the sound, provide it.

Blending Prompt: Encourage your child to blend the sounds. If he or she is unable to blend the sounds, model how to do it. For example, stretch out the sounds /m/ /a/ /p/ slowly at first; then repeat them more quickly /ma/ /p/. See if your child can say the word, *map*. If not, say the word for them and have them repeat.

4.D My Favorite Decodable Book Sets

Use for: Students who need practice applying phonics skills in connected text

Yes, I'm hooked on acquiring decodable books! I have been writing grants and building my collection for almost a decade! I am thrilled with the variety and quality of decodable texts these days, and consider carefully my students' needs when selecting books for small-group lessons. Here are some of my favorite sets.

Dandelion Books

I have three sets of these books: Dandelion Launchers, Dandelion World, and Dandelion Readers. Dandelion Launchers are very beginning books. They start with only five letters: *s, a, t, i,* and *m*, which means you don't have to wait until students know the entire alphabet for them to start reading books. Dandelion World are nonfiction books that follow the same scope and sequence as the Launchers. Dandelion Readers are a bit longer and introduce vowel teams, diphthongs, and *r*-controlled vowels. The series is best for grades K–1 and the beginning of 2.

Express Readers

These books are sturdy and designed with young readers in mind. Students love the characters and storylines. Because I have a limited number of copies of each title, I keep the books in my classroom library for students to read on their own or with a partner, and use them for my take-home books program. They are best for grades K and 1.

Flyleaf

I've been using Flyleaf decodables for a long time. The illustrations are absolutely beautiful and the stories are engaging. These books get quite challenging as you progress through the series, making them a nice choice for first- and second-grade students, as well as for older students who still need decodables.

Geodes

The decodable Geodes books focus on building young readers' knowledge and sparking their curiosity. While these books follow a scope and sequence of phonics skills, they are more difficult than other sets because they are less decodable. As such, they are perfect for preparing students to read regular, authentic texts. I start most students off in books that have a higher percentage of decodable words, and then move them into these books as they are ready, and finally into regular, authentic texts. These books work best in grades 1–3.

Half-Pint Kids

Kindergarten teachers love these books because there are so many at the CVC-word level, plus they are affordable. The pictures are adorable, and the stories are rather short, so students have time to read them a few times during a small-group lesson. With each reading, they tend to be more successful, which boosts their confidence. There are also comprehension questions at the end of each book. They are perfect for grade K and the start of first grade.

Just Right Reader

There are a lot of things to love about these books. There is a QR code in each one that leads to a phonics lesson on the targeted skill, making them wonderful take-home books because students can review or preview phonics skills by watching the lesson. What's even more exciting is that the lessons are in English and Spanish. Also, the books start simply, with only one word per page. Sometimes I give them to students who aren't quite ready to read full sentences so they can read a book like everyone else. These books work well for grades K–2, and for older students who still need decodables.

Laugh-a-Lot Phonics

My students adore the Laugh-a-Lot Phonics readers! The colorful pictures and fun storylines keep their attention. I have three sets: Short Vowels, Long Vowels, and Blends and Digraphs. In first grade, I use the short-vowels set at the beginning of the year and long-vowels set in the middle of the year. The digraphs/blends set contains vowel teams so they're perfect for the end of the year. These sets are great for grades K–2.

Nonfiction Phonics Readers

Who doesn't love a nice selection of nonfiction decodables? They are rather hard to come by, so I was excited to find these sets. Students enjoy looking at the vibrant photographs, and I love the purposeful practice the books provide. I appreciate the fact that the targeted phonics skill is listed in the top-right corner of each book's cover, which enables me to quickly find a book that matches the skill I want students to practice. These sets are appropriate for grades K–2.

Read to Know Text Sets

This beautiful collection focuses on building knowledge. Each set includes three books, two nonfiction and one fiction, that are centered around a common theme. While the books follow a phonics scope and sequence, they are a little less decodable than other sets out there, making them perfect for students who are moving away from decodables and into regular, authentic texts. I also love the companion website, which allows me to print out copies of the books we've read in class for students to read at home. I recommend these books for grades 1–3.

Whole Phonics

One thing I love about the books in this set is that each one contains a true story arc—an exciting flow of events—that captivates students, along with the engaging, comic-book-style illustrations. I remember one of my rambunctious first graders examining a list of titles on the back of one of the books, and exclaiming, "Mrs. Kemeny, I want to read ALL of these!" These books are a bit longer, so I might spend a couple days on the same title, so students can read and reread it to build automaticity. They're best for grades K–2.

*Product availability and format are subject to change.

MOVE 5

Embrace a Better Approach to Teaching "Sight Words"

Move 5 downloadables are available here.

When I was a young teacher, I thought "sight words" were words that could not be sounded out. So, I taught them as whole units to be memorized visually. I have since learned that teaching that way inhibits how the brain learns and stores words. For words to be instantly retrieved when they are encountered in print, their graphemes, phonemes, and meanings need to be linked in long-term memory—or "orthographically mapped." In fact, beginning readers who focus on letter-sound relationships, instead of memorizing whole words, increase activity in the area of the brain best wired for reading (Yoncheva et al., 2015)! And that's what I want! So how we teach words has a wide-ranging and lasting impact.

While many teachers use the term "sight word" to describe a word that appears frequently in texts, researchers use it differently. A sight word is any word readers can recognize immediately, not because they have memorized it, but because the process of orthographic mapping has occurred. As Jan Wasowicz put it, "Every word wants to be a sight word when it grows up!" (Wasowicz, 2020)

Let's review key points about Move 5.

- Memorizing words as a whole unit inhibits the process that is necessary to store words in long-term memory.
- Instead of focusing our efforts on getting students to memorize words, we need to intensify our focus on phonemes and the graphemes that represent them.
- Making sure that words become part of a student's sight-word vocabulary is the goal.
- The process necessary for words to become sight words is called orthographic mapping.
- Orthographic mapping involves the student linking a word's spelling, pronunciation, and meaning.
- High-frequency words can be regular and irregular.
- Irregular high-frequency words can be further categorized by "temporarily irregular" and "permanently irregular." Permanently irregular words will require extra attention and practice.
- We must consider students' phonics knowledge as we choose words to teach.
- Use an explicit protocol to teach high-frequency words—one that helps students map the word's internal sounds to their spellings and meanings.
- Draw students' attention to the word's regular parts and irregular parts.
- Students may need several exposures to a word before they are able to map it.

MOVE 5: Routines and Resources

RESOURCE		PAGE
5.A	High-Frequency Word Routine and Lessons	188
5.B	High-Frequency Words Practice Page	210
5.C	High-Frequency Word Games	212

KEEP  Teaching students irregular high-frequency words.

STOP  Requiring students to memorize large lists of words as whole units, especially those with consistent, reliable spellings (e.g., *that*, *can*).

START  Encouraging students to map words' sounds (phonemes) with their spellings (graphemes) and meanings, whether the words are regular or irregular.

Terms to Know

High-Frequency Word: A word that occurs often in text

Orthographic Mapping: A process that involves connecting pronunciations of phonemes in a word to the graphemes that represent those pronunciations and linking them to the word's meaning to store the word in long-term memory

Sight Word: Any word that can be retrieved from memory instantly because it has been orthographically mapped

Regular High-Frequency Word: A word that occurs often in text and has consistent, reliable sound-spelling correspondences (e.g., can, that)

Temporarily Irregular High-Frequency Word: A word that occurs often in text and is decodable once students have learned the phonics skills it contains (e.g., *like*, *for*)

Permanently Irregular High-Frequency Word: A word that occurs frequently in text and has irregular sound-spelling correspondences (e.g., *said*, *one*)

5.A High-Frequency Word Routine and Lessons

Use for: Students who are learning to read and/or spell high-frequency words

Length of Activity: 5 minutes

Materials:

- Teacher: Lesson Steps Reference Card (page 189), High-Frequency Word Routine Lessons (pages 190–209), dry-erase board and marker
- Students: High-Frequency Words Practice Page (page 211) or dry-erase boards and markers

Drawing on what we know about orthographic mapping, I teach irregular high-frequency words by having students analyze the word all the way through so they anchor the regular spellings and sounds and notice the irregular spellings and sounds. Remember, irregularity exists on a continuum. A word might be phonetically regular, such as *like* and *made*, but isn't for a student who hasn't learned the CVCe phonics skill.

And don't feel compelled to use the term "high-frequency words." I've heard teachers use "tricky words," "heart words," "snap words," "flash words," "red words," and "sticky words." Any term works.

Directions

Follow the routine below (based on the work of Nora Chahbazi and her EBLI program) to teach any high-frequency word. Be sure to model each step for students and have them follow along with you, using their own dry-erase boards or the High-Frequency Words Practice Page on page 211.

1. Say the word and use it in a sentence.
2. Segment and count the sounds.
3. Map the phonemes (sounds) to the graphemes (spellings).
4. Point out the irregular parts.
5. Cover the word and have students rewrite it from memory.
6. Uncover the word and check students' spelling.
7. Have students use the word in a sentence.

Another option is to use one of the pre-made lessons on pages 190–209. For those lessons, I selected 20 words from the Dolch/Fry list: *about, because, come, does, first, friend, for, from, great, laugh, many, of, one, people, said, two, though, what, who,* and *would*. The letters appearing between slashes refer to the sound the letters represent. For example, /d/ means you say the sound of *d*, not the name of the letter.

High-Frequency Word Routine Lesson

about

1. The tricky word we will learn today is: *about*. What word? (*about*) He knew a lot *about* dinosaurs.
2. Tell me the sounds you hear in the word *about* (/u/ /b/ /ou/ /t/). How many sounds? (4) Yes, say the sounds again and draw a line for each sound.

   ___ ___ ___ ___

3. The first sound is /u/. Watch as I write this spelling (*a*). Say /u/ as you write the spelling on the first line. What's the next sound? (/b/) Say /b/ as you write the spelling on the next line (*b*). What's the next sound? (/ou/) Yes, watch as I write this spelling (*ou*). Now say /ou/ as you write the spelling on the line. What's the last sound? (/t/) Say /t/ as you write the spelling on the last line.
4. Which parts are tricky? Yes, the *a* and the *ou*. Circle the *a* and underline it one time because one letter spells that sound. Circle the *ou* and underline it two times because two letters spell that sound. *ou* is a common spelling for /ou/, but we haven't learned that yet.
5. Erase the letters, but leave the lines and circles. (Or fold down the paper.) Now write the word again. See if you can remember the tricky spellings.
6. Here's the correct spelling. Did you get it right? Now erase everything (or fold down the paper) and rewrite the word on the handwriting lines.
7. Tell your neighbor a sentence with the word: *about*. (Optional: Write the sentence on the dry-erase board or worksheet.)

You can lead the lessons yourself or print them out for paraprofessionals or volunteers to use for additional practice with students. The lessons are organized alphabetically for easy access. Teach them in an order that works for you. Or follow the order in which the words are presented in your phonics program.

Differentiation Tips

If students have difficulty, consider the following scaffolds.

- Repeat this lesson in small groups or one-on-one.
- Provide many practice opportunities, allowing students to read and spell these words individually and in connected text.
- Give extra attention to and practice with function words (e.g., *of, to, was*).
- Remember to connect the word to its meaning or use.
- Introduce each high-frequency word slowly, allowing time to practice and review before teaching a new word.
- Encourage successive blending: student blends first two sounds before adding the last sound (e.g., *sat* is read /s/ /a/ /sa/ /t/ /sat/).
- Review, review, review.

To make the activity more challenging, try these.

- Focus more on spelling the word than reading it.
- Introduce words more quickly.
- Encourage students to write sentences containing two or three high-frequency words.

Lesson Steps Reference Card

1. Say the word and use it in a sentence.
2. Segment and count the sounds.
3. Map the phonemes (sounds) to the graphemes (spellings).
4. Point out the irregular parts.
5. Cover the word and have students rewrite it from memory.
6. Uncover the word and check students' spelling.
7. Have students use the word in a sentence.

1. The tricky word we will learn today is: *about*. What word? (*about*) He knew a lot *about* dinosaurs.

2. Tell me the sounds you hear in the word *about* (/u/ /b/ /ou/ /t/). How many sounds? (4) Yes, say the sounds again and draw a line for each sound.

   ____ ____ ____ ____

3. The first sound is /u/. Watch as I write this spelling (*a*). Say /u/ as you write the spelling on the first line. What's the next sound? (/b/) Say /b/ as you write the spelling on the next line (*b*). What's the next sound? (/ou/) Yes, watch as I write this spelling (*ou*). Now say /ou/ as you write the spelling on the line. What's the last sound? (/t/) Say /t/ as you write the spelling on the last line.

4. Which parts are tricky? Yes, the *a* and the *ou*. Circle the *a* and underline it one time because one letter spells that sound. Circle the *ou* and underline it two times because two letters spell that sound. *ou* is a common spelling for /ou/, but we haven't learned that yet.

5. Erase the letters, but leave the lines and circles. (Or fold down the paper.) Now write the word again. See if you can remember the tricky spellings.

6. Here's the correct spelling. Did you get it right? Now erase everything (or fold down the paper) and rewrite the word on the handwriting lines.

7. Tell your neighbor a sentence with the word: *about*. (Optional: Write the sentence on the dry-erase board or worksheet.)

because

1. The tricky word we will learn today is: *because*. What word? (*because*) We couldn't go on the picnic *because* it was raining.

2. Tell me the sounds you hear in the word *because* (/b/ /ee/ /k/ /u/ /z/). How many sounds? (5) Yes, say the sounds again and draw a line for each sound.

   ____ ____ ____ ____ ____

3. The first sound is /b/. Watch as I write this spelling (*b*). Say /b/ as you write the spelling on the first line. What's the next sound? (/ee/) Say /ee/ as you write the spelling on the next line (*e*). What's the next sound? (/k/) Yes, watch as I write this spelling (*c*). Now say /k/ as you write the spelling on the line. What's the next sound? (/u/) Yes, watch as I write this spelling (*au*). Now say /u/ as you write the spelling on the line. What's the last sound? (/z/) Watch as I write the spelling (*se*). Say /z/ as you write the spelling on the last line.

4. Which parts are tricky? Yes, the *au* and the *se*. Circle the *au* and underline it two times because two letters spell that sound. Circle the *se* and underline it two times because two letters spell that sound.

5. Erase the letters, but leave the lines and circles. (Or fold down the paper.) Now write the word again. See if you can remember the tricky spellings.

6. Here's the correct spelling. Did you get it right? Now erase everything (or fold down the paper) and rewrite the word on the handwriting lines.

7. Tell your neighbor a sentence with the word: *because*. (Optional: Write the sentence on the dry-erase board or worksheet.)

1. The tricky word we will learn today is: *come*. What word? (*come*) The dog will *come* when I call him.

2. Tell me the sounds you hear in the word *come* (/k/ /u/ /m/). How many sounds? (3) Yes, say the sounds again and draw a line for each sound.

____ ____ ____

3. The first sound is /k/. Watch as I write this spelling (*c*). Say /k/ as you write the spelling on the first line. What's the next sound? (/u/) Watch as I write this spelling (*o*). Say /u/ as you write the spelling on the next line (*o*). What's the last sound? (/m/) Say /m/ as you write the spelling on the last line (*me*).

4. Which parts are tricky? Yes, the *o* and the *me*. Circle the *o* and underline it one time because one letter spells that sound. Circle the *me* and underline it two times because two letters spell that sound.

5. Erase the letters, but leave the lines and circles. (Or fold down the paper.) Now write the word again. See if you can remember the tricky spellings.

6. Here's the correct spelling. Did you get it right? Now erase everything (or fold down the paper) and rewrite the word on the handwriting lines.

7. Tell your neighbor a sentence with the word: *come*. (Optional: Write the sentence on the dry-erase board or worksheet.)

Explanation: Long ago, scribes wrote books by hand. They used a special way of writing that used a lot of downstrokes. This made it hard to read certain letters when they were next to each other, such as *m*, *n*, *u*, and *v*. To make it easier, they sometimes changed the letter "u" to "o." Even though they spelled it differently, they still said it the same way.

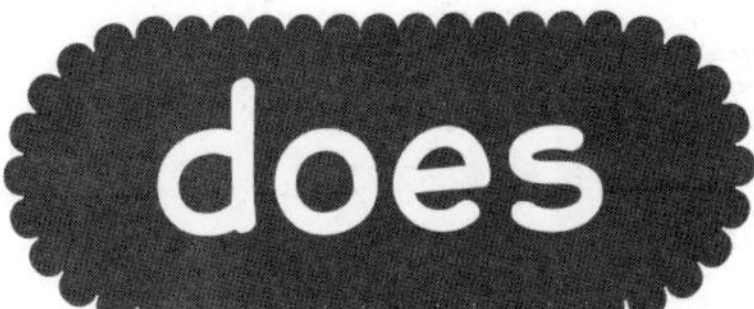

1. The tricky word we will learn today is: *does*. What word? (*does*) The cat *does* not like the water.

2. Tell me the sounds you hear in the word *does* (/d/ /u/ /z/). How many sounds? (3) Yes, say the sounds again and draw a line for each sound.

____ ____ ____

3. The first sound is /d/. Watch as I write this spelling (*d*). Say /d/ as you write the spelling on the first line. What's the next sound? (/u/) Watch as I write this spelling (*o*). Say /u/ as you write the spelling on the next line (*o*). What's the last sound? (/z/) Yes, watch as I write this spelling (*es*). Now say /z/ as you write the spelling on the line.

4. Which parts are tricky? Yes, the *o* and the *es*. Circle the *o* and underline it one time because one letter spells that sound. Circle the *es* and underline it two times because two letters spell that sound.

5. Erase the letters, but leave the lines and circles. (Or fold down the paper.) Now write the word again. See if you can remember the tricky spellings.

6. Here's the correct spelling. Did you get it right? Now erase everything (or fold down the paper) and rewrite the word on the handwriting lines.

7. Tell your neighbor a sentence with the word: *does*. (Optional: Write the sentence on the dry-erase board or worksheet.)

Explanation: *Does* is the third-person present tense of the word *do*. The word *do* means to perform an action. If we talk about something happening right now, we use the present tense. So if we want to say the girl is doing something right now, we use the word *does*. The girl does a flip. These words are related: *do, doing, does, done*.

1. The tricky word we will learn today is: *first*. What word? (*first*) She was the *first* person in line.
2. Tell me the sounds you hear in the word *first* (/f/ /ir/ /s/ /t/). How many sounds? (4) Yes, say the sounds again and draw a line for each sound.

   ____ ____ ____ ____

3. The first sound is /f/. Say /f/ as you write the spelling on the first line (*f*). What's the next sound? (/ir/) Watch as I write this spelling (*ir*). Say /ir/ as you write the spelling on the next line (*ir*). What's the next sound? (/s/) Yes, say /s/ as you write the spelling on the line. What's the last sound? (/t/) Say /t/ as you write the spelling on the last line.
4. Which part is tricky? Yes, the *ir*. Circle the *ir* and underline it two times because two letters spell that sound. *ir* is a common spelling for /ir/, but there are other ways to spell that sound too, so it's a little tricky.
5. Erase the letters, but leave the lines and circles. (Or fold down the paper.) Now write the word again. See if you can remember the tricky spellings.
6. Here's the correct spelling. Did you get it right? Now erase everything (or fold down the paper) and rewrite the word on the handwriting lines.
7. Tell your neighbor a sentence with the word: *first*. (Optional: Write the sentence on the dry-erase board or worksheet.)

1. The tricky word we will learn today is: *friend*. What word? (*friend*) She was such a good *friend*.

2. Tell me the sounds you hear in the word *friend* (/f/ /r/ /e/ /n/ /d/). How many sounds? (5) Yes, say the sounds again and draw a line for each sound.

   ____ ____ ____ ____ ____

3. The first sound is /f/. Say /f/ as you write the spelling on the first line. What's the next sound? (/r/) Say /r/ as you write the spelling on the next line (*r*). What's the next sound? (/e/) Yes, watch as I write this spelling (*ie*). Now say /e/ as you write the spelling on the line. What's the next sound? (/n/) Say /n/ as you write the spelling on the next line (*n*). What's the last sound? (/d/) Say /d/ as you write the spelling on the last line.

4. Which part is tricky? Yes, the *ie*. Circle the *ie* and underline it two times because two letters spell that sound.

5. Erase the letters, but leave the lines and circles. (Or fold down the paper.) Now write the word again. See if you can remember the tricky spellings.

6. Here's the correct spelling. Did you get it right? Now erase everything (or fold down the paper) and rewrite the word on the handwriting lines.

7. Tell your neighbor a sentence with the word: *friend*. (Optional: Write the sentence on the dry-erase board or worksheet.)

1. The tricky word we will learn today is: *for*. What word? (*for*) She made a card *for* her grandpa.

2. Tell me the sounds you hear in the word *for* (/f/ /or/). How many sounds? (2) Yes, say the sounds again and draw a line for each sound.

   ____ ____

3. The first sound is /f/. Say /f/ as you write the spelling on the first line. What's the next sound? (/or/) Yes, watch as I write this spelling (*or*). Now say /or/ as you write the spelling on the line.

4. Which part is tricky? Yes, the *or*. Circle the *or* and underline it two times because two letters spell that sound. *or* is how we spell the sound /or/, but we haven't learned that yet.

5. Erase the letters, but leave the lines and circles. (Or fold down the paper.) Now write the word again. See if you can remember the tricky spellings.

6. Here's the correct spelling. Did you get it right? Now erase everything (or fold down the paper) and rewrite the word on the handwriting lines.

7. Tell your neighbor a sentence with the word: *for*. (Optional: Write the sentence on the dry-erase board or worksheet.)

1. The tricky word we will learn today is: *from*. What word? (*from*) He got a letter *from* his uncle.

2. Tell me the sounds you hear in the word *from* (/f/ /r/ /u/ /m/). How many sounds? (4) Yes, say the sounds again and draw a line for each sound.

    ____ ____ ____ ____

3. The first sound is /f/. Say /f/ as you write the spelling on the first line (*f*). What's the next sound? (/r/) Say /r/ as you write the spelling on the next line (*r*). What's the next sound? (/u/) Yes, watch as I write this spelling (*o*). Now say /u/ as you write the spelling on the line. What's the last sound? (/m/) Say /m/ as you write the spelling on the last line.

4. Which part is tricky? Yes, the *o*. Circle the *o* and underline it one time because one letter spells that sound.

5. Erase the letters, but leave the lines and circles. (Or fold down the paper.) Now write the word again. See if you can remember the tricky spellings.

6. Here's the correct spelling. Did you get it right? Now erase everything (or fold down the paper) and rewrite the word on the handwriting lines.

7. Tell your neighbor a sentence with the word: *from*. (Optional: Write the sentence on the dry-erase board or worksheet.)

1. The tricky word we will learn today is: *great*. What word? (*great*) It was a *great* day to fly a kite.

2. Tell me the sounds you hear in the word *great* (/g/ /r/ /ay/ /t/). How many sounds? (4) Yes, say the sounds again and draw a line for each sound.

   ____ ____ ____ ____

3. The first sound is /g/. Say /g/ as you write the spelling on the first line (*g*). What's the next sound? (/r/) Say /r/ as you write the spelling on the next line (*r*). What's the next sound? (/ay/) Yes, watch as I write this spelling (*ea*). Now say /ay/ as you write the spelling on the line. What's the last sound? (/t/) Say /t/ as you write the spelling on the last line.

4. Which part is tricky? Yes, the *ea*. Circle the *ea* and underline it two times because two letters spell that sound.

5. Erase the letters, but leave the lines and circles. (Or fold down the paper.) Now write the word again. See if you can remember the tricky spellings.

6. Here's the correct spelling. Did you get it right? Now erase everything (or fold down the paper) and rewrite the word on the handwriting lines.

7. Tell your neighbor a sentence with the word: *great*. (Optional: Write the sentence on the dry-erase board or worksheet.)

1. The tricky word we will learn today is: *laugh*. What word? (*laugh*) The joke made her laugh out loud.

2. Tell me the sounds you hear in the word *laugh* (/l/ /a/ /f/). How many sounds? (3) Yes, say the sounds again and draw a line for each sound.

   ____ ____ ____

3. The first sound is /l/. Say /l/ as you write the spelling on the first line (*l*). What's the next sound? (/a/) Watch as I write this spelling (*au*). Say /a/ as you write the spelling on the next line (*au*). What's the last sound? (/f/) Watch as I write this spelling (*gh*). Say /f/ as you write the spelling on the last line (*gh*).

4. Which parts are tricky? Yes, the *au* and the *gh*. Circle the *au* and underline it two times because two letters spell that sound. Circle the *gh* and underline it two times because two letters spell that sound.

5. Erase the letters, but leave the lines and circles. (Or fold down the paper.) Now write the word again. See if you can remember the tricky spellings.

6. Here's the correct spelling. Did you get it right? Now erase everything (or fold down the paper) and rewrite the word on the handwriting lines.

7. Tell your neighbor a sentence with the word: *laugh*. (Optional: Write the sentence on the dry-erase board or worksheet.)

1. The tricky word we will learn today is: *many*. What word? (*many*) There were *many* people in the store.

2. Tell me the sounds you hear in the word *many* (/m/ /e/ /n/ /ee/). How many sounds? (4) Yes, say the sounds again and draw a line for each sound.

   ____ ____ ____ ____

3. The first sound is /m/. Say /m/ as you write the spelling on the first line (*m*). What's the next sound? (/e/) Watch as I write this spelling (*a*). Say /e/ as you write the spelling on the next line (*a*). What's the next sound? (/n/) Say /n/ as you write the spelling on the line. What's the last sound? (/ee/) Yes, watch as I write this spelling (*y*). Say /ee/ as you write the spelling on the last line (*y*).

4. Which parts are tricky? Yes, the *a* and the *y*. Circle the *a* and underline it one time because one letter spells that sound. Circle the *y* and underline it one time because one letter spells that sound. *y* spells the sound /ee/ at the end of words with more than one syllable, but we haven't learned that yet.

5. Erase the letters, but leave the lines and circles. (Or fold down the paper.) Now write the word again. See if you can remember the tricky spellings.

6. Here's the correct spelling. Did you get it right? Now erase everything (or fold down the paper) and rewrite the word on the handwriting lines.

7. Tell your neighbor a sentence with the word: *many*. (Optional: Write the sentence on the dry-erase board or worksheet.)

1. The tricky word we will learn today is: *of*. What word? (*of*)
   She ate a bowl *of* oatmeal.

2. Tell me the sounds you hear in the word *of* (/u/ /v/). How many sounds? (2) Yes, say the sounds again and draw a line for each sound.

   ___ ___

3. The first sound is /u/. Watch as I write this spelling (*o*). Say /u/ as you write the spelling on the first line (*o*). What's the next sound? (/v/) Yes, watch as I write this spelling (*f*). Now say /v/ as you write the spelling on the line (*f*).

4. Which parts are tricky? Yes, the *o* and the *f*. Circle the *o* and underline it one time because one letter spells that sound. Circle the *f* and underline it one time because one letter spells that sound. Both parts of the word are tricky!

5. Erase the letters, but leave the lines and circles. (Or fold down the paper.) Now write the word again. See if you can remember the tricky spellings.

6. Here's the correct spelling. Did you get it right? Now erase everything (or fold down the paper) and rewrite the word on the handwriting lines.

7. Tell your neighbor a sentence with the word: *of*. (Optional: Write the sentence on the dry-erase board or worksheet.)

1. The tricky word we will learn today is: *one*. What word? (*one*) He ate *one* piece of pizza.

2. Tell me the sounds you hear in the word *one* (/w/ /u/ /n/). How many sounds? (3) Yes, say the sounds again and draw a line for each sound.

____ ____ ____

3. The first sound is /w/. What's the next sound? (/u/) Watch carefully. In this word one letter represents two sounds. The letter *o* spells both the /w/ and /u/ in this word so we will write the *o* in between the first two sound lines. Watch me.

__o__

4. Say both sounds /wu/ as you write the spelling between the lines (*o*). What's the last sound? (/n/) Watch as I write this spelling (*ne*). Say /n/ as you write the spelling on the last line (*ne*).

5. Which parts are tricky? Yes, the *o* and the *ne*. Circle the *o* and underline it one time because one letter spells both those sounds. Circle the *ne* and underline it two times because two letters spell that sound.

6. Erase the letters, but leave the lines and circles. (Or fold down the paper.) Now write the word again. See if you can remember the tricky spellings.

7. Here's the correct spelling. Did you get it right? Now erase everything (or fold down the paper) and rewrite the word on the handwriting lines.

8. Tell your neighbor a sentence with the word: *one*. (Optional: Write the sentence on the dry-erase board or worksheet.)

Explanation: This word was originally pronounced with the long *o* as it is in related words: *lone, alone, lonely, only*.

1. The tricky word we will learn today is: *people*. What word? (*people*) The *people* at the park were having fun.
2. Tell me the sounds you hear in the word *people* (/p/ /ee/ /p/ /ul/). How many sounds? (4) Yes, say the sounds again and draw a line for each sound.

   ____ ____ ____ ____

3. The first sound is /p/. Say /p/ as you write the spelling on the first line (*p*). What's the next sound? (/ee/) Watch as I write this spelling (*eo*). Say /ee/ as you write the spelling on the next line (*eo*). What's the next sound? (/p/) Yes, say /p/ as you write the spelling on the line (*p*). What's the last sound? (/ul/) Watch as I write this spelling (*le*). Say /ul/ as you write the spelling on the last line (*le*).
4. Which parts are tricky? Yes, the *eo* and the *le*. Circle the *eo* and underline it two times because two letters spell that sound. Circle the *le* and underline it two times because two letters spell that sound. You will often see *le* at the end of a word, but we're still learning that.
5. Erase the letters, but leave the lines and circles. (Or fold down the paper.) Now write the word again. See if you can remember the tricky spellings.
6. Here's the correct spelling. Did you get it right? Now erase everything (or fold down the paper) and rewrite the word on the handwriting lines.
7. Tell your neighbor a sentence with the word: *people*. (Optional: Write the sentence on the dry-erase board or worksheet.)

1. The tricky word we will learn today is: *said*. What word? (*said*) She *said* hi to me in the hall.

2. Tell me the sounds you hear in the word *said* (/s/ /e/ /d/). How many sounds? (3) Yes, say the sounds again and draw a line for each sound.

   ___ ___ ___

3. The first sound is /s/. Say /s/ as you write the spelling on the first line (*s*). What's the next sound? (/e/) Watch as I write this spelling (*ai*). Say /e/ as you write the spelling on the next line (*ai*). What's the last sound? (/d/) Say /d/ as you write the spelling on the last line (*d*).

4. Which part is tricky? Yes, the *ai*. Circle the *ai* and underline it two times because two letters spell that sound.

5. Erase the letters, but leave the lines and circles. (Or fold down the paper.) Now write the word again. See if you can remember the tricky spellings.

6. Here's the correct spelling. Did you get it right? Now erase everything (or fold down the paper) and rewrite the word on the handwriting lines.

7. Tell your neighbor a sentence with the word: *said*. (Optional: Write the sentence on the dry-erase board or worksheet.)

Explanation: *Said* is the past-tense form of the word *say*. Other similar words: *pay—paid, lay—laid*.

two

1. The tricky word we will learn today is: *two*. What word? (*two*) She gave away two cookies.
2. Tell me the sounds you hear in the word *two* (/t/ /oo/). How many sounds? (2) Yes, say the sounds again and draw a line for each sound.

   ____ ____

3. The first sound is /t/. Watch as I write this spelling (*tw*). Say /t/ as you write the spelling on the first line. What's the next sound? (/oo/) Watch as I write this spelling (*o*). Say /oo/ as you write the spelling on the next line (*o*).
4. Which parts are tricky? Yes, the *tw* and the *o*. Circle the *tw* and underline it two times because two letters spell that sound. Circle the *o* and underline it one time because one letter spells that sound.
5. Erase the letters, but leave the lines and circles. (Or fold down the paper.) Now write the word again. See if you can remember the tricky spellings.
6. Here's the correct spelling. Did you get it right? Now erase everything (or fold down the paper) and rewrite the word on the handwriting lines.
7. Tell your neighbor a sentence with the word: *two*. (Optional: Write the sentence on the dry-erase board or worksheet.)

Explanation: "tw" generally means two, split, separate. For example: *twin, twice, twist, twelve, twenty, between*.

1. The tricky word we will learn today is: *though*. What word? (*though*) I want to go to the park even *though* it's raining.
2. Tell me the sounds you hear in the word *though* (/th/ /oe/). How many sounds? (2) Yes, say the sounds again and draw a line for each sound.

   ____ ____

3. The first sound is /th/. Watch as I write this spelling (*th*). Say /th/ as you write the spelling on the first line. What's the next sound? (/oe/) Yes, watch as I write this spelling (*ough*). Now say /ough/ as you write the spelling on the line.
4. Which part is tricky? Yes, the *ough*. Circle the *ough* and underline it four times because four letters spell that sound.
5. Erase the letters, but leave the lines and circles. (Or fold down the paper.) Now write the word again. See if you can remember the tricky spellings.
6. Here's the correct spelling. Did you get it right? Now erase everything (or fold down the paper) and rewrite the word on the handwriting lines.
7. Tell your neighbor a sentence with the word: *though*. (Optional: Write the sentence on the dry-erase board or worksheet.)

1. The tricky word we will learn today is: *what*. What word? (*what*) I wonder *what* she is doing.

2. Tell me the sounds you hear in the word *what* (/w/ /u/ /t/). How many sounds? (3) Yes, say the sounds again and draw a line for each sound.

   ____ ____ ____

3. The first sound is /w/. Watch as I write this spelling (*wh*). Say /w/ as you write the spelling on the first line. What's the next sound? (/u/) Watch as I write this spelling (*a*). Say /u/ as you write the spelling on the next line (*a*). What's the last sound? (/t/) Say /t/ as you write the spelling on the last line.

4. Which parts are tricky? Yes, the *wh* and the *a*. Circle the *wh* and underline it two times because two letters spell that sound. Circle the *a* and underline it one time because one letter spells that sound. *wh* is a common spelling for /w/, but we need help remembering when to use it.

5. Erase the letters, but leave the lines and circles. (Or fold down the paper.) Now write the word again. See if you can remember the tricky spellings.

6. Here's the correct spelling. Did you get it right? Now erase everything (or fold down the paper) and rewrite the word on the handwriting lines.

7. Tell your neighbor a sentence with the word: *what*. (Optional: Write the sentence on the dry-erase board or worksheet.)

1. The tricky word we will learn today is: *who*. What word? (*who*) *Who* wants to go to recess?
2. Tell me the sounds you hear in the word *who* (/h/ /oo/). How many sounds? (2) Yes, say the sounds again and draw a line for each sound.

   ____ ____

3. The first sound is /h/. Watch as I write this spelling (*wh*). Say /h/ as you write the spelling on the first line (*wh*). What's the next sound? (/oo/) Watch as I write this spelling (*o*). Say /oo/ as you write the spelling on the next line (*o*).
4. Which parts are tricky? Yes, the *wh* and the *o*. Circle the *wh* and underline it two times because two letters spell that sound. Circle the *o* and underline it one time because one letter spells that sound.
5. Erase the letters, but leave the lines and circles. (Or fold down the paper.) Now write the word again. See if you can remember the tricky spellings.
6. Here's the correct spelling. Did you get it right? Now erase everything (or fold down the paper) and rewrite the word on the handwriting lines.
7. Tell your neighbor a sentence with the word: *who*. (Optional: Write the sentence on the dry-erase board or worksheet.)

1. The tricky word we will learn today is: *would*. What word? (*would*) *Would* you help me clean the table?

2. Tell me the sounds you hear in the word *would* (/w/ /o͝o/ /d/). How many sounds? (3) Yes, say the sounds again and draw a line for each sound.

   _____ _____ _____

3. The first sound is /w/. Say /w/ as you write the spelling on the first line. What's the next sound? (/o͝o/) Watch as I write this spelling (*oul*). Say /o͝o/ as you write the spelling on the next line (*oul*). What's the last sound? (/d/) Say /d/ as you write the spelling on the last line.

4. Which part is tricky? Yes, the *oul*. Circle the *oul* and underline it three times because three letters spell that sound.

5. Erase the letters, but leave the lines and circles. (Or fold down the paper.) Now write the word again. See if you can remember the tricky spellings.

6. Here's the correct spelling. Did you get it right? Now erase everything (or fold down the paper) and rewrite the word on the handwriting lines.

7. Tell your neighbor a sentence with the word: *would*. (Optional: Write the sentence on the dry-erase board or worksheet.)

5.B High-Frequency Words Practice Page

Use for: Students who are learning to read and/or spell high-frequency words

Length of Activity: 5 minutes

Materials:

Students: High-Frequency Words Practice Page (page 211), pencil

Directions

Use this page instead of dry-erase boards for the High-Frequency Word Routine. Or use it as a tool for students to review words you've taught.

1. Write the target word in the space at the top of the sheet and make a copy for each student.
2. Distribute the sheet to students, have them read the target word, segment its sounds, then draw a line for each sound.
3. Have them write the corresponding spelling on each line, circling the tricky part.
4. Ask students to fold down the sheet to cover what they wrote.
5. Have them segment and say the sounds again as they write the spelling of each part in the sound boxes. If they need help, let them unfold their paper to take a peek at the word.
6. Ask them to fold down the sheet again to cover what they wrote.
7. In the third section, have students write the word on the handwriting lines. Remind them to use the lines correctly and to write neatly.
8. Ask them to compose a sentence, using the word.

High-Frequency Words Practice Page

TARGET WORD:

Draw the sound lines. Then write the spellings on the correct lines. Circle the tricky spellings.

Cover the word and write it again in the sound boxes.

Write the word two times on these lines.

Write the word in a sentence.

Differentiation Tips

If students have difficulty, consider the following scaffolds.

- Have students complete the page with a teacher or helpful peer.
- Provide more practice opportunities reading and writing the word with guidance from the teacher or volunteer.
- Give extra attention and practice to function words (e.g., *of, to, was*).
- Remember to connect the word to its meaning or use.
- Allow more time to practice and review the word before teaching a new one.
- Review, review, review.

To make the activity more challenging, try these.

- Focus more on spelling the word than reading it.
- Introduce words more quickly.
- Encourage students to compose a sentence containing two or three high-frequency words.
- Have students complete the page independently after you have taught the word.

TARGET WORD:

Draw the sound lines. Then write the spellings on the correct lines. Circle the tricky spellings.

Cover the word and write it again in the sound boxes.

Write the word two times on these lines.

Write the word in a sentence.

5.C High-Frequency Word Games

Use for: Students who are learning to read and/or spell high-frequency words accurately

Length of Activity: 10–15 minutes

Some students need more practice opportunities than others. Games are a fantastic way to provide those opportunities! They keep students engaged, while giving them extra time to interact with and map important words.

Spin, Say, Write

Materials: Spin, Say, Write page (page 215), pencils, paper clips

Prep: Choose six high-frequency words, write on the pie chart, and make a copy for each student.

How to Play: Take turns spinning a paper clip, using the pencil tip to anchor it on the pie chart. Once the paper clip lands on a word, say it aloud, and write it down correctly as you say the sounds.

Race to the Finish

Materials: copy of game board (pages 216–217), playing pieces (counters, Unifix cubes), dice

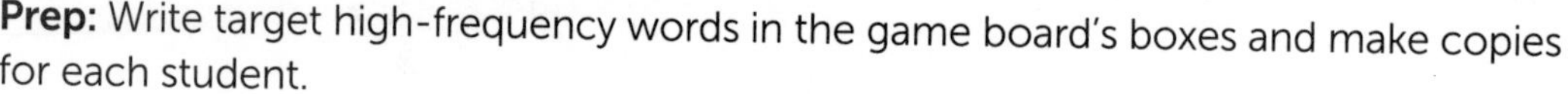

Prep: Write target high-frequency words in the game board's boxes and make copies for each student.

How to Play: Players take turns moving their piece the number of spaces rolled on a die. When they land on a space, they read aloud (or write) the word. The first player to get to the finish wins!

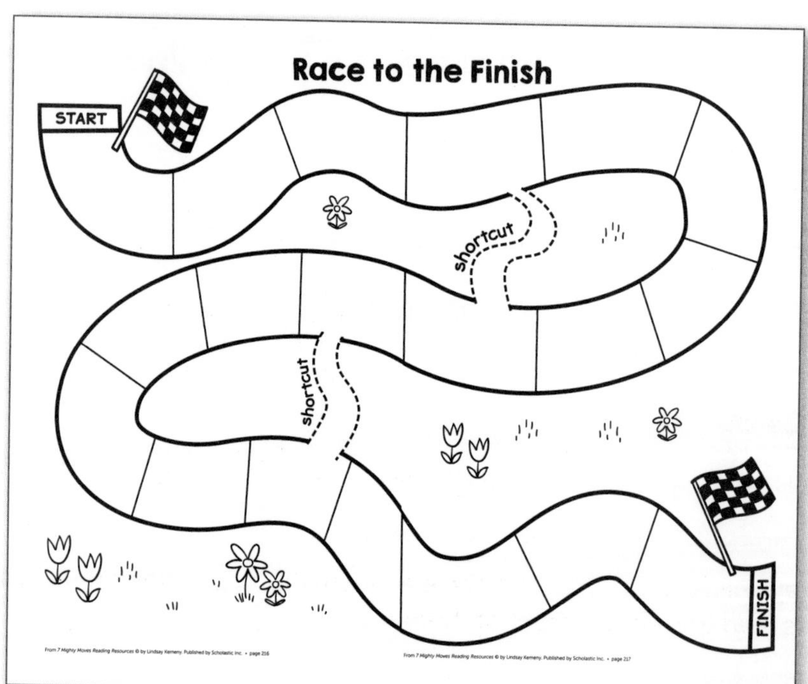

Bingo

Materials: Blank Bingo Boards (pages 168–169), Bingo chips, pencils

Prep: Make a copy of the Bingo Board for each student.

How to Play: Distribute the boards and chips to players. Dictate high-frequency words one at a time. Players will spell each word anywhere on their Bingo Board. Once completed, play Bingo! Call out high-frequency words one at a time. Players mark the words they hear on their cards. The first player to get a full row, column, or diagonal line calls out "Bingo!" and wins.

Pop!

Materials: High-Frequency Word Cards (pages 218–226), "Pop!" word cards (page 226)

Prep: Copy the "Pop!" word cards and the high-frequency word cards

How to Play: Shuffle all cards and place them face down. Players take turns drawing a card and reading it. If they read it correctly, they keep it. If players draw a "Pop!" card, they have to return all their collected cards to the bottom of the stack. The player with the most cards at the end of the game wins!

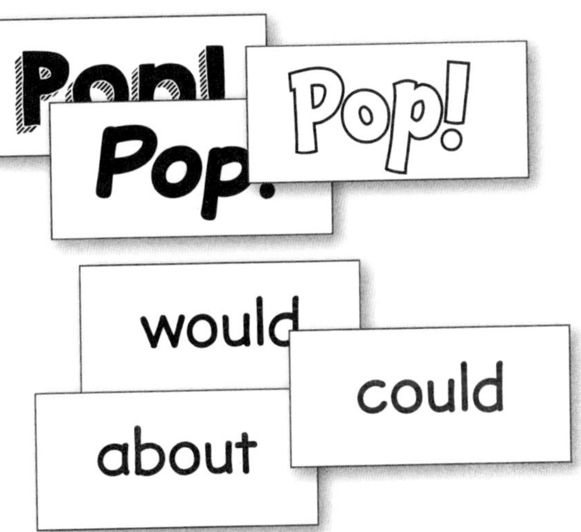

Memory Match Mayhem

Materials: High-Frequency Word Cards (pages 218–226)

Prep: Print and cut out pairs of high-frequency word cards

How to Play: Shuffle the cards and lay them face down. Students take turns flipping over two cards at a time. They read the words aloud. If they find a match (both cards have the same word), they keep the pair and get another turn. The player with the most pairs at the end wins.

Musical Cards

Materials: High-Frequency Word Cards (pages 218–226), music

Prep: Print and cut out high-frequency word cards

How to Play: Place word cards in a circle and turn on music. When music stops, all students read the word in front of them.

Word Builder Blitz

Materials: High-Frequency Word Cards (pages 218–226), sound boxes (page 227), magnetic letters or dry-erase boards and markers

Prep: Print and cut out the cards. Print, cut, and laminate the sound boxes.

How to Play: Shuffle and place word cards face down. First player picks a card and reads it to his or her partner. The partner segments the sounds while placing a manipulative in each sound box, then puts magnet letters (or writes) the letters in the corresponding box. Partner checks he or she spelled it correctly and then players switch roles.

Go Fish

Materials: High-Frequency Word Cards (pages 218–226)

Prep: Print and cut out two copies of the cards.

How to Play: Shuffle and deal five cards each. Players take turns asking others for cards matching their own. If the asked player has the card, he or she gives it to the asker. If not, the asker draws a card from the deck (Go Fish!). The player with the most matches wins.

Differentiation Tips

If students have difficulty, consider the following scaffolds.

- Pair students with classmates who can help them.
- Use a smaller deck of high-frequency words for each game.
- Repeat the same high-frequency word several times during the game.
- Mix in regular decodable words with a few target high-frequency words.
- Focus on reading the words rather than spelling.
- Repeat the High-Frequency Word Routine.

To make the games more challenging, try these.

- Use a larger deck of words.
- Focus on spelling the words.
- Replace "easier" high-frequency words with more sophisticated ones.

Spin, Say, Write

Race to Ⓐ

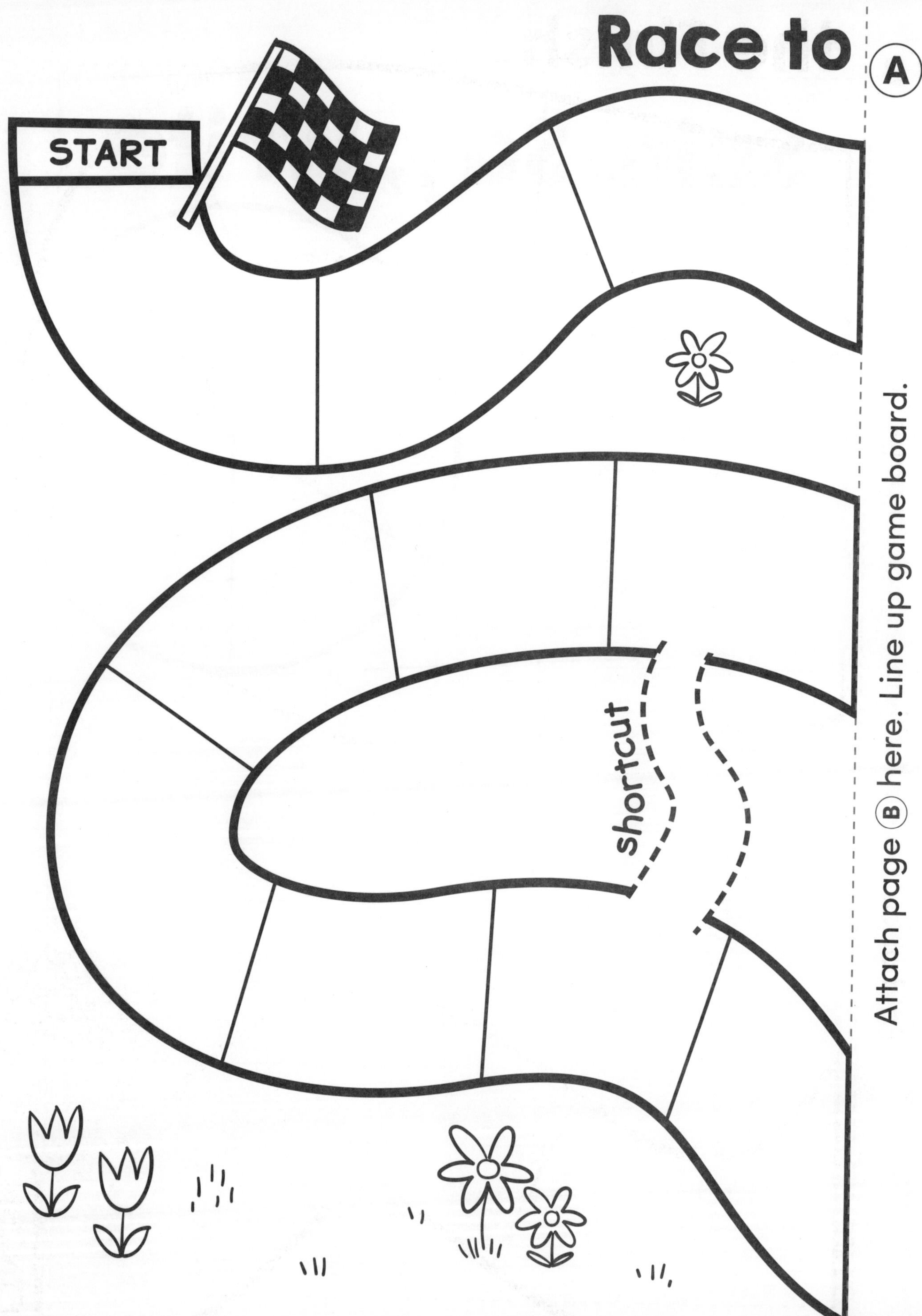

Attach page Ⓑ here. Line up game board.

B

the Finish

Fold or cut on dotted line. Attach to page A.

shortcut

FINISH

about	again
around	all
always	away
any	are
because	been
before	both

by	buy
carry	come
could	do
does	done
draw	each
eight	find

first	friend
for	from
give	goes
good	great
have	her
hurt	how

into	its
kind	know
laugh	little
live	like
long	look
many	move

more	my
now	of
one	once
only	open
or	other
people	play

please	pretty
put	right
said	saw
see	should
some	start
the	their

there	three
they	to
two	too
today	thank
think	though
use	very

walk	was
way	were
what	when
which	where
who	why
want	work

would	write
you	your
Pop!	Pop!
Pop!	Pop!
Pop!	Pop!
Pop!	Pop!

MOVE 6

Move 6 downloadables are available here.

Focus on Meaningful Fluency Practice

Sometimes we think reading fluency will develop on its own, but it would be shortsighted to expect a student's dysfluency to improve by reading silently. We need to give students plenty of opportunities to read aloud with the opportunity for feedback. Reading fluency is a result of our explicit, systematic instruction combined with "carefully orchestrated reading practice" (Hudson et al., 2009). I'm always thinking about how to orchestrate that targeted practice.

Fluency is most often described as a combination of accuracy, rate, and prosody (Hasbrouck, 2020).

Accuracy: Accuracy, the foundation of fluency, refers to the extent to which students read the words correctly. A reasonable target for accuracy is 98 percent, which is high enough for students to maintain comprehension of most texts.

Rate: Rate refers to the speed at which students read words. We don't need speed readers, but we do need students to develop automaticity at the letter, letter-pattern, word, and sentence levels so they can devote attention to the text's meaning.

Prosody: Prosody refers to the expression and phrasing students use as they read. It also includes their intonation and volume, and the degree to which they emphasize words and phrases.

Let's review key points about Move 6.

- Fluency is a complex skill that requires students to read accurately, with appropriate rate and expression, to make meaning.
- Fluency has a direct impact on students' comprehension.
- When students are not fluent, and have to focus intensely on retrieving sound-symbol correspondences from memory, they do not have much cognitive space left to think about what they are reading.
- Systematic and explicit phonics is effective as long as it is not taught in isolation. Students need plenty of opportunities to read continuous text to internalize the phonics concepts we teach.
- Whole-group, round-robin reading creates an unnecessary emotional toll on students that can lead to devastating effects. It is an ineffective practice and has extremely limited practice opportunities for students.
- Students who struggle to read texts orally do not become good readers if left to read silently.
- We must address the foundational subskills of reading, so that fluency can evolve from there.
- Research has consistently found that repeated oral reading is effective for developing fluency.
- Students must have multiple, meaningful practice opportunities to improve fluency.
- Choral reading, cloze reading, echo reading, partner reading, performing, text scooping, and timed repeated reading are effective techniques for improving fluency.

MOVE 6: Routines and Resources

RESOURCE		PAGE
6.A	Partner Reading Routine	230
6.B	Timed Repeated Reading Chart	234
6.C	Scooping Phrases Practice Page	237
6.D	Poems to Read and Perform	243

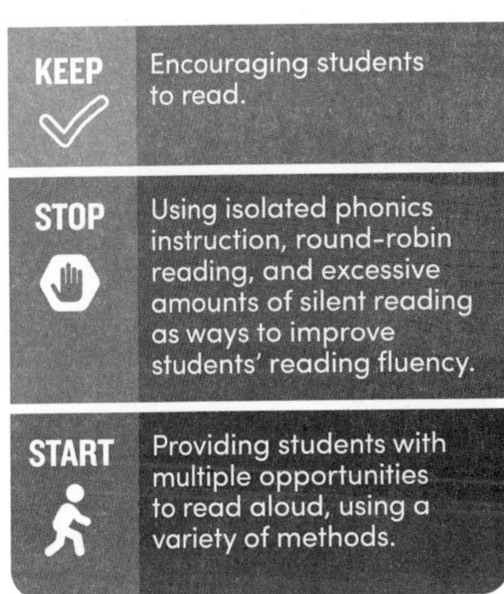

6.A Partner Reading Routine

Use for: Students who are working on becoming more fluent readers

Length of Activity: 20 minutes

Materials:

- Teacher: partner list, Partner Reading Rules (page 232)
- Students: folders with fluency passages, Ask, Then Tell handout (page 233), Paragraph Shrinking Card (page 257), partner labels (optional, online)

One way I orchestrate oral reading practice is with partner reading. It's an excellent way for students to practice their reading skills. I'm intentional when assigning partners. I list students in order, from least fluent to most fluent. Then I split the list in half, assigning the most fluent reader in one half to the most fluent in the second half; the second most fluent in one half with the second most fluent in the second half, and so on, and assign each pair "Reader 1" and "Reader 2." (Feel free to get creative with naming: "Milk" and "Cookies" or "Chips" and "Salsa," for example.) I have the more fluent student read first to provide a model for the other student. Of course, do not reveal the weaker and stronger readers to students.

There are many ways to structure partner reading. After pairing up students, you might assign them a certain amount of text to read before switching. For example, they might switch off every other sentence, paragraph, or page. Or you might have Reader 1 model each page or paragraph, and then have Reader 2 read the same page or paragraph afterward.

Directions

One of my favorite ways to structure partner reading is using an evidence-based routine called Partner Reading Paragraph Shrinking (Fuchs et al., 2008; Burns et al., 2015).

Watch a presentation on Partner Reading Paragraph Shrinking here:

1. Give each student a folder with reading passages, Ask, Then Tell handout (page 233), and Paragraph Shrinking Card (page 257).
2. On the first day, explain the rules, and the error-correction guidelines. Then ask students to practice. Have Reader 1 read for five minutes while Reader 2 follows along. Then have Reader 2 go back to the beginning of the passage and read for five minutes, while Reader 1 follows along.

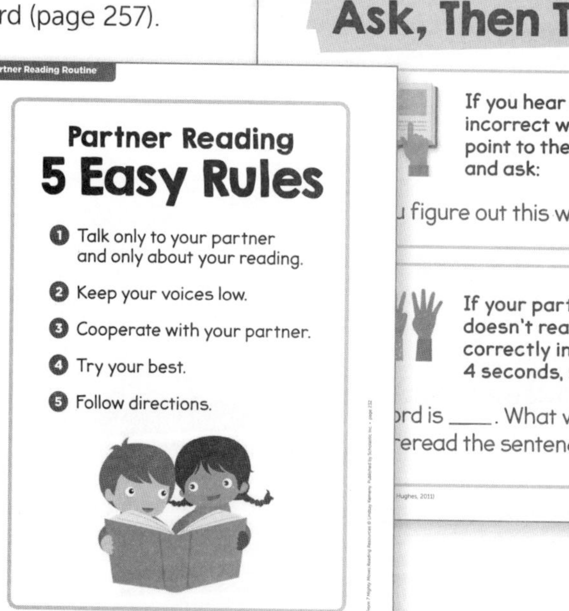

3. On the second day, teach and model Paragraph Shrinking (see Move 7.A), a three-step process to help students summarize each paragraph. Students identify who or what the paragraph is about, say the most important idea about the "who" or "what," and then say the main idea in 10 words or less.
4. Ask students to practice: Have Reader 1 read for five minutes, stopping after each paragraph to summarize. Then have Reader 2 pick up wherever Reader 1 left off, continuing to read for five minutes and stopping to summarize each paragraph.
5. Repeat the activity, with different texts, on Days 2 to 10. (Extend the activity beyond two weeks, if you desire.)

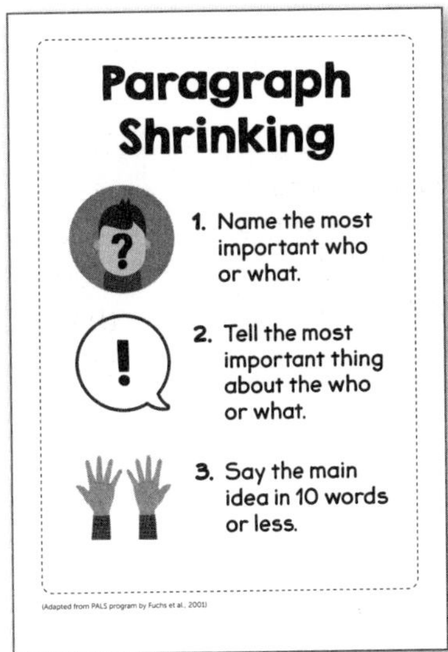

Quick Overview

- Reader 1 reads the text for five minutes.
- Reader 2 reads the same text for five minutes.
- Reader 1 continues reading for five minutes where Reader 2 left off, stopping at the end of each paragraph to summarize it.
- Reader 2 continues reading for five minutes where Reader 1 left off, stopping at the end of each paragraph to summarize it.

Differentiation Tips

If students have difficulty, consider the following scaffolds.

- Preview unfamiliar words before students read.
- Use simpler passages.
- Use decodable texts instead of regular texts.
- Place student in a triad instead of a pair. Assign that student to be Reader 2 along with another student. Have Reader 1 read aloud first, and then have both Reader 2s read aloud together.
- Provide a separate intervention for students during this time.

To make the activity more challenging, try this.

- Use more complex passages.

Partner Reading
5 Easy Rules

1. Talk only to your partner and only about your reading.
2. Keep your voices low.
3. Cooperate with your partner.
4. Try your best.
5. Follow directions.

Ask, Then Tell

If you hear an incorrect word, point to the word and ask:

"Can you figure out this word?"

If your partner doesn't read it correctly in 4 seconds, say:

"This word is ____. What word? Now reread the sentence."

(based on material from Archer & Hughes, 2011)

6.B Timed Repeated Reading Chart

Use for: Individual students in second grade and above who are accurate, but need help with rate

Length of Activity: 5–15 minutes, at least three times a week

Materials:

- Teacher: copy of a passage, timer
- Students: Timed Repeated Reading Chart (page 236), crayons, copy of passage

Timed Repeated Reading (Hudson et al., 2022) is a one-on-one intervention for students in second grade and above who are reading accurately, but could use help with rate.

Directions

Choose a passage between 50 and 200 words that the student can read with at least 90 percent accuracy. Choosing the right passage is the key to students' motivation (Hudson et al., 2022).

1. **Preview Material** Let the student practice reading the passage before being timed. Encourage her to read the text accurately. Model correct pronunciations of words or sounds that may be difficult for her.
2. **Set Goals and Review Graph** Have the student review her WCPM graph from previous sessions (see steps 8 and 9) and set a Words-Correct-per-Minute (WCPM) goal for the session. For example, the goal might be to read five more words correctly in one minute—and/or even more words by the end of the week. Keep goals realistic and the discussion positive, aiming to encourage and motivate the student.
3. **Read and Record for One Minute** Have the student read aloud for one minute, keeping your timer out of the student's view. As the student reads, mark any errors. If she pauses and doesn't know the word, tell it to her and count it as an error. Wait only three seconds before providing the word to keep her momentum going.
4. **Provide Constructive Feedback** Offer praise and advice. Give time for the student to practice any words missed.
5. **Calculate Score** To determine the WCPM score, subtract the number of errors from the total number of words read in one minute. For example, if she read 86 words in a minute, but missed 5 of the words, her WCPM would be 81.

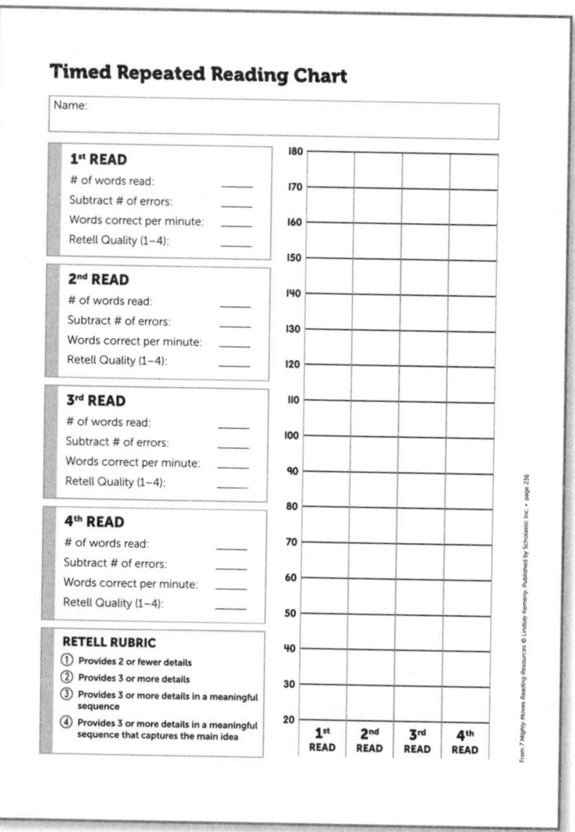

Timed Repeated Reading Chart

Name:

1st READ
# of words read: ____
Subtract # of errors: ____
Words correct per minute: ____
Retell Quality (1–4): ____

2nd READ
# of words read: ____
Subtract # of errors: ____
Words correct per minute: ____
Retell Quality (1–4): ____

3rd READ
# of words read: ____
Subtract # of errors: ____
Words correct per minute: ____
Retell Quality (1–4): ____

4th READ
# of words read: ____
Subtract # of errors: ____
Words correct per minute: ____
Retell Quality (1–4): ____

RETELL RUBRIC
① Provides 2 or fewer details
② Provides 3 or more details
③ Provides 3 or more details in a meaningful sequence
④ Provides 3 or more details in a meaningful sequence that captures the main idea

180
170
160
150
140
130
120
110
100
90
80
70
60
50
40
30
20

1st READ | 2nd READ | 3rd READ | 4th READ

6. **Graph Data** Help the student fill out the graph to represent the WCPM score. She would color the graph up to 81.
7. **Repeat Steps 3–6** Time the student for one minute as she rereads aloud the passage to give her a chance to improve her score. While Hudson and colleagues don't include this step, I find it motivates students because they almost always do better on the second read. Calculate and graph the data again.
8. **Analyze Trends and Check Goals** Check the student's rate and accuracy goals and any trends you notice. The student should reach both goals before moving on to a new passage. Make adjustments if her rate is not improving. For example, sometimes I have the student practice reading the passage aloud with me, as part of Step 1.
9. **Celebrate and Support!** Congratulate students when they meet or get close to their goals. Set future goals.

Differentiation Tips

If students have difficulty, consider the following scaffolds.

- Use a simpler passage.
- Preview difficult or unfamiliar words before reading.
- Keep the timer out of view of the student.
- Set appropriate, realistic goals.
- Remember to keep your attitude upbeat and relaxed.
- Instead of timing students on the whole passage, choose a part of the passage (e.g., the first two paragraphs) for them to read untimed. Calculate and graph how many words they are able to read correctly within that portion of the text.
- If this activity causes anxiety in a student, discontinue it.

To make the activity more challenging, try these.

- Use a more complex passage.
- Focus on suitable expression.
- Have students retell what they read immediately after Step 3, and focus on the quality of the retelling.

Timed Repeated Reading Chart

Name:

1st READ

# of words read: ______

Subtract # of errors: ______

Words correct per minute: ______

Retell Quality (1–4): ______

2nd READ

# of words read: ______

Subtract # of errors: ______

Words correct per minute: ______

Retell Quality (1–4): ______

3rd READ

# of words read: ______

Subtract # of errors: ______

Words correct per minute: ______

Retell Quality (1–4): ______

4th READ

# of words read: ______

Subtract # of errors: ______

Words correct per minute: ______

Retell Quality (1–4): ______

RETELL RUBRIC

① Provides 2 or fewer details

② Provides 3 or more details

③ Provides 3 or more details in a meaningful sequence

④ Provides 3 or more details in a meaningful sequence that captures the main idea

180				
170				
160				
150				
140				
130				
120				
110				
100				
90				
80				
70				
60				
50				
40				
30				
20				
	1st READ	2nd READ	3rd READ	4th READ

Scooping Phrases Practice Page

Phrase scooping is a way of chunking text into meaningful units by clustering groups of words that naturally go together, meaning where there's a natural pause or a change in tone or emphasis. It encourages students to read fluently, instead of word by word, which can lead to better comprehension.

Use for: Students who read word by word and need to work on fluency

Length of Activity: 5–10 minutes

Materials:

- Students: a reading fluency passage or a Scooping Phrases Practice Page (pages 238–242)

Directions

Begin by having students scoop just a few words at a time. As students improve, gradually increase the number of words.

Here are some options for scooping phrases:

- Mark scoops for students. Have them read the words within each scoop smoothly.
- Read a sentence aloud fluently as students listen. Then have students mark scoops that match how you read the sentence. Then have them to read it aloud, using the scoops as a guide.
- Invite students to mark scoops on their own. Then have them partner up and take turns reading.

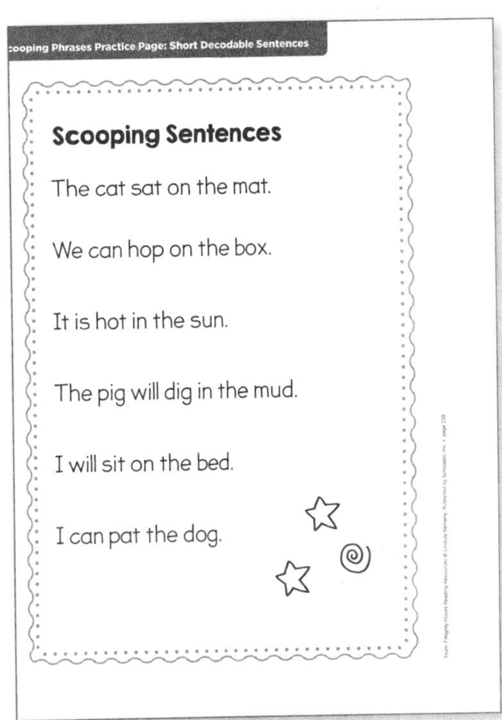

Scooping Phrases Practice Page: Short Decodable Sentences

Scooping Sentences

The cat sat on the mat.

We can hop on the box.

It is hot in the sun.

The pig will dig in the mud.

I will sit on the bed.

I can pat the dog.

Differentiation Tips

If students have difficulty, consider the following scaffolds.

- Have students scoop fewer words at first.
- Use a simpler text.
- Pair the student with an adult reader, rather than a peer.
- Start by modeling the activity for the student.
- Have students read aloud with you, encouraging them to keep pace.

To make the activity more challenging, try these.

- Have students scoop longer phrases.
- Use a more complex text.
- Focus on expression.

Scooping Sentences

The cat sat on the mat.

We can hop on the box.

It is hot in the sun.

The pig will dig in the mud.

I will sit on the bed.

I can pat the dog.

Scooping Sentences

The big dog can run fast.

I like to eat ice cream.

They want to watch a movie.

Can you please help me?

He loves to ride his bike.

The horse jumped over the fence.

Scooping Sentences

My friend likes to ride his red bike.

We will go to the park later today.

The brown bear caught a fish in the river.

She read a book about space to the class.

They played tag at the park down the street.

The black cat meowed loudly
because he was hungry.

We love to build sandcastles at the beach.

My favorite color is blue, but green is nice.

After school, I will go to soccer practice.

Scooping Sentences

When it rains, we stay inside
and play board games.

Because she studied hard,
she got a good grade on her test.

Although the cookies were tempting,
he resisted and ate an apple instead.

The lost puppy wandered through
the park until it found its owner.

We dug a moat around the sandcastle
we built at the beach.

They explored the dark forest with flashlights
in hand, searching for owls.

continued on next page

continued from previous page

The pirate with the patched eye told a story about a hidden treasure.

The girl who loves to read borrowed a stack of books from the library.

The spaceship that traveled to Mars carried a crew of brave astronauts.

Poems to Read and Perform

Reading and performing poems is an enjoyable, invigorating way for students to improve their reading fluency. Preparing for a performance gives student an authentic reason to read a text multiple times, and develops prosody.

Use for: Students who are developing their reading fluency

Length of Activity: 5–10 minutes

Materials:

- Students: Poems to Read and Perform (pages 244–253 and online)

Directions

Give students a new poem at the start of the week. Read aloud the poem while students follow along silently. Then have students choral-read it aloud with you, as a class. Throughout the week, whenever you have a few extra minutes in your day, read the poem by choral reading, echo reading (i.e., you read and then the class reads), and partner reading (i.e., students read to one another). At the end of the week, have students volunteer to perform the poem in front of the whole class or for a small group.

Consider giving each student a poetry folder to collect poems each week. Have students read and review the poems throughout the year, at school and at home for their families.

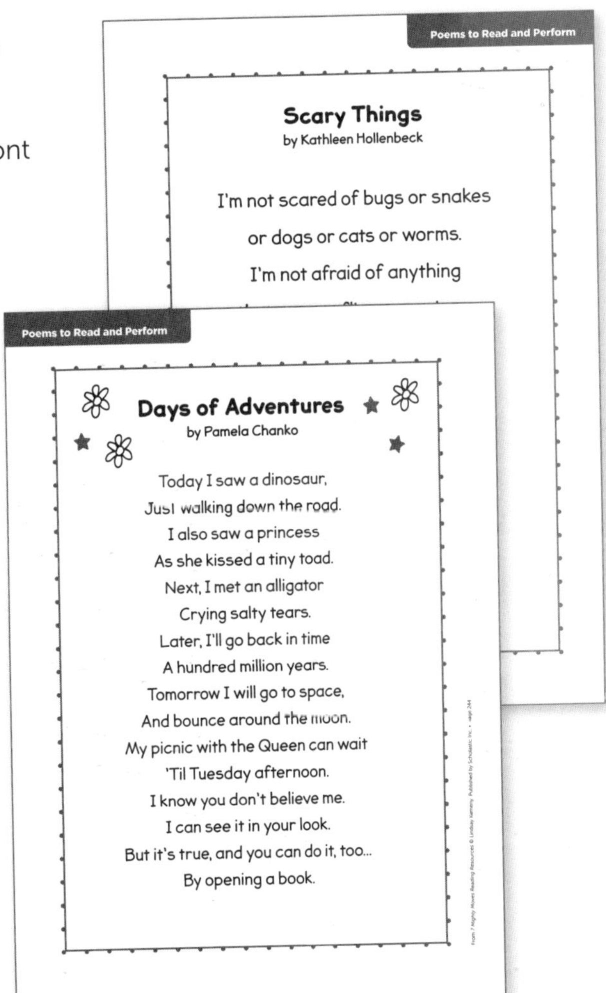
Poems to Read and Perform

Scary Things
by Kathleen Hollenbeck

I'm not scared of bugs or snakes
or dogs or cats or worms.
I'm not afraid of anything

Poems to Read and Perform

Days of Adventures
by Pamela Chanko

Today I saw a dinosaur,
Just walking down the road.
I also saw a princess
As she kissed a tiny toad.
Next, I met an alligator
Crying salty tears.
Later, I'll go back in time
A hundred million years.
Tomorrow I will go to space,
And bounce around the moon.
My picnic with the Queen can wait
'Til Tuesday afternoon.
I know you don't believe me.
I can see it in your look.
But it's true, and you can do it, too...
By opening a book.

Differentiation Tips

If students have difficulty, consider the following scaffolds.

- Use a simpler poem with more decodable words
- Allow more time for rehearsal.
- Have students perform the poem with a partner or in a group.

To make the activity more challenging, try these.

- Use a more complex poem.
- Encourage student to read more expressively and use hand gestures.

Days of Adventures

by Pamela Chanko

Today I saw a dinosaur,
Just walking down the road.
I also saw a princess
As she kissed a tiny toad.
Next, I met an alligator
Crying salty tears.
Later, I'll go back in time
A hundred million years.
Tomorrow I will go to space,
And bounce around the moon.
My picnic with the Queen can wait
'Til Tuesday afternoon.
I know you don't believe me.
I can see it in your look.
But it's true, and you can do it, too...
By opening a book.

Scary Things

by Kathleen Hollenbeck

I'm not scared of bugs or snakes
or dogs or cats or worms.
I'm not afraid of anything
that runs or flies or squirms.
I'm not scared of thunderstorms
or wind that bends the trees,
but I don't like the darkness.
May I keep a light on, please?

My Lunch Box

by Kathleen Hollenbeck

My lunch box sits
upon the shelf.
I look with longing eyes.
It sits there like
a treasure box
that holds a great surprise.
The lunch bell rings.
I race across
and grab my box and then
I open it. . .
excitement fades. . .
it's tuna fish again.

Amazing Changes

by Dexter Twisdale

Sitting on a grassy patch
A tiny egg's about to hatch.
Can you guess what will come out
To eat the leaves and crawl about?
A caterpillar, yes, that's right!
It sees a leaf and takes a bite.
And then, can you imagine this?
It spins itself a chrysalis!
It sits so still, but by and by
It grows into a butterfly.
So watch and wait, and then one day
That butterfly will fly away.

My Teddy

by Kathleen Hollenbeck

Sometimes when I am feeling sad
and things just don't seem right,
I find my favorite teddy bear
and hold my teddy tight.
My teddy's face is furry.
His eyes are bright and black,
and teddy always listens well,
although he can't talk back.

The Substitute Teacher

by Kathleen Hollenbeck

When I got to school today,
my teacher wasn't there.
Someone else was at her desk
and sitting in her chair.
She didn't have my teacher's smile
or hands
or hair
or voice.
She didn't ask if she could stay.
I didn't have a choice.
Her smile was warm and friendly.
She told us all her name.
She taught us math and phonics.
We played a spelling game.
She read a funny chapter book
and had us read some, too.
She did just about everything
our own teacher would do.
I learned a lot at school today.
I had a lot of fun.
If my teacher's out again,
I hope we get this one!

What Does It Mean to Be Responsible

by Kathleen Hollenbeck

It's really very simple.
If you start it, see it through.
If you make a mess, then clean it.
Pick up what belongs to you.
If you have a job to do,
get it done before you play.
If you hurt a person's feelings,
say "I'm sorry" right away.
If you break it, try to fix it
or replace it if you must.
Keep a promise. Be a person
others know that they can trust.

All About Us

by Kathleen Hollenbeck

Our hair is brown
or blond
or black
or any shade of red.
It might be long
or short
or straight
or curly on our heads.
Our eyes are brown
or blue
or green
or hazel, black, or gray.
We're tall. We're short.
We're in between.
That's how we look today.

Mary's Lamb

by Sarah Josepha Hale

Mary had a little lamb,
Its fleece was white as snow,
And everywhere that Mary went
The lamb was sure to go;
He followed her to school one day—
That was against the rule,
It made the children laugh and play,
To see a lamb at school.

And so the Teacher turned him out,
But still he lingered near,
And waited patiently about,
Till Mary did appear;
And then he ran to her, and laid
His head upon her arm,
As if he said—"I'm not afraid—
You'll keep me from all harm."

"What makes the lamb love Mary so?"
The eager children cry—
"O, Mary loves the lamb, you know,"
The Teacher did reply;—
"And you each gentle animal
In confidence may bind,
And make them follow at your call,
If you are always kind."

The Three Little Kittens

attributed to Eliza Lee Cabot Follen

Three little kittens
They lost their mittens,
And they began to cry,
Oh, mother dear,
We sadly fear,
Our mittens we have lost.
What! Lost your mittens,
You naughty kittens!
Then you shall have no pie.
Mee-ow, mee-ow, mee-ow.
No, you shall have no pie.

The three little kittens
They found their mittens,
And they began to cry,
Oh, mother dear,
See here, see here,
Our mittens we have found.
Put on your mittens,
You silly kittens,
And you shall have some pie.
Purr-r, purr-r, purr-r,
Oh, let us have some pie.

MOVE 7

Improve Comprehension by Developing Vocabulary and Background Knowledge

Reading comprehension is complex! It is not a single "skill," but an "orchestrated product of a set of linguistic and cognitive processes" (Castles et al., 2018). There are so many factors in play as our students read. Earlier in my career, I didn't understand the critical roles background knowledge and vocabulary play. Now I do. In addition to some strategy instruction, I also need to focus my instruction on those two critical areas.

Vocabulary: Students need to understand the meanings of words, as well as relationships between and among them, and the context in which they appear. We can implement an instructional routine that introduces the word's pronunciation and meaning, and provides examples and opportunities for students to practice and interact with it throughout the week.

Background Knowledge: We can begin building background knowledge from the time students enter kindergarten. Besides teaching critical content in our science and social studies lessons, we can engage them in rich texts on a variety of important topics, in ELA and other points in our day. We can help them deepen their knowledge through writing in response to these texts.

While Move 7 focuses on developing vocabulary and background knowledge, it includes some strategy instruction–instruction in the service of building knowledge. Some important strategies include summarizing, generating and responding to questions, writing main idea sentences, and self-monitoring.

MOVE 7: Routines and Resources

RESOURCE		PAGE
7.A	Paragraph Shrinking Card	256
7.B	Nonfiction Reading Passages and Key Word Outline	258
7.C	Sentence Combining Routine	278
7.D	Vocabulary Routine	282
7.E	Three-Column Notes	286
7.F	Shades-of-Meaning Vocabulary Cards	288
7.G	Academic Vocabulary Reference Cards	306

Ways Students Can Write About Their Reading

- Personally react to the text
- Analyze and interpret it
- Summarize it
- Notate it
- Question it—and find answers (Graham & Hebert, 2010)

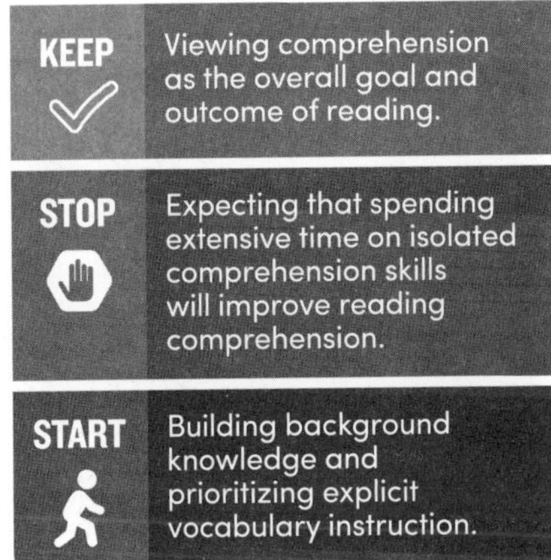

Let's review key points about Move 7.

- Reading comprehension is complex and multifaceted.
- There is a correlation between good reading comprehension and how much vocabulary and content knowledge you have on the subject.
- There is no comprehension strategy powerful enough to compensate for the fact that you can't read the words (Archer, 2011).
- Support comprehension by making time for social studies and science instruction.
- Integrate content in your literacy block.
- Rich read-alouds help students learn new information, see alternative perspectives, and think critically.
- Using multiple texts on the same topic is a great way to deepen knowledge and acquire vocabulary.
- Wide reading enables students to gain information about their world and others' worlds, build content knowledge, learn words, consider new perspectives, and gain new insights.
- Support comprehension by having students generate questions and practice paragraph shrinking (page 257).
- Intentionally teaching vocabulary words with a systematic routine before students encounter them in a text helps them comprehend the text and the words.
- Support vocabulary development by using sophisticated language, having students create three-column notes, allowing them to act out words, and encouraging them to write stories using them.
- Students deepen their knowledge by writing about what they read.

7.A Paragraph Shrinking Card

Use for: All students

Length of Activity: 5 minutes

Materials:

- Students: reading passage, Paragraph Shrinking Card (page 257)

Paragraph shrinking, developed by Peer Assisted Learning Strategies (Fuchs et al., 2001) at Vanderbilt University, is an excellent way for students to attend to meaning, while they read. Specifically, it's an evidence-based activity that helps students determine a text's main idea, and can be done with the whole class, in small groups, or in pairs. I also love to use it as part of a partner-reading routine (page 230) and with the Key Word Outlines (pages 260–262).

Directions

Read a paragraph or passage, such as an informational piece on sloths, and then ask students to:

1. Name the most important "who" or "what." In this case, the what is the sloth.
2. Explain the most important detail about the who or what. For example, the most important thing about the sloth is that it doesn't get much energy from the food it eats, so it moves really slowly to save energy.
3. Say the main idea in 10 words or less: "Sloths move slowly to save their energy."

Use the Paragraph Shrinking Card for students to refer to as they do this activity in pairs.

Differentiation Tips

If students have difficulty, consider the following scaffolds.

- Start by using simpler passages.
- Model the activity—with any text, across subjects and throughout the day.
- Do the activity several times as a whole class before having students do it in pairs or on their own.

To make the activity more challenging, try these.

- Use more complex passages.
- Have students write their main-idea sentences.

Paragraph Shrinking

1. Name the most important who or what.

2. Tell the most important thing about the who or what.

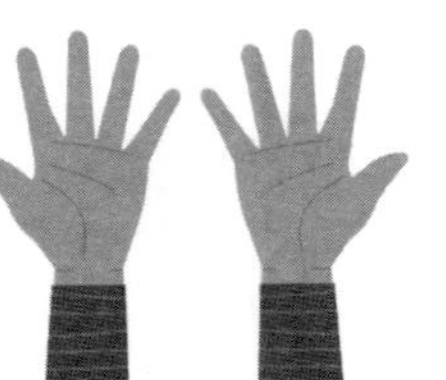

3. Say the main idea in 10 words or less.

(Adapted from PALS program by Fuchs et al., 2001)

Paragraph Shrinking

1. Name the most important who or what.

2. Tell the most important thing about the who or what.

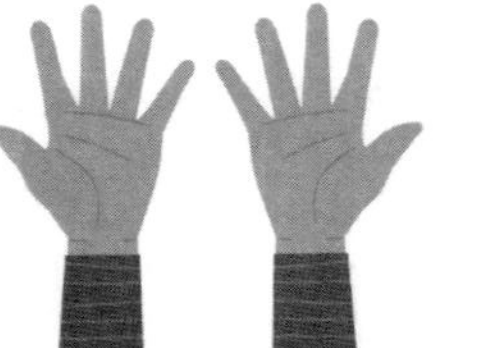

3. Say the main idea in 10 words or less.

(Adapted from PALS program by Fuchs et al., 2001)

7.B Nonfiction Reading Passages and Key Word Outline

Use for: Students who need support in sentence and paragraph composition

Length of Activity: 30 minutes

Materials:

- Teacher: Key Word Outline Template (page 260), Blank Writing Pages (pages 261–262), marker or pencil, a short nonfiction passage (pages 263–277 and online)
- Students: Key Word Outline Template (page 260), Blank Writing Pages (pages 261–262), pencils, short nonfiction passages (pages 263–277 and online)

When students write about what they read, they deepen their knowledge and, therefore, their comprehension. That's why I love having them do it! I combine Paragraph Shrinking (page 257) with a writing technique I learned from the Institute for Excellence in Writing. After determining the passage's main idea by shrinking the passage, students create key word outlines and use them to write their own paragraphs. I love that they can focus on the process of writing, without getting stuck on what to write about. The topic and ideas are already right there in their outline! It encourages students to craft coherent sentences using the words in their outlines and forces them to consider the knowledge they gained through their reading.

Directions

1. Give each student a copy of a short nonfiction passage i.e., about six sentences long). Ideally, the passage you choose aligns with topics students are learning about in your core reading program, social studies, science, etc. You can use passages from your program, create your own, or use the passages I created (pages 263–277). My passages are made up of about six sentences, making them easy to outline and, therefore, great for beginners. If you use a longer passage, have students choose up to six interesting facts or ideas from it to create the outline.
2. Read the passage to students and then read it together.
3. Guide students to find the main idea by asking the "Paragraph Shrinking" questions on page 257. Their main idea sentence can be their writing's topic sentence.
4. Reread the first sentence aloud and ask, "What do you think are the three most important words in this sentence?" Have students discuss possible words in pairs and then as a class. Have them circle the three words they chose.
5. Have students create a key word outline by putting the topic of the passage at the top of the template (page 260). Under that, next to the *T* (for topic sentence), have them write the three words from the first sentence or from their "Paragraph Shrinking" sentence.

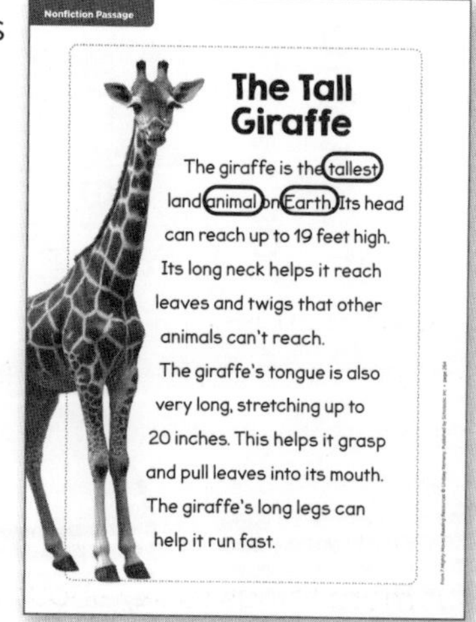

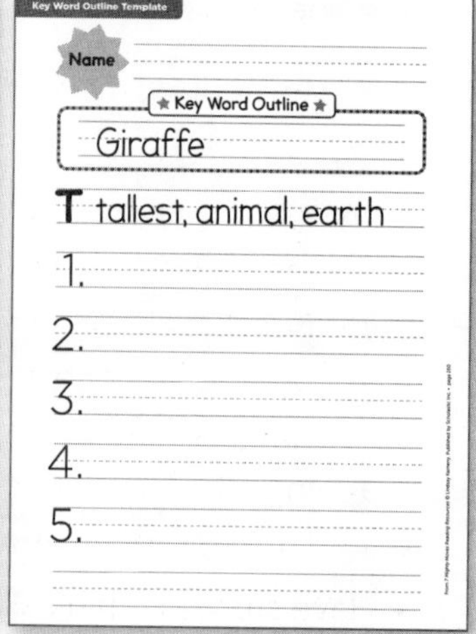

6. Reread the second sentence and ask students to circle the three most important words and then write them on line 1 of the template. Repeat the process for the rest of the sentences. These will be the supporting details of the paragraph students write.
7. Set the passage aside. Have students create and say sentences from each line of key words, which prompts them to attend to meaning and develops their knowledge of syntax and semantics.
8. Have them use the outline to compose a paragraph. This is an excellent way to support students' comprehension and writing skills.

Nonfiction Passage

The Tall Giraffe

The giraffe is the tallest land animal on Earth. Its head can reach up to 19 feet high. Its long neck helps it reach leaves and twigs that other animals can't reach. The giraffe's tongue is also very long, stretching up to 20 inches. This helps it grasp and pull leaves into its mouth. The giraffe's long legs can help it run fast.

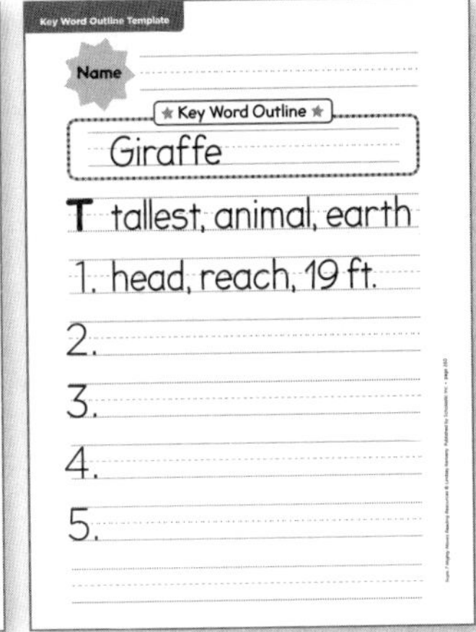

Key Word Outline Template

Name

Key Word Outline

Giraffe

T tallest, animal, earth
1. head, reach, 19 ft.
2.
3.
4.
5.

Nonfiction Passage

The Tall Giraffe

The giraffe is the tallest land animal on Earth. Its head can reach up to 19 feet high. Its long neck helps it reach leaves and twigs that other animals can't reach. The giraffe's tongue is also very long, stretching up to 20 inches. This helps it grasp and pull leaves into its mouth. The giraffe's long legs can help it run fast.

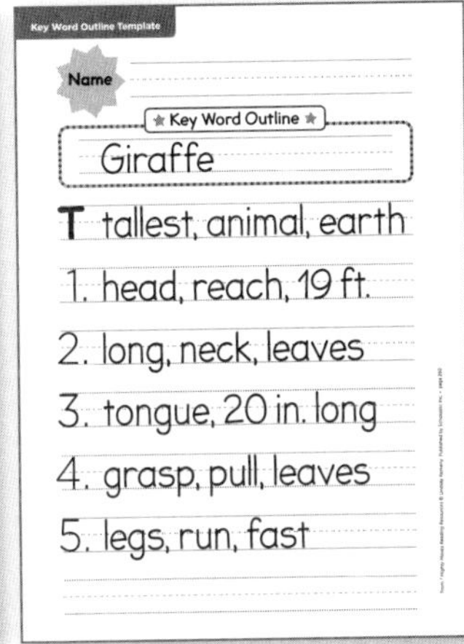

Key Word Outline Template

Name

Key Word Outline

Giraffe

T tallest, animal, earth
1. head, reach, 19 ft.
2. long, neck, leaves
3. tongue, 20 in. long
4. grasp, pull, leaves
5. legs, run, fast

Differentiation Tips

If students have difficulty, consider the following scaffolds.

- Read the passage to students.
- Allow students to create their key word outlines along with you.
- After creating the outline, have students create their sentences orally, rather than writing them.
- Lean in and help students craft each sentence orally from their notes. You might start the sentence for them, allowing them to "fill in the blank" or partially compose the sentence.
- Create the key word outline and paragraph as a class. Have students share their ideas orally as you act as the scribe.
- Model, model, model.

To make the activity more challenging, try these.

- Allow students to read the passage, create their outlines, and write their paragraphs independently.
- Choose a longer, more complex passage. Students can select six or more interesting facts or ideas to write about.
- Encourage students to include more advanced words in their writing.
- Encourage students to embellish their writing by including more details, adding a hook, sharing their opinions, etc.
- Teach students to add a concluding sentence that wraps up the paragraph.
- Have students think about more things to say about the topic and write multiple paragraphs.

Name

★ Key Word Outline ★

T

1.

2.

3.

4.

5.

Name

Name

Beautiful Butterflies

Butterflies are amazing insects with a special life cycle. They start as tiny eggs. These eggs hatch into hungry caterpillars. Caterpillars munch on

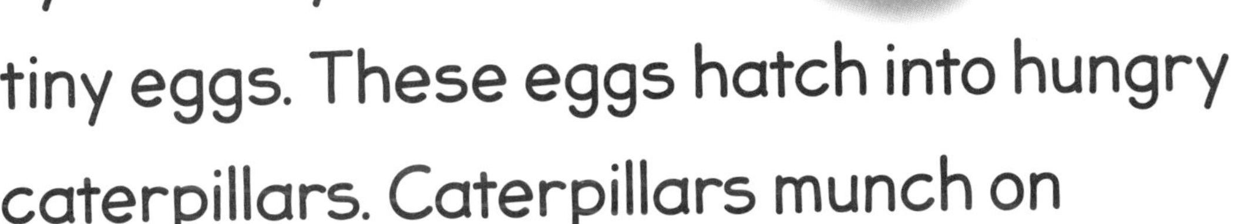

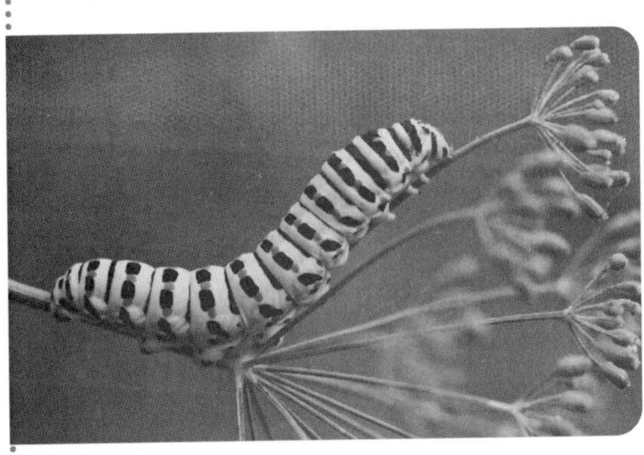

leaves until they're ready to build a chrysalis. Inside, they transform into beautiful butterflies! Finally, they emerge with wings and flutter away.

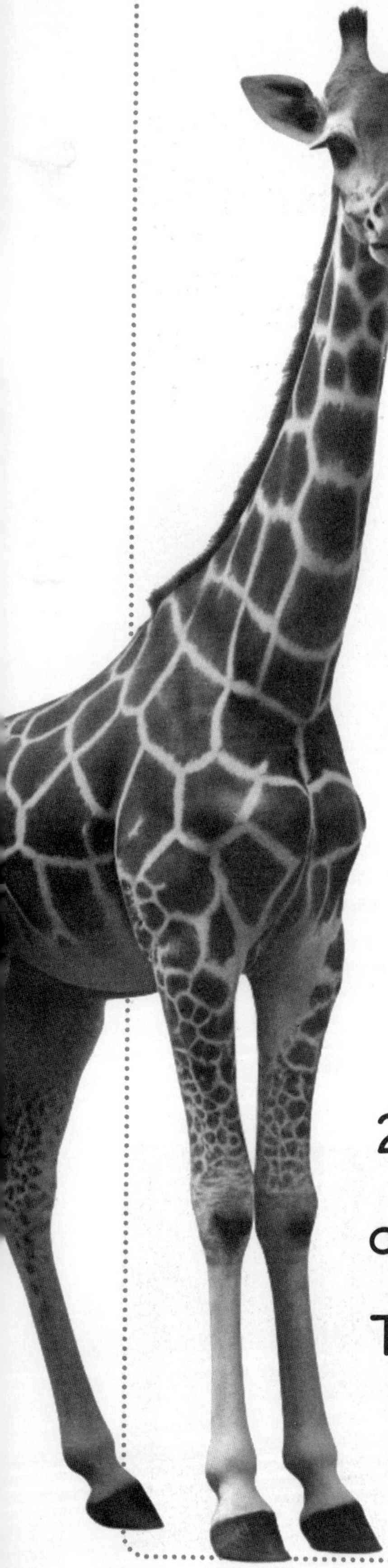

The Tall Giraffe

The giraffe is the tallest land animal on Earth. Its head can reach up to 19 feet high. Its long neck helps it reach leaves and twigs that other animals can't reach.

The giraffe's tongue is also very long, stretching up to 20 inches. This helps it grasp and pull leaves into its mouth. The giraffe's long legs can help it run fast.

Rain

Rain is so helpful for the earth. When it rains, the clouds sprinkle the earth with fresh water. This water helps plants grow big and strong, like giving them a yummy drink! Rain also fills up rivers and lakes. The clean water helps us take showers, brush our teeth, and have water to drink. Rain is like a gift for the earth!

Muscles

Our bodies are full of amazing muscles that help us move! We use muscles to jump, run, play, and even smile. Did you know you even have muscles in your tongue and face? They help you move your tongue and lips to form words as you talk. When we exercise, our muscles get stronger. Eating healthy foods like fruits and vegetables gives our muscles the energy they need to work hard all day.

Amazing Ants

Ants are tiny insects that live together in big colonies. Each ant has a job to do. Some ants go around finding food, others take care of the baby ants, and some strong ants help build the nest. Ants can't talk the way we do, but they can still communicate with each other. They tap their legs and antennae to tell each other where to find food or if there is danger. Ants work together as a team to keep their colony strong.

Night Lights

When the sun goes down at night, we see stars shining in the dark sky. Stars are giant balls of burning gas. They look small, but they are way bigger than Earth. Even though stars seem close, they are millions of miles away! Stars seem to twinkle at night, but they're not really blinking! It's the air wiggling a bit that makes them look like they're twinkling.

Dynamic Dinosaurs

Millions of years ago, giant creatures called dinosaurs lived on Earth. These enormous animals came in all shapes and sizes. Some dinosaurs were even bigger than a school bus! We learn about dinosaurs by studying fossils. Fossils are the bones and leftover parts of dinosaurs and plants. They can help us learn more about what dinosaurs looked like and how they lived.

Spider Webs

Spider webs are amazing structures made of thin, sticky silk. These webs can be different shapes. Some look like circles, some look like funnels, and some even look like sheets!

Spiders spin these webs to catch their prey, like flies and mosquitoes. When an insect gets stuck in the web, it wiggles around and the spider can feel its vibrations. The spider uses its eight legs to capture and eat it.

Let's Recycle!

We can help the earth by recycling. Recycling means turning old items into something new. When we throw things away, they pile up in a big mountain of trash. Recycling helps make that mountain smaller, which is good for the earth. Many things we use every day can be recycled, like

plastic bottles, paper, and aluminum cans. You can help recycle at home by sorting your trash!

Community Helpers

Our community is full of helpful people who work hard to keep us safe and healthy. Firefighters put out fires. Police officers keep us safe. Doctors take care of our health. Teachers help us learn new things every day! All these people help make our community a wonderful place.

The Mighty Lion

Lions are big cats that live in Africa. They live in groups called prides. These prides work together to hunt big animals. They chase their prey into a corner and then use their sharp teeth and claws to catch it. Lions also work together to raise their cubs. Lions rely on teamwork to survive.

Shining Sun

The sun is a giant star in the center of our solar system. It's about a hundred times bigger than Earth! This giant ball of burning gas gives us light and heat, which helps plants grow and keeps us warm. The sun is millions of degrees hot! It's much too bright to look at directly. Even though it's far away, we need to protect our eyes with sunglasses to avoid damage.

Busy Bees

Bees are tiny insects with a big job! They zoom from flower to flower collecting pollen, a yellow dust that

helps plants make seeds. Bees use the pollen to make honey, a delicious and sweet treat we love to eat. As bees flit between flowers, some pollen sticks to their fuzzy bodies. When they land on another flower, some of that pollen rubs off, helping the new flower make seeds. Bees are busy helpers for both plants and us!

The Desert

Deserts are hot, dry places with very little rain. Many different kinds of plants and animals live in the desert. Look closely and you might see a tiny lizard hiding in the rocks, or a beautiful flower blooming after a rare rain shower! Animals that live in the desert have to be clever to survive the heat and lack of water. They have special features that help them. Camels store fat in their humps for energy, and snakes can slither through sand to find shade.

The Five Senses

Our bodies have five amazing senses that help us explore the world around us. We can see with our eyes and hear with our ears. We can smell things with our noses and taste with our tongues. We can touch and feel things with our skin. These senses help us enjoy delicious food, listen to music, and discover new places! They let us know when something is fun, yummy, or even dangerous.

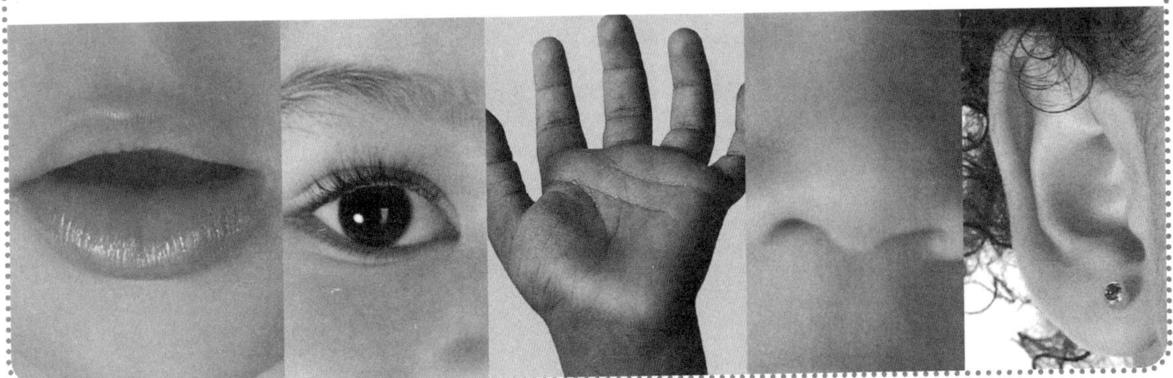

7.C Sentence Combining Routine

Use for: All students

Length of Activity:
10–15 minutes

Materials:

- Teacher: Lesson Plan Template (page 280), Sentence Combining Cue Card (page 281)
- Students: paper and pencils

For this powerful strategy (Graham & Perin, 2007; Hochman & Wexler, 2017), you give students two short declarative sentences and ask them to find ways to combine them into longer, more complex sentences. I've found that teaching students to write complex sentences enhances their comprehension of such structures when they encounter them in text. I usually choose sentences from a grade-level text that we are reading, but you can write your own, inspired by a topic you're covering in science, social studies, etc. Then I walk students through a sentence-combining process described below, which I learned from Dr. Deborah Glaser.

Directions

Use the template on page 280 to plan your lesson, along with the cue card on page 281 to help you remember the steps as you teach.

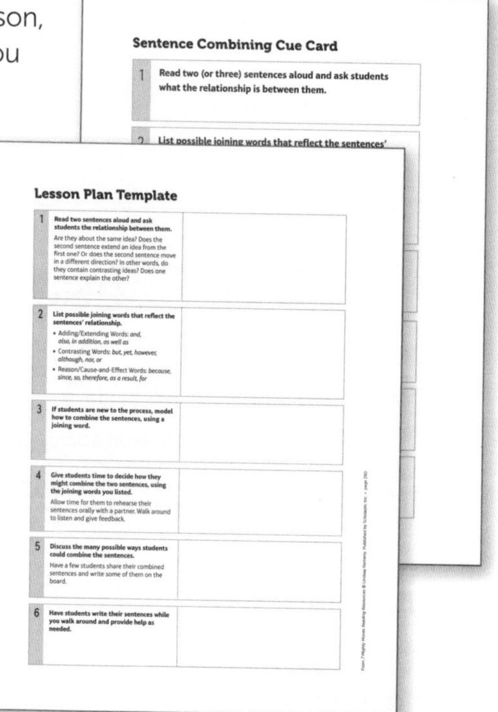

Sentence Combining Cue Card

1	**Read two (or three) sentences aloud and ask students what the relationship is between them.**
2	**List possible joining words that reflect the sentences'**

Lesson Plan Template

1	**Read two sentences aloud and ask students the relationship between them.** Are they about the same idea? Does the second sentence extend an idea from the first one? Or does the second sentence move in a different direction? In other words, do they contain contrasting ideas? Does one sentence explain the other?	
2	**List possible joining words that reflect the sentences' relationship.** • Adding/Extending Words: *and, also, in addition, as well as* • Contrasting Words: *but, yet, however, although, nor, or* • Reason/Cause-and-Effect Words: *because, since, so, therefore, as a result, for*	
3	**If students are new to the process, model how to combine the sentences, using a joining word.**	
4	**Give students time to decide how they might combine the two sentences, using the joining words you listed.** Allow time for them to rehearse their sentences orally with a partner. Walk around to listen and give feedback.	
5	**Discuss the many possible ways students could combine the sentences.** Have a few students share their combined sentences and write some of them on the board.	
6	**Have students write their sentences while you walk around and provide help as needed.**	

1. **Read the two sentences aloud to students and ask them what the relationship is between them.** Are they about the same idea? Does the second sentence extend an idea from the first one? Or does the second sentence move in a different direction? In other words, do they contain contrasting ideas? Does one sentence explain the other?
2. **List possible joining words that reflect the sentences' relationship.** For example, if both sentences are about the same idea, and the second one extends the idea in the first, you might list these words: *and, in addition*, or *also*. If the two sentences contain contrasting ideas, you might list these words: *but, yet, however*, or *although*. If the sentences have a cause-and-effect relationship, you might list these words: *because, since, therefore*, or *so*.
3. **If students are new to the process, model how to combine the sentences using one of the joining words.**
4. **Give students time to decide how they might combine the two sentences, using the possible joining words that you listed.** Allow time for them to rehearse their sentences orally with a partner. Walk around to listen and give feedback.

5. **Discuss with students the many possible ways they could combine the sentences.** Have a few students recite their combined sentences, as you write some of them on the board.
6. **Have students write their sentences while you provide help as needed.** Students may need scaffolding at first. With my first graders, I spend several lessons combining sentences with the words *and* or *also* before moving on to sentences with the words *but* or *however*. Don't rush the process, and do provide as much help as students need.

This activity is a great way for students to review content you are teaching across subject areas. You might choose to write sentences that review content you taught in your science lesson. At the conclusion of your lesson, students can combine these sentences to deepen their knowledge of the topic as well as strengthen their sentence composition skills. Consider having them write their combined sentence as part of an exit ticket. You might also practice combining sentences within the context of an essay or paragraph students are composing. Try to find ways to integrate sentence combining in your classroom so it is not thought of as an isolated skill.

Differentiation Tips

If students have difficulty, consider the following scaffolds.

- Give more time for students to practice combining sentences with similar ideas, using the words *and* or *also* before moving on to combining contrasting or cause/effect sentences.
- Have student work with a positive peer.
- Provide a sentence starter and have the student complete the sentence.
- Keep the sentence construction verbal, without assigning the written component. Or have students write their sentence with a partner.
- Make sure to walk through the entire process with the student.
- List possible joining words for students to select from. Keep the list of possibilities small and simple, at first.
- Model, model, model.

To make the activity more challenging, try these.

- Allow students to complete more steps of the process independently.
- Give more advanced joining words to use, such as *nor* or *although*.
- Encourage them to construct several different possibilities to combine their sentences.
- Have them combine three sentences instead of two.
- Provide longer, more complex sentences to combine.

Lesson Plan Template

1	**Read two sentences aloud and ask students the relationship between them.** Are they about the same idea? Does the second sentence extend an idea from the first one? Or does the second sentence move in a different direction? In other words, do they contain contrasting ideas? Does one sentence explain the other?	
2	**List possible joining words that reflect the sentences' relationship.** • Adding/Extending Words: *and, also, in addition, as well as* • Contrasting Words: *but, yet, however, although, nor, or* • Reason/Cause-and-Effect Words: *because, since, so, therefore, as a result, for*	
3	**If students are new to the process, model how to combine the sentences, using a joining word.**	
4	**Give students time to decide how they might combine the two sentences, using the joining words you listed.** Allow time for them to rehearse their sentences orally with a partner. Walk around to listen and give feedback.	
5	**Discuss the many possible ways students could combine the sentences.** Have a few students share their combined sentences and write some of them on the board.	
6	**Have students write their sentences while you walk around and provide help as needed.**	

Sentence Combining Cue Card

1 **Read two (or three) sentences aloud and ask students what the relationship is between them.**

2 **List possible joining words that reflect the sentences' relationship.**

- Adding/Extending Words: *and, also, in addition, as well as*
- Contrasting Words: *but, yet, however, although, nor, or*
- Reason/Cause-and-Effect Words: *because, since, so, therefore, as a result, for*

3 **Model how to combine the sentences using one of the joining words.**

4 **Give students time to decide how they might combine the two sentences and allow time for them to rehearse and discuss with a partner.**

5 **Have a few students share their sentences and discuss with students the many possible ways they could combine the sentences.**

6 **Have students write down their sentences.**

7.D Vocabulary Routine

Use for: All students

Length of Activity:
3–5 minutes

Materials:

- Teacher: Vocabulary Lesson Plan Template (page 284), Vocabulary Routine Reference Card (page 285)

I love the simplicity of this vocabulary routine, which I learned from Dr. Anita L. Archer, co-author, with Dr. Charles A. Hughes, of *Explicit Instruction: Effective and Efficient Teaching* (2011). Archer is a master of effective vocabulary instruction, and I recommend watching online videos of her teaching this routine.

Directions

Use the Vocabulary Lesson Plan Template (page 284) and Vocabulary Routine Reference Card (page 285) to help you plan and carry out the lesson.

1. **Introduce the word and its pronunciation.** Display the word and have the students repeat it. Have students tap, clap, or pound the syllables of the word.

   This word is *frigid*. What word? *frigid*.
   Tap and say the parts: *fri-gid*.
   Again: *fri-gid*.
   frigid is an adjective, a describing word.

2. **Present a student-friendly definition.** Tell students the definition or have them read it with you.

   frigid means very cold; freezing.

3. **Illustrate the word with examples:**
   - Concrete examples (act it out or use an object)
   - Visual examples
   - Verbal examples

   When the air outside is *frigid*, you are so cold you can barely move. You'd shiver and move around to try to keep yourself warm. (Use hands and arms to pretend to shiver.)

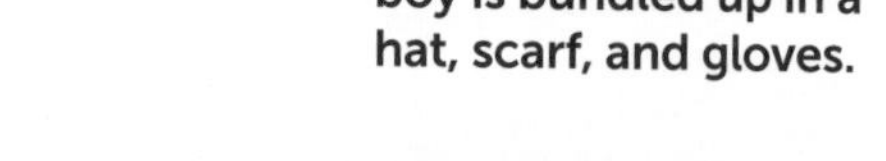

It is frigid outside, so this boy is bundled up in a hat, scarf, and gloves.

4. **Check students' understanding, using one of these options:**

   Ask deep-processing questions:

   > How do animals survive when it's frigid outside? Begin by saying: When it is frigid, animals...

   Have students discern between non-examples and examples:

   > Tell me *frigid* or *not frigid*.
   > We see huge icicles outside. (*frigid*)
   > We go swimming on a sunny day. (*not frigid*)

   Have students compare the word to other words:

   > Last week we learned the word *chilly*. How are *chilly* and *frigid* similar? How are they different?

The penguins love to swim in the frigid ocean water.

Differentiation Tips

If students have difficulty, consider the following scaffolds.

- Repeat the routine in small groups.
- Provide picture supports to demonstrate the word's meaning.
- Provide more examples.
- Review the word frequently throughout the week.
- Connect the word with similar words that the student is familiar with.
- Choose easy-to-explain, high-utility words.

To make the activity more challenging, try these.

- Encourage students to use the word in conversations.
- Encourage students to use the word in their writing.
- Share additional meanings and uses of the word.

Vocabulary Lesson Plan Template

1

Introduce the word's pronunciation.

- Display the word and have the students repeat it.
- Have students tap, clap, or pound the syllables of the word.

2

Introduce the word's meaning.

Make sure it's a student-friendly, easy-to-understand definition.

3

Illustrate the word with examples (and non-examples, when helpful).

- Concrete examples (act it out or use an object)
- Visual examples
- Verbal examples

4

Check students' understanding.

Be sure to:

- Ask deep-processing questions.
- Have students discern between non-examples and examples.
- Have students compare the word to other words.

Vocabulary Routine Reference Card

1

Introduce the word's pronunciation.

- Display the word and have the students repeat it.
- Have students tap, clap, or pound the syllables of the word.

2

Introduce the word's meaning.

Make sure it's a student-friendly, easy-to-understand definition.

3

Illustrate the word with examples
(and non-examples, when helpful).

- Concrete examples. (Act out the word or use a representative object.)
- Visual examples
- Verbal examples

4

Check understanding. Be sure to:

- Ask deep-processing questions.
- Have students discern between non-examples and examples.
- Have students compare the word to other words.

7.E Three-Column Notes

Use for: Students who are learning new vocabulary words

Length of Activity: 10 minutes

Materials:

- Teacher: Three-Column Notes Page (page 287), music (optional)
- Students: Three-Column Notes Page (page 287), pencils

Three-Column Notes comes from Dr. Deborah Glaser's Top Ten Tools professional training. It is one of my favorite ways to provide my students with multiple exposures to our vocabulary words throughout the week.

Directions

1. Pass out a copy of the Three-Column Notes Page to each student.
2. Have them write the target word in the first column, write a definition in the second column (with your help, if necessary), and draw a picture that illustrates the word in the third column.
3. Have students fold the picture column back so it's directly behind the definition column. Then have them fold the first column back so it's on top of the picture column. After making the two folds, students should see the column of words on one side and the column of definitions on the other.
4. Have them stand up, push in their chairs, and walk around the room until you say "stop." You could play music while they're walking around.
5. When the music stops, or when you say "stop," have each student buddy-up with a classmate. Then choose one of these options:
   - Ask one partner to choose a word from the first column and the other partner to give the definition.
   - Ask one partner to choose a word and the other partner to use the word in a sentence, instead of giving the definition.
   - Ask one partner to share the definition, and the other partner to determine what word is being defined.

   Have partners check their responses by referring to their notes and then switch roles.
6. Ask them to continue quizzing each other until the music starts again, or you say "go." Then have all students walk around again and repeat the process.

Differentiation Tips

If students have difficulty, consider the following scaffolds.

- Remember to complete the page as a class.
- Give students a copy of the page with the word and definition already written for them. They fill in only the third column: adding a picture to illustrate the word.
- Provide plenty of instruction and review of the words' definitions before having students work with their partners.
- Remind students they can review their notes.

To make the activity more challenging, try these.

- Encourage students to say the definition without looking at their notes.
- Have students use the word in a sentence, instead of sharing the definition. Encourage them to use a different sentence each time.
- Have students use two of the words in a sentence.

Word	Definition	Picture

7.F Shades-of-Meaning Vocabulary Cards

Use for: Students who are learning and deepening their vocabulary knowledge

Length of Activity: 10–15 minutes

Materials:

- Teacher: Shades-of-Meaning Vocabulary Cards (page 290–305)
- Students: set of vocabulary cards, Shades-of-Meaning Worksheet (online, optional)

Think of words with similar meanings as existing on a gradient, similar to arranging colors on a spectrum. For example, think of the word *ecstatic* on one end of a spectrum and *disappointed* on the other. As you move along the spectrum, the words' meanings change slightly: *ecstatic, happy, content, satisfied, sad, disappointed*. This activity demonstrates how words can have similar meanings with varying degrees of intensity. Introducing shades of meaning to your students will spark rich conversations about vocabulary. As they talk through and explain their thinking, they think more deeply and critically about the meaning of words.

Directions

Preparation

1. **Choose Vocabulary Words:** Select two opposite words from your reading program or texts students are reading, such as *miniscule* and *colossal*.
2. **Create a Semantic Gradient:** Brainstorm words that fall between those two words, creating shades of meaning.
3. **Prepare the Activity:** Write each word on a separate card, using the template on page 305. Decide on your number of student groups and create one set of words for each group. Cut the cards apart and place them in envelopes or secure them with rubber bands.

You can skip these steps and use the word lists starting on page 290. Be sure to choose a list with at least one word that connects to a topic you're currently covering.

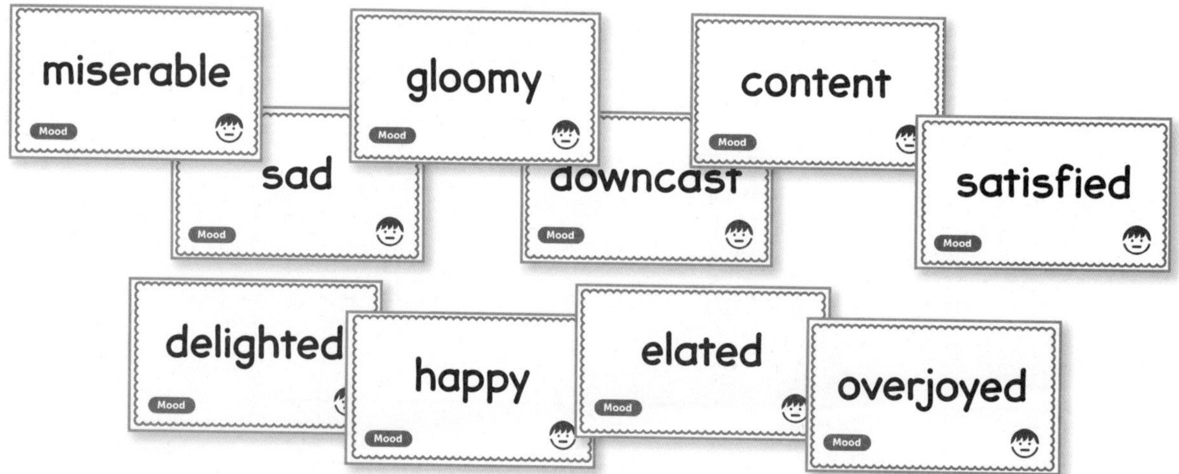

With Students

1. **Form Groups:** Pair up students or put them into small groups of three to five.
2. **Sort the Words:** Give each pair or group a set of cards. Have students work together to arrange the words in a logical order that reflects the increasing or decreasing intensity of meaning.
3. **Facilitate Discussion:** Circulate the room, asking questions and encouraging students to explain their reasoning as they arrange the words. Offer assistance as needed.
4. **Gather the Class:** Once all groups are finished, discuss as a class how various groups ordered the words. Explore the reasoning behind their choices and any interesting choices.

Optional Activities

- Have students use the Shades-of-Meaning Worksheet (online) instead of doing the card-sorting activity.
- When they complete the card-sorting activity, have students use their understanding to fill out the worksheet.

Differentiation Tips

If students have difficulty, consider the following scaffolds.

- Start with fewer words.
- Define any unfamiliar words at the start of the activity.
- Adjust the word lists to ensure that most of the words are familiar to students. Include just a couple of new or slightly more challenging words within each list.
- Group students so that each group contains a student with stronger vocabulary skills who can offer guidance and discussion during the sorting process.
- Provide pictures or simple drawings to represent the words.
- Complete the activity as a whole class so you can guide the discussion and decisions.

To make the activity more challenging, try these.

- Use more advanced vocabulary words.
- Increase the number of words.
- Instead of providing the full spectrum of words, give students the starting and ending words and have them brainstorm words in between to fill out the gradient.
- Give students a couple blank cards and have them brainstorm additional words to add in.
- Provide students with a sentence frame where one of the words on the spectrum could fit in the blank space. Have them discuss which word would fit best, based on the overall meaning of the sentence.

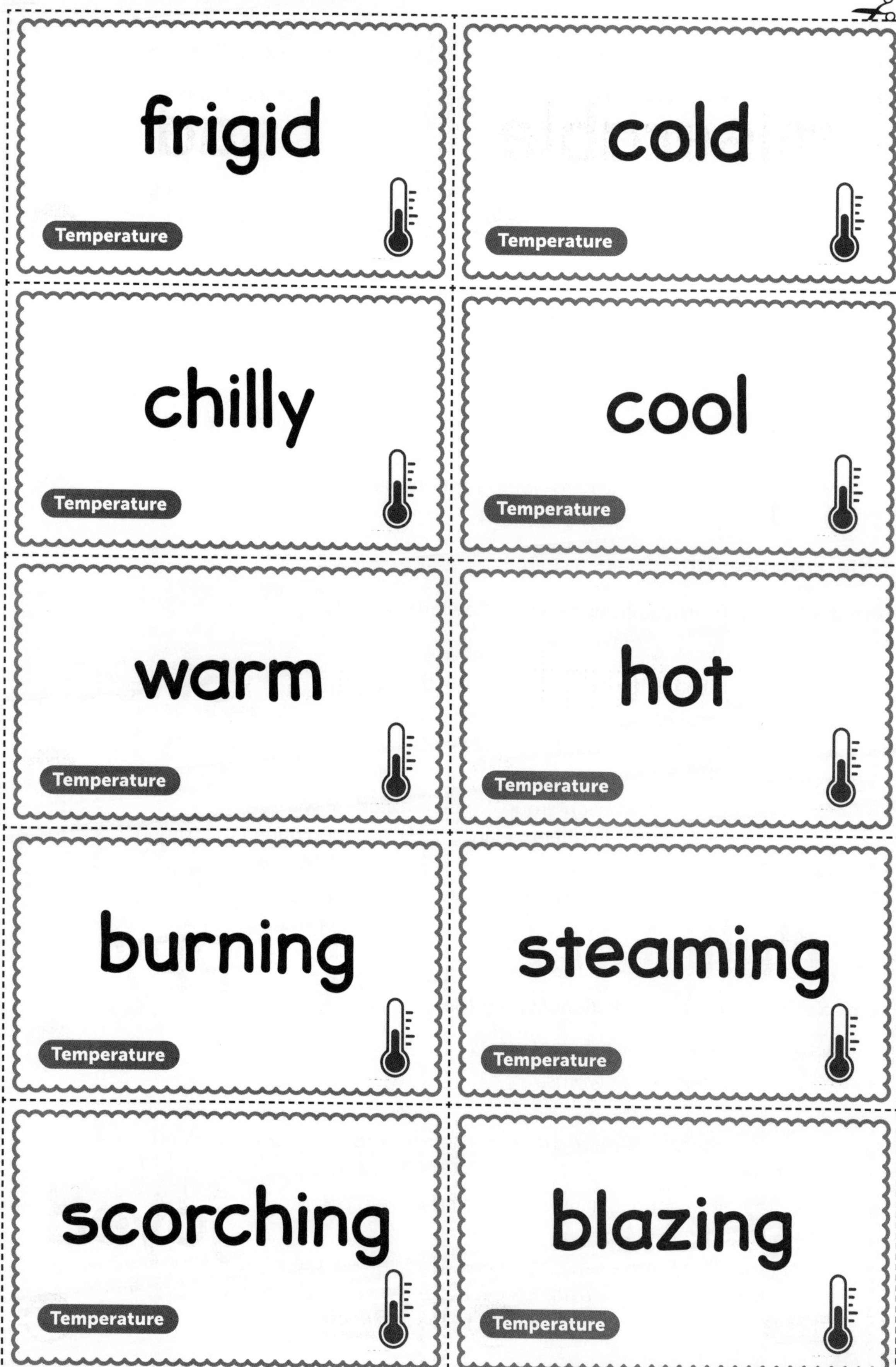
frigid
Temperature
cold
Temperature
chilly
Temperature
cool
Temperature
warm
Temperature
hot
Temperature
burning
Temperature
steaming
Temperature
scorching
Temperature
blazing
Temperature

miserable
Mood
sad
Mood
gloomy
Mood
downcast
Mood
content
Mood
satisfied
Mood
delighted
Mood
happy
Mood
elated
Mood
overjoyed
Mood

pitch-black

Light

dark

Light

dim

Light

dusky

Light

glowing

Light

bright

Light

sunny

Light

shiny

Light

dazzling

Light

blinding

Light

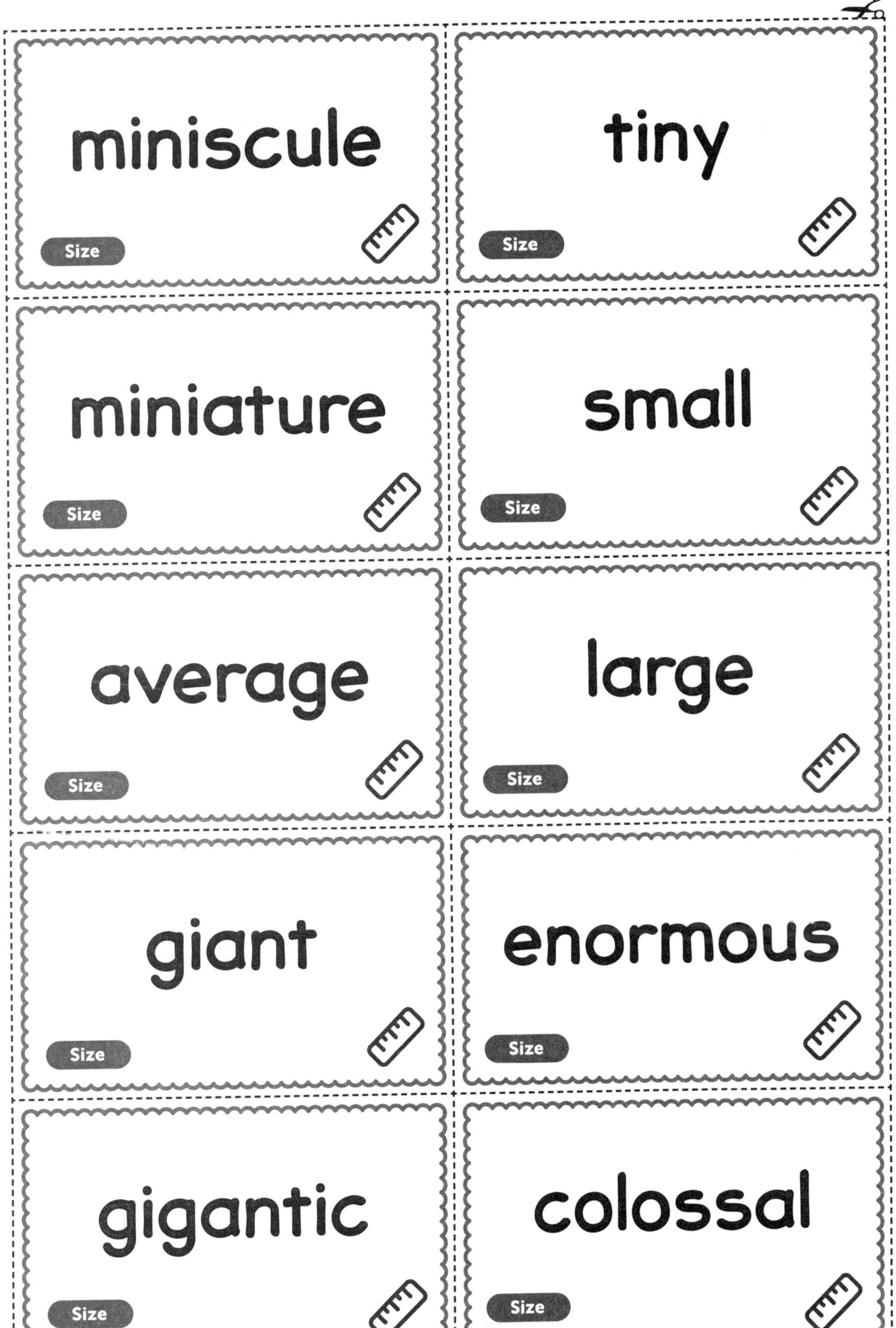
miniscule
Size
tiny
Size
miniature
Size
small
Size
average
Size
large
Size
giant
Size
enormous
Size
gigantic
Size
colossal
Size

sluggish

Speed

slow

Speed

poky

Speed

moderate

Speed

brisk

Speed

fast

Speed

rushing

Speed

rapid

Speed

swift

Speed

racing

Speed

silent

Sound

muffled

Sound

quiet

Sound

soft

Sound

moderate

Sound

loud

Sound

yelling

Sound

shouting

Sound

roaring

Sound

boisterous

Sound

disgusting

Flavor

yucky

Flavor

bland

Flavor

okay

Flavor

good

Flavor

yummy

Flavor

flavorful

Flavor

delicious

Flavor

scrumptious

Flavor

mouthwatering

Flavor

calm

Fear

uneasy

Fear

worried

Fear

nervous

Fear

scared

Fear

frightened

Fear

terrified

Fear

petrified

Fear

paralyzed with fear

Fear

panic-stricken

Fear

filthy Cleanliness	grimy Cleanliness
dirty Cleanliness	messy Cleanliness
untidy Cleanliness	tidy Cleanliness
clean Cleanliness	sparkling Cleanliness
spotless Cleanliness	perfect Cleanliness

infant
Age

young
Age

little
Age

immature
Age

middle-aged
Age

mature
Age

grown-up
Age

old
Age

elderly
Age

ancient
Age

smooth
Texture
polished
Texture
glossy
Texture
sleek
Texture
soft
Texture
bumpy
Texture
wavy
Texture
uneven
Texture
rough
Texture
jagged
Texture

frail
Strength

feeble
Strength

wimpy
Strength

weak
Strength

average
Strength

strong
Strength

sturdy
Strength

powerful
Strength

forceful
Strength

invincible
Strength

soaked

Wetness

drenched

Wetness

dripping

Wetness

wet

Wetness

moist

Wetness

damp

Wetness

dry

Wetness

baked

Wetness

parched

Wetness

dehydrated

Wetness

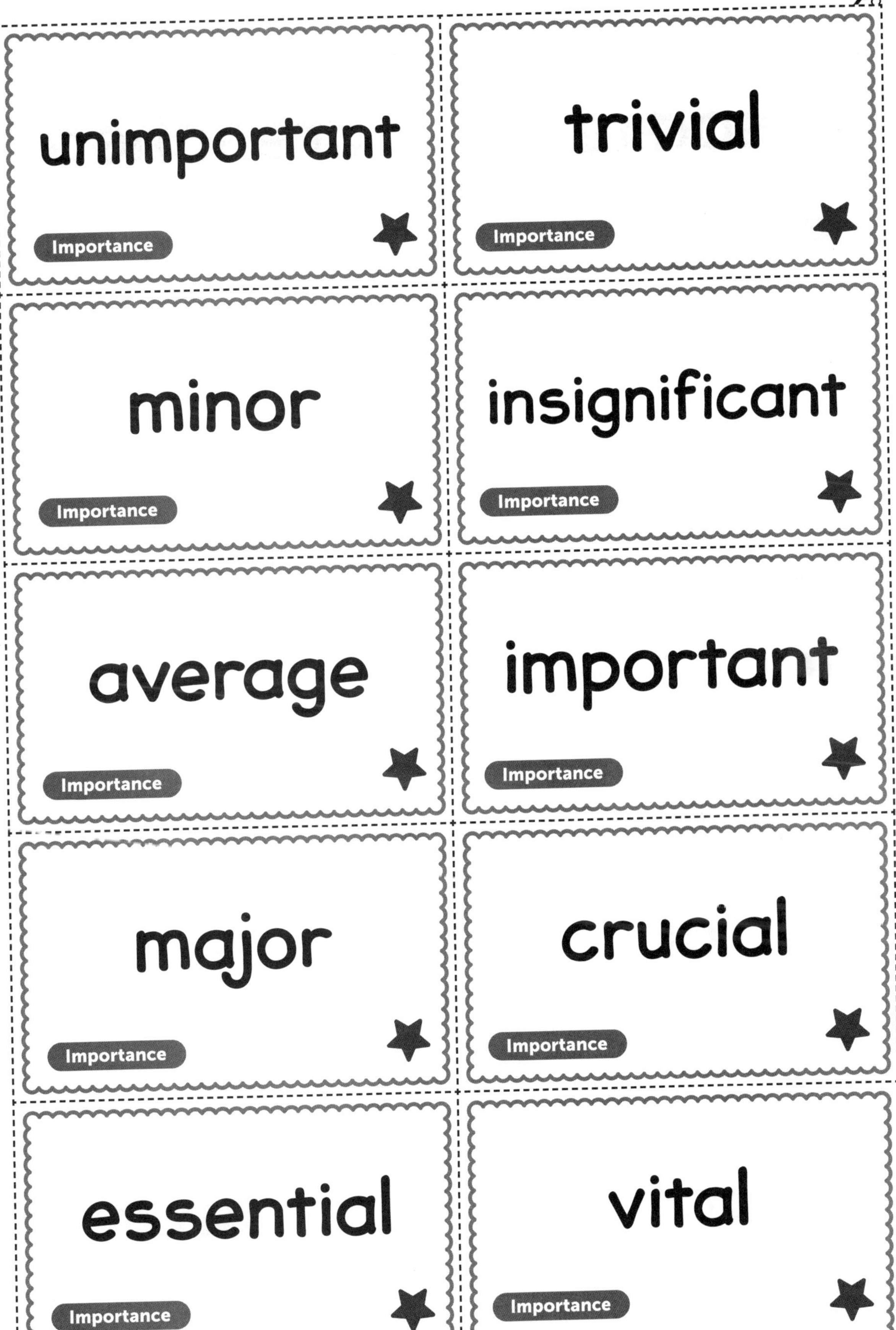
unimportant
Importance
trivial
Importance
minor
Importance
insignificant
Importance
average
Importance
important
Importance
major
Importance
crucial
Importance
essential
Importance
vital
Importance

alert

Energy Level

wide-awake

Energy Level

energetic

Energy Level

peppy

Energy Level

lively

Energy Level

tired

Energy Level

sluggish

Energy Level

sleepy

Energy Level

drowsy

Energy Level

exhausted

Energy Level

7.G Academic Vocabulary Reference Cards

Use for: All students

Length of Activity: Any spare minute throughout your day

Materials:

Teacher: Academic Vocabulary Reference Cards (pages 307–317), binder ring

One of the best ways I know to get students to use academic language when they speak and write is by using it myself with them. Find ways to incorporate sophisticated words throughout your day. For example, instead of asking students, "Please get out your 'big books,'" I say, "Please get out your anthologies." The first time I did that, my students looked around the room, clearly perplexed. I explained, "An anthology is a collection of stories. Can you get out your anthology so we can find our story in it and read it?" Not long afterward, my students were using the word "anthology" themselves. Lane and Allen (2010) encourage us to elevate the language we use with students to enhance their vocabulary. In their article, they share many sophisticated words you can introduce at various points in the day, which I've used for this routine.

Directions

Print out the cards on pages 307–317 and thread them on a binder ring. Each day, choose a sophisticated word from the ring. Throughout your day, use the word and encourage students to use it, too. Be ready to explain the word with a student-friendly definition, if necessary.

Differentiation Tips

If students have difficulty, consider the following scaffolds.

- Focus on repetition. It may take multiple encounters with the word before students understand its meaning completely.
- Provide picture supports.
- Remember that this practice is about exposing students to sophisticated vocabulary, not requiring mastery of it.
- Select words that are accessible and "just right" for your students, and introduce them gradually.

To make the activity more challenging, try these.

- Encourage students to use the word in conversation and writing.
- Introduce words more quickly.
- Choose more sophisticated words.

Accumulate

To gather things together over time.

Example: "Our class has accumulated a lot of crayons over the year."

Classroom Supplies

Arrange

To put things in a specific order or place.

Example: "Before you leave, please arrange your desks back into neat rows."

Classroom Supplies

Allocate

To give a specific amount of something to someone or something.

Example: "For today's art project, I'm allocating five markers to each of you."

Classroom Supplies

Collect

To gather things from different places.

Example: "It's time to collect your writing assignments. Please place them in the basket."

Classroom Supplies

Allot

To give a specific amount of something, often used for time or space.

Example: "Each group is allotted 15 minutes to work on their project. Please use your time wisely."

Classroom Supplies

Deplete

To use up something completely.

Example: "We've depleted our supply of markers. I need to order some more."

Classroom Supplies

Amass

To collect a large amount of something, often in a short period.

Example: "We need to amass a lot of construction paper for our upcoming art project. Can everyone bring some in next week?"

Classroom Supplies

Dispense

To give out something in small amounts.

Example: "If you need a tissue, just let me know and I'll be happy to dispense one for you."

Classroom Supplies

Distribute

To give out something to everyone.

Example: "After I distribute the books, please turn to page 35."

Classroom Supplies

Reserve

To set aside something for someone or something specific.

Example: "I've reserved a few extra notebooks in case anyone forgot theirs."

Classroom Supplies

Gather

To bring things together from different places.

Example: "Let's gather around the rug."

Classroom Supplies

Stockpile

To collect and store a large amount of something in preparation for future use.

Example: "To be on the safe side, I've stockpiled some extra paper towels so we won't run out."

Classroom Supplies

Hoard

To collect and keep a large amount of something for yourself, often more than you need.

Example: "It's not nice to hoard all the markers when others need them too. Remember to share!"

Classroom Supplies

Adjacent

Next to or close by.

Example: "Make sure you're standing adjacent to your classmate in line, with no big gaps."

Words Related to Walking in Line

Replenish

To refill or fill up something that has been used up.

Example: "It looks like some game pieces are missing from the math manipulatives bin. Let's work together to replenish the bin."

Classroom Supplies

Approach

To come closer to something in a controlled way.

Example: "As we approach the library, please approach quietly so we don't disturb others."

Words Related to Walking in Line

Disorderly

Not neat or organized, chaotic.

Example: "Let's avoid any disorderly conduct while we wait."

Words Related to Walking in Line

Linger

To stay somewhere longer than necessary.

Example: "Please avoid lingering at the water fountain. We need to keep the line moving smoothly."

Words Related to Walking in Line

Efficiently

In a well-organized way that doesn't waste time.

Example: "If we line up efficiently, we will get to the lunchroom faster."

Words Related to Walking in Line

Orderly

Neat, organized, and well-behaved.

Example: "Let's line up in an orderly fashion."

Words Related to Walking in Line

File

A line of people or things one behind the other.

Example: "Line up in a single file, please."

Words Related to Walking in Line

Parallel

Running alongside something else in the same direction, but not touching.

Example: "Let's line up in two parallel lines."

Words Related to Walking in Line

Halt

To stop moving.

Example: "Halt for a moment when we reach the end of the hall."

Words Related to Walking in Line

Pause

To stop for a moment.

Example: "Let's pause for a moment while the other class goes by."

Words Related to Walking in Line

Perpendicular

Forming a right angle (90 degrees) with something else.

Example: "When we get to the hallway, turn perpendicular to the main line and head toward the exit doors."

Words Related to Walking in Line

Queue

A line of people waiting.

Example: "Remember to wait patiently in the queue for the water fountain."

Words Related to Walking in Line

Proceed

To move forward in a particular direction.

Example: "Once you've received your lunch, you can proceed to your table."

Words Related to Walking in Line

Rapidly

Very quickly.

Example: "There's no need to run rapidly through the halls."

Words Related to Walking in Line

Procession

A formal line of people moving slowly.

Example: "Let's line up and form a quiet procession as we head to the library."

Words Related to Walking in Line

Swiftly

Quickly and smoothly.

Example: "Let's line up swiftly."

Words Related to Walking in Line

Proximity

How close something is to something else.

Example: "Please be mindful of your proximity to the person in front of you. Leave enough space."

Words Related to Walking in Line

Vicinity

The general area around a place.

Example: "Once we get outside, please stay in this vicinity until you are picked up."

Words Related to Walking in Line

Articulate

To speak clearly.

Example: "Try to be as articulate as possible so everyone can understand your ideas."

Words Related to Group Time

Contribute

To give something in order to help.

Example: "Make sure everyone in your group is contributing."

Words Related to Group Time

Ascertain

To find out something for sure.

Example: "Before we begin, let's ascertain everyone has the materials they need."

Words Related to Group Time

Converse

To have a conversation with someone.

Example: "Please converse with your partner."

Words Related to Group Time

Assemble

To gather together.

Example: "Let's assemble at the carpet."

Words Related to Group Time

Convey

To communicate or express something.

Example: "Please convey your ideas to your group."

Words Related to Group Time

Coherent

Clear, logical, and easy to understand.

Example: "Make sure your ideas are coherent so we can understand them."

Words Related to Group Time

Cooperate

To work together with others toward a common goal.

Example: "Remember to cooperate and listen to one another."

Words Related to Group Time

Deliberate

To discuss something carefully before making a decision.

Example: "Let's take some time to deliberate as a group before we decide on our plan."

Words Related to Group Time

Elucidate

To explain something clearly and in detail.

Example: "Do you understand or do I need to elucidate further?"

Words Related to Group Time

Determine

To decide or choose something.

Example: "Let's work together to determine the best way to solve this problem."

Words Related to Group Time

Express

To communicate your thoughts and feelings.

Example: "You may express your opinions and ideas freely."

Words Related to Group Time

Disperse

To scatter or spread out.

Example: "Now you may disperse and find a quiet spot to begin your work."

Words Related to Group Time

Oblige

To agree to do something, especially as a favor.

Example: "I'm happy to oblige and answer your question."

Words Related to Group Time

Elaborate

To explain something in more detail.

Example: "That's a great idea! Can you elaborate on your thoughts a little more for the group?"

Words Related to Group Time

Participate

To take part in an activity.

Example: "I would like everyone to participate in the discussion."

Words Related to Group Time

Portray

To describe or show something in a particular way.

Example: "Let's draw a picture to portray this idea."

Words Related to Group Time

Compassionate

Caring for and understanding others' feelings.

Example: "If someone is hurt, let's be compassionate and help them."

Words Related to Harmony

Verbalize

To express something using words.

Example: "Can you verbalize how that made you feel?"

Words Related to Group Time

Considerate

Thinking about how your actions affect others.

Example: "That was so considerate of you to stay quiet while I was talking."

Words Related to Harmony

Agreeable

Willing to go along with others' ideas.

Example: "Let's try to be agreeable when we work together in our groups."

Words Related to Harmony

Courteous

Polite and respectful toward others.

Example: "Let's remember to use courteous language."

Words Related to Harmony

Amiable

Friendly and likable.

Example: "It was so amiable of you to invite her to play."

Words Related to Harmony

Gracious

Polite and kind, especially when accepting something.

Example: "If someone helps you, be gracious and say thank you."

Words Related to Harmony

Pleasant

Agreeable and enjoyable to be around.

Example: "I love being part of such a pleasant class."

Words Related to Harmony

Bicker

To argue over something unimportant.

Example: "Let's stop bickering and find a way to work together."

Words Related to Conflict

Respectful

Showing regard for others and their feelings.

Example: "Let's think of ways that we can be respectful."

Words Related to Harmony

Quarrel

A heated argument or disagreement.

Example: "Let's remember to talk kindly to each other and try not to quarrel."

Words Related to Conflict

Sympathetic

Understanding and caring about someone else's misfortune.

Example: "If someone is feeling sad, be sympathetic and kind."

Words Related to Harmony

Rectify

To fix a mistake or problem.

Example: "If you make a mistake, you can rectify the problem."

Words Related to Conflict

Amends

Making things right after a disagreement.

Example: "If you have a disagreement with a friend, try to talk it out and make amends."

Words Related to Conflict

Resolve

To find a solution to a problem.

Example: "Remember, there's always a way to resolve our problems in a kind way."

Words Related to Conflict

Squabble

A minor argument or disagreement.

Example: "Small squabbles can happen sometimes. Take a deep breath and we'll try to work it out."

Words Related to Conflict

Vulgar

Rude and offensive, often using swear words or inappropriate language.

Example: "Vulgar language has no place in our classroom. Let's speak kindly and clearly."

Words Related to Manners

Discourteous

Rude and impolite.

Example: "Interrupting others or speaking out of turn is discourteous."

Words Related to Manners

Accomplished

Successfully completed a task or goal.

Example: "You've accomplished a lot today. Keep up the great work!"

Words Related to Being Correct

Impolite

Lacking good manners or courtesy.

Example: "It's impolite to speak to your friend that way."

Words Related to Manners

Appropriate

Suitable or fitting for the situation.

Example: "You chose appropriate words to describe the character in your story."

Words Related to Being Correct

Offensive

Causing someone to feel upset or insulted.

Example: "Using offensive language or jokes is not appropriate in our classroom. Let's treat each other with kindness and respect."

Words Related to Manners

Exemplary

Serving as a model of excellence.

Example: "Your work on this project is exemplary. I'd love to share it with the class."

Words Related to Being Correct

Masterful

Having or showing great skill or competence.

Example: "The way you explained that concept was truly masterful."

Words Related to Being Correct

Suitable

Right or fitting for a particular purpose.

Example: "This book is a suitable choice for your book report. It seems interesting."

Words Related to Being Correct

Precise

Exact and accurate.

Example: "I love your precise answer to the question. It shows that you really understand the concept."

Words Related to Being Correct

Inaccurate

Not exact or correct.

Example: "This information seems a bit inaccurate. Let's find a reliable source to locate the most up-to-date facts."

Words Related to Being Incorrect

Proficient

Having or showing a good level of skill or knowledge.

Example: "You've become proficient in solving these types of problems."

Words Related to Being Correct

Inadequate

Not enough.

Example: "I planned for us to complete this project in 30 minutes, but I can see that is inadequate. I'll give you some more time tomorrow."

Words Related to Being Incorrect

Proper

Correct or appropriate according to the rules or standards.

Example: "You used proper punctuation in your writing. Excellent job!"

Words Related to Being Correct

Invalid

Not having legal or logical force.

Example: "This source seems a bit invalid. Let's look for a different website that is more accurate."

Words Related to Being Incorrect

References

Archer, A. L., & Hughes, C. A. (2011). *Explicit instruction: Effective and efficient teaching (What works for special-needs learners).* The Guilford Press.

Blachman, B. A., Tangel, D. M., Ball, E. W., Black, R., & McGraw, C. K. (1999). Developing phonological awareness and word recognition skills: A two-year intervention with low-income, inner-city children. *Reading and Writing: An Interdisciplinary Journal, 11*(3), 239–273.

Brady, S. (2020). A 2020 perspective on research findings on alphabetics (phoneme awareness and phonics): Implications for instruction. *The Reading League, 1*(3) (September/October), 20–28.

Burns, M. K., Karich, A. C., Maki, K. E., Anderson, A., Pulles, S. M., Ittner, A., McComas, J. J., & Helman, L. (2015). Identifying classwide problems in reading with screening data. *Journal of Evidence-Based Practices for Schools, 14*(2), 186–204.

Castles, A., Rastle, K., & Nation, K. (2018). Ending the reading wars: Reading acquisition from novice to expert. *Psychological Science in the Public Interest, 19*(1), 5–51.

Fuchs, D., Fuchs, L. S., Otaiba, S. A., Thompson, A., Yen, L., McMaster, K. N., Svenson, E., & Yang, N. J. (2001). K-PALS: Helping kindergartners with reading readiness: Teachers and researchers in partnerships. *TEACHING Exceptional Children, 33*(4), 76–80.

Fuchs, D., Fuchs, L. S., Simmons, D. C., & Mathes, P. G. (2008). *Peer assisted learning strategies: Reading methods for grades 2–6*. Vanderbilt University.

Graham, S., & Hebert, M. A. (2010). *Writing to read: Evidence for how writing can improve reading—A report to Carnegie Corporation of New York.* Alliance for Excellent Education.

Graham, S., & Perin, D. (2007). *Writing next: Effective strategies to improve writing of adolescents in middle and high schools—A report to Carnegie Corporation of New York.* Alliance for Excellent Education.

Hasbrouck, J. (2020). An update to the national reading panel report: What we know about fluency in 2020. *The Reading League Journal, 1*(3), 29–31.

Hochman, J. C., & Wexler, N. (2017). *The writing revolution: A guide to advancing thinking through writing in all subjects and grades (1st ed.).* Jossey-Bass.

Hudson, R. F., Anderson, E. M., McGraw, M., Ray, R., & Wilhelm, A. (2022). Structured literacy interventions for reading fluency. In L. Spear-Swerling (Ed.), *Structured literacy interventions* (pp. 102–107). The Guilford Press.

Hudson, R. F., Pullen, P. C., Lane, H. B., & Torgesen, J. K. (2009). The complex nature of reading fluency: A multidimensional view. *Reading & Writing Quarterly, 25*(1), 4–32.

Kilpatrick, D. A. (2016). *Equipped for reading success: A comprehensive, step-by-step program for developing phonemic awareness and fluent word recognition*. Casey & Kirsch Publishers.

Lane, H. B., & Allen, S. A. (2010). The vocabulary-rich classroom: Modeling sophisticated word use to promote word consciousness and vocabulary growth. *The Reading Teacher, 63*(5), 362–370.

Mesmer, H. A. E. (2000). Decodable text: A review of what we know. *Reading Research and Instruction, 40*(2), 121–141.

National Reading Panel (2000). *Teaching children to read: An evidence-based assessment of the scientific research literature on reading and its implications for reading instruction*. National Institute of Child Health and Human Development.

Reutzel, P., Mohr, K. A. J., & Jones, C. D. (2019). Exploring the relationship between letter recognition and handwriting in early literacy development. *Journal of Early Childhood Literacy, 19*(3), 349–374.

Stone, L. (2018). *Reading for life: High quality literacy instruction for all (1st ed.).* Routledge.

Wasowicz, J. (2020). Every word wants to be a sight word when it grows up [webinar]. Learning By Design, Inc.

Yoncheva, Y. N., Wise, J., & McCandliss, B. (2015). Hemispheric specialization for visual words is shaped by attention to sublexical units during initial learning. *Brain and Language, 145–146,* 23–33.

Index